José Napoleón Duarte and
the Christian Democratic Party
in Salvadoran Politics

STEPHEN WEBRE

José Napoleón Duarte and the Christian Democratic Party in Salvadoran Politics 1960–1972

Louisiana State University Press
Baton Rouge and London

Design: Albert Crochet
Type face: VIP Melior
Composition: The Composing Room of Michigan, Inc.
Printing and Binding: Thomson-Shore, Inc.

LIBRARY OF CONGRESS CATALOGING IN PUBLICATION DATA

Webre, Stephen, 1946–
  José Napoleón Duarte and the Christian Democratic
Party in Salvadoran Politics, 1960–1972

  Bibliography: p.
  Includes index.
  1. Partido Demócrata Cristiano (Salvador)
2. Duarte, José Napoleón. 3. Salvador—Politics
and government—1944–   I. Title.
JL1579.A53W4   320.9'7284'05   78–14746
ISBN 0–8071–0462–0

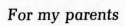

For my parents

Contents

Preface

In the years immediately following the Cuban Revolution of 1959, progressives at home and abroad argued that other Latin American countries must soon put behind them their heritage of economic and social injustice, arbitrary rule, and patterns of political violence if they hoped to avoid almost certain Communist takeover. In Washington, the administration of President John F. Kennedy, acting as much from strategic cold war concerns as from genuine sensitivity to the tribulations of the Latin American masses, sought to promote such a transition through the Alliance for Progress. Local rulers soon perceived that support from the United States came more readily when they showed evidence of soundness on the issue of Cuba and Communist subversion, a willingness to enact social and economic reforms designed to elevate the masses within a framework of capitalist development, and respect for the norms of democratic government as understood by North Americans.

"Social democrats," who had distinguished themselves in the struggle against dictatorship at a time when "revolution" was a simpler and less wicked concept in Latin America, enjoyed great prestige in this era, as did a new movement which seemed to appear from nowhere in the 1960s—Christian Democracy. The rapid expansion of Christian Democratic parties during the decade seemed to confirm the optimistic predictions of those who equated political development with "democracy" and conceived its progress to be linear and irreversible.

This study is an account of El Salvador's "democratic" era between 1960 and 1972 with primary emphasis upon the development and role of that country's most important opposition movement, the Salvadoran Christian Democratic party (PDC). The feature which characterized this twelve-year period in the minds of many observers in the United States was a political "liberalization" that included a commitment on the part of the government to social and economic reform and to relatively free and open competition for power on the part of opposition parties. Most writers attributed this development to the policies of Julio Adalberto Rivera, who came to power by force in 1961 and served as constitutional president from 1962 to 1967. Rivera publicly committed his regime to the ideals of the Alliance for Progress, and North American officials, journalists, and scholars generally hailed him as a champion of democracy and reform.

Viewed superficially, the career of the Christian Democratic party offered evidence in support of this interpretation. Founded in late 1960 in the midst of the turmoil that followed the overthrow of the authoritarian regime of José María Lemus, the PDC emerged in the Rivera period as El Salvador's most successful opposition party. But while the party's early victories seemed to demonstrate the success of the democratic experiment, the optimism did not last. In the final analysis, the rapid rise and sudden decline of the Christian Democratic party reflected the uneasy course of the tenuous Salvadoran democracy itself from its origins in crisis in late 1960, through its years of success and confidence, to its collapse into violence and repression in 1972. This period in Salvadoran history provides something of a microcosm of the broader Latin American experience with reformism in the sixties—an experience that began to turn bitter as early as 1964 with the failure of the Brazilian democracy and can perhaps be said to have ended for all practical purposes with the dissolution in 1973 of one of the region's oldest, most respected, but least understood democratic systems, that of Chile.

A major difficulty of North American discussions of Latin American politics has always been the confusion of ideological labels. The overuse of the terms liberal and democracy, in particular, has often contributed to misconceptions. In this study, *liberal* is used to describe that position which it has traditionally described, and continues to describe, in El Salvador. A liberal is understood to be one who opposes state intervention in the economy or in social relations. Salvadoran liberals believe essentially that the market place should regulate the economy and that the state should be weak and passive, exerting itself only in defense of economic liberty (understood as "property and the rights of the owner") and in prohibition of such artificial devices as unions designed to interfere with the smooth and favorable operation of the "invisible hand." That in times of crisis these liberals are the first to demand government action to drive up prices of their products on the world market, depress wages, or provide easy credit may seem an inconsistency to the casual observer but not to the Salvadoran liberal, whose ideology is, after all, a highly complex series of rationalizations of his privileged position within a blatantly inequitable system.

Liberals tend to be political *democrats* in the sense that they favor freedom of speech and press, the rule of law, the separation of powers, and a system of checks and balances. These ideals are part of the heritage of Salvadoran liberalism from the days when it was the vanguard in a stage of development that was imitative of Anglo-American political and economic institutions, but there is a practical value to them as well in that they facilitate obstruction of government actions against particular economic and social interests. Opposition to "tyranny" in El Salvador has often been inextricably bound with opposition to social and economic reforms and this has been a constant source of confusion, especially to North Americans who tend to cherish the myth of democracy as a holistic good and do not generally distinguish, as Latin Americans often do, between political and social democracy. When the term democracy is used in this study it is restricted to its political sense. A Salvadoran democrat is anyone who believes in civilian control, regular elections, and the political and civil rights generally recognized in the western world, without reference to his or her position on social and economic change.

Liberals in El Salvador, thus, are what we might call conservatives in the United States. The term conservative itself is little used in El Salvador, however. Liberals call themselves liberals; and their opponents call them *reactionaries*—or worse. There are several varieties of Salvadoran conservative, though, and not all qualify as liberals. There is, for instance, a small group that looks for its inspiration not to nineteenth-century laissez-faire doctrines but to El Salvador's Hispanic, Catholic heritage. These types, if called upon to label their position, would probably choose *traditionalist.* They are less concerned with democratic forms than liberals and can even be frankly authoritarian. They also differ from many liberals in their elevation of the church to the role of moral arbiter in politics, economics, and society—something liberals find difficult to accept because of their philosophical commitment to separation of church and state and because of the strong strain of anticlericalism in the Salvadoran liberal tradition. In spite of these differences, liberals and traditionalists generally find themselves in agreement on major issues because of their common belief that Salvadoran society is quite fragile and that social disintegration is a constant threat. The possible agents of such a disintegration are perceived as multitudinous and in the main extra-Salvadoran; both liberals and traditionalists subsume them within the vague blanket concept of *communism.* In this study, the term *conservative* is taken to refer collectively to all elements who, for whatever reason, deny the desirability or the possibility of social and economic change.

That position which insists upon the feasibility, the desirability, and even the necessity of social and economic change, accomplished generally within a capitalist framework but largely through active state intervention, is called herein, as in El Salvador, *progressive.* Progressives (sometimes called *neo-liberals*), of course, are not necessarily democrats. Progressive governments since 1948, for example, have maintained democratic façades but their actual behavior has tended to authoritarianism. This should not be surprising since the most dynamic agents of progressive ideas have been military officers, and since opposition to these ideas has long been identified with the liberal tradition of civil supremacy and political democracy. Opposition progressive groups, of course, do tend to be democratic since their political role would make little sense otherwise. Progressives are not *revolutionaries;* there are very few of the latter in Salvadoran politics in spite of the fact that many politicians choose to describe themselves as such.

The ideological position of the Christian Democratic party is discussed in Chapter 3. It is essentially a blend of the democratic, traditionalist, and progressive strains, a circumstance which partially accounts for the ideologically heterogeneous following it attracted in its early days.

The author owes thanks to many without whose assistance this study could never have appeared. Professor Roland H. Ebel of Newcomb College, Tulane University, provided materials and advice. The Brandt Dixon Scholarship Fund of Newcomb College made possible José Napoleón Duarte's visit to the United States in 1973 and, thereby, the two-week series of interviews used extensively here as documentation. Professor Ralph Lee Woodward, Jr., of Tulane directed the work in its original form as an M.A. thesis, and Professor Gertrude Matyoka Yeager read an earlier version. Professors Richard E. Greenleaf and Gene S. Yeager of the Tulane Center for Latin American Studies provided material and moral support when it was most needed. Professors Glen S. Jeansonne of Williams College, Herbert M. Levine of the University of Southwestern Louisiana, and Raymond McGowan and James T. Bain of St. Mary's Dominican College read portions of the final version, as did Arthur White of Isidore Newman School. Special thanks are due Jo Anne Weaver Bain, formerly of the Tulane Latin American Library, and in particular to Kathy Spas of the Howard-Tilton Library, who selflessly and carefully read the manuscript in its entirety. Finally, anyone who has worked at Tulane University will appreciate the author's obligation to the late Marjorie E. LeDoux, director until her untimely death in 1976 of the Latin American Library. None of these persons, of course, is responsible for those errors of fact or interpretation that more thorough research in better sources with more advanced techniques, not to mention longer historical perspective, will, in the future, inevitably reveal.

Chapter I

Salvadoran Politics to 1960

The Central American republic of El Salvador is the smallest and at the same time the most densely populated state on the American continent. In 1971, 3,541,000 persons lived within its 8,260 square miles and this figure was rapidly increasing.[1] The population is almost uniformly *mestizo*, or what Central Americans call *ladino*. Although there are isolated cases of Indian cultural survivals in the western zone, these are much reduced from the earlier decades of the century and are in no way comparable to the vast non-Hispanic population that characterizes neighboring Guatemala.[2] Although the population of El Salvador is ethnically, linguistically, and—because of its effective occupation of such a small territorial area—geographically unified, only in the loosest sense does it constitute a nation. Perhaps the greatest cultural gap is that between the city and the countryside. In spite of El Salvador's high population density, it remains a predominantly rural and agricultural society. Sixty percent of the population was classified as rural in 1971, and agriculture

1. El Salvador, Dirección General de Estadística y Censos, *Cuarto censo nacional de población: Cifras preliminares* (San Salvador, 1971), 2. The population of El Salvador had grown from 2,510,984 in 1961 and was expected to reach eight to ten million by the year 2000. José Arnoldo Sermeño Lima, "El Salvador, 1985–2000: Población y recursos naturales," *Estudios Sociales Centroamericanos,* III (September–December, 1974), 213–16. For an excellent introduction in English to the social, economic, and political context of contemporary Salvadoran history, see Alastair White, *El Salvador* (New York, 1973).

2. Franklin D. Parker, *The Central American Republics* (London, 1964), 145. See also the classic study by Rodolfo Barón Castro, *La población de El Salvador: Estudio acerca de su desenvolvimiento desde la época prehispánica hasta nuestros días* (Madrid, 1942), especially pp. 523–32.

employed more than one-half the work force and accounted for nearly 70 percent of all exports. Still, it is that 40 percent of Salvadorans living in urban areas who have benefited most from the country's rapid but uneven and often painful integration into the modern world. One illustration of this is the matter of literacy. Whereas only 20 percent of urban residents were considered illiterate in 1971, the corresponding figure for the rural population was 56 percent.[3]

Clearly dominant among Salvadoran urban communities is the capital city, San Salvador, which, with a reported population of 337,171 in 1971, was more than three times the size of the next largest city, Santa Ana. The capital is more than the administrative center of the country; it is the commercial, financial, industrial, social, and cultural hub as well. The capital elite is the national elite and capital politics is national politics. Local landed families with any sort of standing at all maintain establishments in the capital, and "national" political parties draw their leadership from San Salvador's professional community. Relatively short distances and good transportation facilities connecting it to all regions of the country have contributed to San Salvador's primacy and to the corresponding eclipse, since the 1920s, of competing regional centers.[4]

Poor in mineral resources, what prosperity El Salvador has known over the years has come from agricultural production for export. During the colonial period, the chief product was indigo. Since the second half of the nineteenth century it has been coffee. Because of the country's geographic limitations, an essentially conservative belief has prevailed that it has no option in this regard and that the health of the economy in general depends almost exclusively upon the health of the coffee industry. As one of El Salvador's most distinguished students of agricultural economics wrote in 1950, "It is in the end axiomatic, at least for now, that in El Salvador only coffee

3. Inter-American Development Bank, *Economic and Social Progress in Latin America: Annual Report, 1972* (Washington, D.C., 1972), 198–205.

4. Dirección de Estadística, *Cuarto censo*, 1; Everett A. Wilson, "The Crisis of National Integration in El Salvador, 1919–1935" (Ph.D. dissertation, Stanford University, 1969), 135–36, 142–44, and *passim*. For the argument that the politics of a country of El Salvador's size and characteristics should be thought of in terms of city rather than nation, see Roland H. Ebel, "Governing the City-State: Notes on the Politics of the Small Latin American Countries," *Journal of Inter-American Studies and World Affairs*, XIV (1972), 325–46.

will resolve our social and economic problems."[5] Despite recent trends in agricultural diversification and industrialization, this belief remains for many Salvadorans an article of faith that is not lightly challenged.[6]

The dramatic expansion of coffee culture in the late nineteenth and early twentieth centuries was accompanied by the concentration of large expanses of the republic's most desirable agricultural land into a very few hands. A review of land tenure patterns in El Salvador reveals the familiar unbalanced distribution of property considered characteristic of Latin America as a whole. In 1971, according to the government's own figures, out of 270,868 exploitations some 250,539, or 92.5 percent, were less than ten hectares and the vast majority of these were less than three hectares. These small farms accounted, however, for only 27.1 percent of the total land under cultivation while the 63 largest individual exploitations (those of 1000 hectares or more) by themselves account for 8.5 percent.[7] The size of the country and the density of its population have tended to aggravate this already difficult situation. In El Salvador, virtually alone among Latin American countries, land is genuinely a scarce resource. There is no frontier to be opened, settled, and developed.[8]

The virtual monopolization of the most valuable productive land by a few families has contributed to the development of a relatively compact economic elite proprietary in its attitude toward national policy and defensive of its advantages almost to the point of paranoia. The vast economic power of this "oligarchy" is, along with the country's demographic problems and the high level of politicization within its military establishment, one of the most centrally important realities of Salvadoran politics. The popular label "fourteen families" may not be strictly accurate, but a small network of fami-

5. Félix Choussy, Economía agrícola salvadoreña: Producción agrícola e industrias conexas (San Salvador, 1950), 361.

6. See, for example, Rafael Huezo Selva, El espacio económico más singular del continente americano (San Salvador, 1972). Even an observer critical of monocultural dependence and the inequitable distribution of benefits associated with coffee culture concedes its great ecological suitability to Salvadoran conditions. See the indispensable work of David Browning, El Salvador: Landscape and Society (Oxford, 1971), 222–26.

7. El Salvador, Dirección General de Estadística y Censos, Tercer censo nacional agropecuario, 1971 (2 vols.; San Salvador, 1974–75), II, xxxi, 1.

8. Ernest Feder, The Rape of the Peasantry: Latin America's Landholding System (Garden City, N.Y., 1971), 48.

lies, linked together by marital as well as corporate alliances, does control a disproportionate share of production, commerce, and finance.[9] In its campaigns against social and economic change, the oligarchy has taken advantage of its ability to co-opt the political elite, drawn increasingly since the 1930s from the military and the professions, through such devices as social preferment and pecuniary largesse. In the public arena, the defenders of privilege have alternated between obfuscatory, legalistic delaying tactics and frankly emotional appeals to popular fears and anxieties. A measure of their success is the fact that, although the oligarchy has not directly administered the country since 1931, and although since 1948 Salvadoran governments have been openly committed to the ideals of economic and social reform, very few measures have in fact been enacted without at least the tacit approval of the wealthiest families. In the 1960s, El Salvador, unlike other Latin American countries, still lacked land reform legislation or legally sanctioned peasant organizations of any sort.[10]

Before 1931, the families that in effect owned the country also governed it. In those less complex times, the presidential chair was occupied by a succession of representatives of the Dueñas, Regalado, Escalón, and other wealthy families. This trend reached its ultimate expression under the Meléndez-Quiñónez "dynasty." Carlos Meléndez (1912–1919) passed the presidency to his brother Jorge Meléndez (1919–1923) and in turn to his brother-in-law Alfonso Quiñónez Molina (1923–1927). Throughout this period, the outward forms of political democracy were observed although there were occasional breaches, such as the assassination of President Manuel Enrique Araujo in 1912. The gap between form and substance was wide, however. From 1903 through 1927, presidential elections in El Sal-

9. Any list would necessarily include the Alfaro, Alvarez, Battle, Borgonovo, Deininger, De Sola, Dueñas, Durán, Escalón, Guirola, Hill, Llach, Magaña, Mathies, Meléndez, Menéndez, Meza Ayau, Parker, Quiñónez, Regalado, Salaverría, Sol Millet, and Wright families. The presence of non-Hispanic names represents naturalized immigrant elements rather than foreign participation. Unlike other Central American countries, native capital has always provided the primary source of investment for economic development in El Salvador. Robert T. Aubey, "Entrepreneurial Formation in El Salvador," *Explorations in Entrepreneurial History*, 2nd ser., VI (1968–69), 268–85; Eduardo Colindres, "La tenencia de la tierra en El Salvador," *Estudios Centro Americanos*, XXXI (1976), 463–72.

10. Feder, *Rape of the Peasantry*, 161, 183.

vador were staged performances organized by the government in power for the purpose of installing its chosen candidate. The Meléndez-Quiñónez dynasty in particular, in spite of its patriarchal liberal demeanor and certain populist pretensions, such as the "Red League" organized by Quiñónez in 1917, was little other than a series of civilian dictatorships which freely employed censorship and physical intimidation against their critics, while vigorously defending and perpetuating a labor-repressive economic regime.[11]

Oligarchic domination of Salvadoran politics began to weaken during the administration of Quiñónez's chosen successor, lawyer Pío Romero Bosque (1927–1931). Romero Bosque is warmly remembered in El Salvador for his independence, ability, honesty, and integrity. Buoyed by the remarkable prosperity of the late 1920s, he summoned the courage to break with the elements that had installed him. No more receptive to innovation in social or economic matters than his predecessors, Romero Bosque turned his attention to political reform; but the rapid decline in world coffee prices beginning in 1929 badly undercut his position. The 1920s had seen the rapid emergence of labor organizations and leftist groups, and in 1930 came the first appearance above ground of the Salvadoran Communist party. Romero Bosque had no solution for the economic crisis that beset El Salvador and he vacillated uneasily between concession and repression in his approach to the political troubles it generated. As the end of his term approached, he made the fateful decision to break completely with the past and deliver upon his campaign promise to allow an open election to choose his successor.[12] Whether the president acted from a sincere commitment to democracy, concern for his historical reputation, or simply frustration in the face of multiplying problems, a period of deepening social and economic crisis was probably not the most propitious moment for experimentation with so totally unfamiliar a political procedure.

11. White, El Salvador, 87–97. For a sanguine portrait of El Salvador in the golden age of coffee and liberalism, see Percy F. Martin, Salvador of the Twentieth Century (London, 1911).

12. Thomas P. Anderson, Matanza: El Salvador's Communist Revolt of 1932 (Lincoln, Neb., 1971), 1–39. For an uncritical but detailed account of the Romero Bosque administration, see Jacinto Paredes, Vida y obras del doctor Pío Romero Bosque: Apuntes para la historia de El Salvador (San Salvador, 1930). The social and economic history of this period is well presented in Wilson, "Crisis of Integration."

The election of 1931 was one of only four genuinely meaningful presidential campaigns in Salvadoran history.[13] A host of candidates appeared carrying the standards of hastily organized "parties," but in the end the victory went to Arturo Araujo. Himself a wealthy landowner with a reputation for treating his peasants fairly, Araujo ran a frankly populist campaign calling for sweeping change, including land reform, although he avoided the revolutionary rhetoric of the Marxists in favor of the more moderate *vitalista* philosophy of Alberto Masferrer.[14]

Once in office, Araujo proved unwilling or unable to deliver upon his promises. The oligarchy withheld its support and thus made it difficult for him to recruit experienced ministers. In addition, the president himself gave evidence of personal incapacity to meet the demands of the general economic crisis.[15] On December 2, 1931, the army overthrew Araujo and installed in his place his vice-president, General Maximiliano Hernández Martínez, whose enigmatic personality would dominate El Salvador for the next thirteen years. Although men with military titles and combat experience from civil or isthmian warfare had held the presidency on many occasions in the past, Martínez was the first professional soldier in a modern sense to achieve the position, and the coup which installed him was itself the first successful military revolt since the one that brought Tomás Regalado to power in 1898.

That the Salvadoran army emerged as a political actor of prime importance only at this moment was partially due to its rather late professionalization, beginning only in the early twentieth century. The representatives of the oligarchy, seeking to employ the armed

13. The other three were those of 1950, 1967, and 1972. The criteria for "meaningfulness" here are, of course, subjective. In all four elections there were active, serious opposition, a major option involved, and some, although not always overwhelming, doubt as to the outcome.

14. One of Araujo's key supporters, Masferrer (1868–1932) was a Salvadoran journalist and man of letters best known for his works of social criticism which defined national problems in moral terms and called for a social order in which the wealthy would recognize an ethical obligation to concede the poor sufficient means and opportunity to insure a life above what Masferrer considered the "minimum" standards of dignity and productivity. The handiest compendium of Masferrer's social thought is that published by the Guatemalan government during the presidency of Juan José Arévalo: Alberto Masferrer, *El mínimum vital y otras obras de carácter sociológico* (Guatemala, 1950).

15. Wilson, "Crisis of Integration," 208–18.

forces as merely an instrument of their own power, had maintained civilian control and a tight budgetary policy. Pío Romero Bosque had himself served as minister of war under Quiñónez and during his own presidency maintained civilians, including his son, in that post. Arturo Araujo, however, owed his electoral victory in great part to the agreement of General Martínez to abandon his own presidential campaign, in which he represented the emerging corporate interest of the army. The price for this agreement was the assignment of the war ministry to a soldier. The job went to Martínez himself and, since December, 1931, elements of the military have, with only momentary and inconsequential exceptions, never failed to control both the presidency and the portfolio of defense.[16]

Martínez had no sooner assumed the presidency than he faced a crisis whose legacy continues to weigh heavily upon the Salvadoran political consciousness. On January 22, 1932, Indian and *ladino* peasants in the country's western zone rose in rebellion under nominal Communist leadership and swept through the district looting, pillaging, and on occasion killing local officials and landowners. Government troops turned the rebels back at Sonsonate and quickly suppressed the movement. Retribution following the restoration of order was swift and brutal. Local civilians lynched some leaders before they could be taken by authorities, but those who fell into official hands fared little better; execution was generally immediate. Identifying and punishing the followers was more difficult than liquidating the leaders, and the authorities consequently resorted to arbitrary methods. In most areas it was apparently sufficient proof of guilt to be noticeably an Indian or a peasant or to be unable to show a safe-conduct pass. Most of the official murder in the period following the rebellion occurred in the small towns and rural areas of the West, but in the capital as well authorities used voting lists and informers to identify and exterminate urban "Communists." Estimates of the number killed in the revolt and the repression that followed vary wildly. The most reliable study concludes as a "reasonable estimate" that between eight thousand and ten thousand rebels (or suspected rebels) died, probably more than 90 percent of them in the

16. Robert Varney Elam, "Appeal to Arms: The Army and Politics in El Salvador, 1931–1964" (Ph.D. dissertation, University of New Mexico, 1968), 1–26.

repression rather than in the fighting itself. By contrast, victims of rebel violence amounted to perhaps one hundred, most of whom were soldiers or local officials.[17]

From different perspectives the revolt of 1932 exhibits characteristics of race warfare as well as of a classic *jacquerie*. Certainly, it was only in part the highly organized Communist revolution the Martínez government claimed. Such a revolution had indeed been planned by leftist leaders incensed by the regime's intervention to prevent Communist party victories in municipal and Legislative Assembly elections held in January. The intellectual authors of the conspiracy hoped to coordinate the peasant rising in the West with a revolt in the capital by radical students, workers, and soldiers from the barracks. The government, however, knew of the plans and by January 19 had arrested the student leaders and neutralized the barracks. When the Indians and peasants—most of whom had been recruited into the movement on the basis of local resentments or immediate grievances and were, in John Gunther's colorful phrase, "no more communists than Martínez is an eskimo"[18]—did revolt, their movement was socially and geographically isolated and the result was largely uncoordinated violence.

Out of the rebellion and subsequent hecatomb have emerged myths that remain salient in Salvadoran political culture to this day, especially among conservatives. The historical judgment upon the revolt in El Salvador has been, until quite recently, almost universally negative, and only the radical Left has dared openly to make heroes of the martyred student leaders—Augustín Farabundo Martí, Alfonso Luna, and Mario Zapata. General awareness that thousands of Salvadorans died as a result of Communist agitation has obscured the fact that the greater part of the killing was the work of the regime and not of the rebels. It has generally been repeated that hundreds of property-owners lost their lives, although a recent study has established that the total number of all civilian victims could hardly have been more than thirty-five.[19] The revolt and its aftermath still hover

17. Anderson, *Matanza*, 134–36. Other accounts, much less objective than that of Anderson and varying dramatically in their points of view, include: Joaquín Méndez (h.), *Los sucesos comunistas en El Salvador* (San Salvador, 1932); Jorge Schlesinger, *Revolución comunista* (Guatemala, 1946); Roque Dalton, *Miguel Mármol: Los sucesos de 1932 en El Salvador* (San José, Costa Rica, 1972).
18. John Gunther, *Inside Latin America* (New York, 1941), 127.
19. Anderson, *Matanza*, 136.

like a brooding incubus over the collective consciousness of the Salvadoran political class. Any party which advocates social justice, especially if its program involves change in the agrarian sector, must suffer the endless repetition of accusations that such proposals are impractical and hopelessly visionary in a country as small and as poor as El Salvador and that to speak of them publicly as though they were attainable serves only to inflame the masses. And it is, after all, only irresponsible Red deceit of the masses that leads them to violence in the pursuit of such chimeras as social and economic justice.

Times of crisis seemed to call for a strong hand and Martínez's response to the events of 1932 suggested the oligarchy could expect to benefit from its surrender of political responsibility to the army. Even so, the economic elite was never completely comfortable with the Martínez regime. For one thing, the dictator was not one of them. Unlike his predecessors in office, Martínez was of humble, Indian parentage and had chosen a military career as an avenue of social mobility. Trained in military academies in Guatemala and El Salvador, Martínez harbored intellectual pretensions as a philosopher. He was largely an autodidact, and brought with him to the presidency a number of bizarre beliefs and eccentricities. Martínez cultivated theosophy, was a vegetarian and a non-drinker, preferred being called *maestro* (teacher) to *presidente*, and lectured and wrote prolifically on a number of moral and philosophical questions. El Salvador's refined oligarchy, as suspicious of him as he was of them, dismissed him socially in a way they could not politically as "the crazy Indian" (*el indio chiflado*).[20]

Most of the measures Martínez took early in the 1930s benefited the landowners at the expense of the workers. He outlawed both urban and rural labor organizations and enacted "vagrancy" laws designed to insure coffee growers and other large agriculturalists a ready supply of cheap workers. Coffee prices hit a record low in 1932. In order to protect growers from the loss of their lands through

20. William Krehm, *Democracia y tiranías en el Caribe,* ed. Vicente Sáenz (Mexico, 1949), 44–49; John Martz, *Central America: The Crisis and the Challenge* (Chapel Hill, N.C., 1959), 82. In spite of its importance to an understanding of twentieth-century El Salvador, the Martínez regime has received little scholarly attention. Wilson ("Crisis of Integration," 233–72) has an excellent account of the first four years and offers some provocative interpretations that have greatly influenced the approach adopted herein. See also David Luna, "Análisis de una dictadura fascista latinoamericana: Maximiliano Hernández Martínez, 1931–1944," *La Universidad* (San Salvador), XCIV (September–October, 1969), 38–130.

credit foreclosure, Martínez decreed a moratorium on the collection of debts and arbitrarily reduced prevailing interest rates. In El Salvador, measures taken in defense of coffee are understood to be in defense of the nation, and certainly it was not only the oligarchy that benefited. By keeping the existing system of coffee production, processing, and marketing intact until world prices recovered, Martínez protected not only latifundists but also small and medium producers as well as public and commercial employees whose jobs depended upon the surpluses generated by the export trade.

Martínez also contributed to the institutionalization of the coffee system, particularly in the crucial area of credit. The creation of the Central Reserve Bank (Banco Central de Reserva) as the republic's sole bank of issue, the establishment of a national mortgage bank (Banco Hipotecario) and a federation of savings associations (Federación de Cajas de Crédito), and finally the organization of the Salvadoran Coffee Company (Compañía Salvadoreña de Café) as a source of credit and an exporter in its own right, all helped bring order to an anachronistic system and served to protect the interests of property-owners at all levels. The fact that all these institutions, although organized on state initiative to serve public functions, were in fact private corporations subscribed by private capital indicates that the advance in El Salvador from the sacred principles of laissez-faire liberalism to the concept of the economically active state was still quite tentative. Although these reforms were prejudicial to the interests of individual oligarchic families heavily engaged in banking and finance who might have hoped to profit from a credit squeeze upon less dynamic landholders, they were beneficial to the industry as a whole. During the Martínez period and for years thereafter, oligarchs dominated these new organizations and operated them to their benefit. Future governments, however, would take advantage of their existence to increase state participation in the economy and augment the capacity of the state to function as a defender and promoter of capitalism as a system rather than the not infrequently contradictory interests of a few individual capitalists.[21]

---

21. On the relationship between the political evolution of the Salvadoran state and its economic role, see Rubén Zamora, "¿Seguro de vida ó despojo? Análisis político de la transformación agraria," *Estudios Centro Americanos*, XXXI (1976), 530 and *passim*. This essay contains one of the most thoughtful and provocative analyses of contemporary Salvadoran politics the author has seen.

A nationalist, almost isolationist, mentality accompanied this vigorous effort to protect and strengthen the coffee industry. Throughout most of its history, El Salvador has looked beyond its borders in search of ways to transcend its geographic limitations. It has, for instance, always been in the vanguard of movements for the political or economic integration of the Central American isthmus. During the 1930s, however, the economic crisis along with political and diplomatic difficulties frustrated efforts to come to agreement with the other Central American countries.[22] At a crucial point in its development, El Salvador thus became convinced that it would have to survive by doing what it did best with the limited resources at hand. Thus Martínez's domestic economic policy was one of re-trenchment and contraction. Coffee was reliable, so all the efforts of the state were directed to expanding the return from the coffee crop.[23] The dictator gave no encouragement to development in any other area of the economy. He believed that the Salvadoran economy should first of all be Salvadoran and he therefore opposed foreign loans and issued decrees restricting the entrepreneurial activities of immigrant minorities. In order to protect local artisans Martínez set limits on the level of capitalization of manufacturing enterprises, thereby discouraging industrial development.[24] To provide for peasants displaced by the continued emphasis upon coffee, he organized a state-inspired private agency, Social Improvement (Mejoramiento Social, S.A.), which purchased some agricultural land for distribution. This program did not have a major claim on the government's revenues, however, and the few peasants who benefited from it received nothing in the way of technical or credit assistance.[25]

Those who in the 1960s still believed that El Salvador must look only to itself and learn to live with its limitations remembered Martínez as the only Salvadoran president who understood this.[26] While

22. Sandas Lorenzo Harrison, "The Role of El Salvador in the Drive for Unity in Central America" (Ph.D. dissertation, Indiana University, 1962), especially Chap. 4; Thomas L. Karnes, The Failure of Union: Central America, 1824–1960 (Chapel Hill, N.C., 1961), 227–28.
23. Wilson, "Crisis of Integration," 244.
24. Luna, "Dictadura fascista," Chap. 3.
25. Browning, Landscape and Society, 274–80.
26. See, for example, Roberto López Trejo, Realidad dramática de la república: 25 años de traición a la fuerza armada y a la patria (San Salvador, 1974); and Alberto Peña Kampy, El general Martínez: Un patriarcal presidente dictador (San Salvador, n.d.).

subsequent administrations, especially those after 1948, have built upon Martínez's institutional contributions, they have moved progressively away from his narrow economic vision. They have promoted industrialization, agricultural diversification, and the development of lands, such as those on the Pacific Coast, previously ignored because they were unsuited to coffee. They have also sought regional integration and foreign, especially North American, investment. But they have never abandoned the rhetorical shibboleth of Salvadoran solutions for Salvadoran problems. Proposals for social and economic reforms inevitably describe themselves as "truly Salvadoran," and all suggestion of foreign inspiration, be it from Washington, Moscow, or elsewhere, is roundly denied. Even in the 1960s when the two most consequential progressive forces in the country were a government closely identified with the Alliance for Progress and an opposition Christian Democratic party with formal and informal ties to sister parties throughout Latin America, each would find it necessary to insist upon the uniqueness of the Salvadoran condition and the consequent necessity of purely national solutions.

Salvadoran leaders seldom address themselves to the question of whether this nationalism is truly compatible with Central Americanism. Both have become hallowed precepts. The only way in which El Salvador has ever hoped to transcend its geographic and demographic limitations is through integration with the other isthmian republics. From the 1920s, the republic's northern neighbor, Honduras, absorbed surplus peasants and workers, functioning as the Caribbean frontier El Salvador alone among the Central American states lacked. Beginning in 1960, the inauguration of the Central American Common Market opened an important outlet for Salvadoran manufactured goods and spurred an industrial "boom" that momentarily led Salvadoran leaders to believe that the republic could in fact live beyond its means. These hopes suffered a severe reversal with the so-called "Football War" between El Salvador and Honduras in 1969. Once again, the country would feel isolated and sense the need to fall back upon its own resources. The major point of contention between conservatives and progressives in the postwar period would be whether El Salvador should emphasize the institutions which had proven reliable in the past, as Martínez had done, or whether it should seek new solutions. The fact that abnormally high coffee prices helped speed economic recovery seemed to give the advantage in this argument to the conservatives.

Martínez successfully defied the United States when he came to power. Throughout the 1930s he was an unashamed admirer of Hitler and Mussolini, whose historical situations he saw as analogous to his own.[27] El Salvador, however, fell dutifully into line with the Allies when the United States entered World War II. There was, of course, a fundamental contradiction between the nature of the Martínez regime and the prodemocracy propaganda of the Rockefeller Committee. The dictator's newly found friendship with the United States contributed in part to the irony that the coalition of opponents that ultimately accomplished his downfall consisted of civilian democrats, pro-Axis officers, entrepreneurs and bankers frustrated by his economic restrictions, and coffee producers incensed by his decision in 1943 to increase revenues by raising the tax on exports.[28]

The conspirators sprang their coup on April 2, 1944, while Martínez was out of the capital on holiday. The effort was badly coordinated and loyal troops managed to stifle it after considerable violence. Martínez responded with customary harshness, sending the major participants in the revolt before a firing squad. The capital remained restless, however, and a paralyzing general strike soon broke out supported by government, bank, and commercial employees, by students, and by professionals. Recognizing his position as hopeless, Martínez announced his resignation on May 8, and departed the country. Probably not intending his absence to be permanent, he deposited the presidency into the hands of General Andrés Ignacio Menéndez, an honest, unambitious officer who had loyally stood in as interim president on a previous occasion. This time, however, Menéndez named a broadly representative cabinet, restored freedom of the press, and issued a call for elections. Had the election been held when Menéndez intended, and had it been fair, the victor would likely have been Arturo Romero, a popular young physician

27. On Washington's attitude, see Kenneth J. Grieb, "The United States and the Rise of General Maximiliano Hernández Martínez," *Journal of Latin American Studies*, III (1971), 151–72.
28. The events surrounding the overthrow of Martínez receive detailed treatment in Krehm, *Democracia y tiranías*, 49–68.

who had been a central figure in the April 2 conspiracy. But many of the officers involved in the coup attempt had perished in the repression, and their alliance with the dictator's civilian opponents was largely a matter of convenience anyway. Romero stood for a return to civilian rule and by 1944 military men did not have to be intransigent *martinistas* to oppose that. In October, before the election could be held, a second coup displaced Menéndez.[29]

The politics of the next four years were essentially the politics of the Salvadoran army. At least three broad groupings seem to have emerged within the officer corps. The one that appeared to be in ascendancy following the coup against Menéndez consisted of senior officers of Martínez's generation and outlook and included the new president, Colonel Osmín Aguirre y Salinas, director of the national police and a principal figure in the massacre of 1932. A second faction, whose importance increased steadily during the late 1940s, represented junior officers, better trained and more widely traveled than their seniors, more progressive in their political views, and more frustrated in their personal careers. Finally, there was a fading minority of patrician liberals such as Colonel José Asencio Menéndez, the son of a former president, who opposed military rule and became minister of war in the government-in-exile Arturo Romero established under the aegis of the revolutionary regime in neighboring Guatemala.[30]

Aguirre proceeded with the postponed elections, but close governmental control of the electoral machinery left little doubt as to the outcome. The army's candidate, General Salvador Castaneda Castro, easily defeated Arturo Romero. Castaneda's candidacy had met considerable opposition within the officer corps but, in the end, he seemed the least objectionable alternative. His presidency was not particularly effective, although he did assert his independence of Aguirre. A new constitution promulgated in 1945 to replace the traditional liberal charter of 1886, which had been restored upon Martínez's fall, was of little importance since Castaneda maintained a state of siege throughout most of his period in office. The president's primary difficulty was keeping peace within the military; during his term, he had to suppress several coup attempts. He was especially

29. *Ibid.*, 107–23.
30. *Ibid.*; Elam, "Appeal to Arms," 95–115.

distrustful of the junior officers and sent many of them out of the country for training or on diplomatic missions. One measure that made him particularly unpopular among this group was the establishment of limits on the number of officers in each grade that heavily weighted the officer corps in favor of the senior ranks and at the same time blocked opportunities for promotion. On December 14, 1948, the morning after Castaneda called for a constitutional amendment to permit the extension of his term, the junior officers overthrew him.[31]

The December 14 movement described itself as a revolution of the "military youth" (juventud militar). The Revolutionary Council established to rule the country included three middle-ranked officers and two civilian professionals. Lieutenant Colonel Manuel de Jesús Córdova, the initial spokesman for the movement, was subdirector of the military academy. Major Oscar Bolaños was a former professor of logistics and military history. Major Oscar Osorio was a former subdirector of the academy and was attached to the embassy in Washington at the time of the coup. Of the two civilians, Humberto Costa was an attorney and Reynaldo Galindo Pohl was a schoolteacher and part-time law student. The aims of the new junta were similar to those of democratic revolutionary movements operating throughout the Caribbean area in the late 1940s. It promised a return to political democracy as well as social and economic reform and appointed a cabinet dominated, with the important exception of the defense ministry, by young civilians, many of whom were associated with the university.[32]

Very soon after the establishment of the Revolutionary Council, Major Osorio emerged as the dominant figure in the December 14 movement—to the point that Colonel Córdova resigned within the month and took up exile in Honduras. In October, Osorio himself left the council in order to campaign for the presidency as the candidate of the official party of the "revolution," the Revolutionary Party of Democratic Unification (Partido Revolucionario de Unificación Democrática, PRUD). Osorio's principal opponent was Colonel José

31. Elam, "Appeal to Arms," 115–29.
32. Ibid., 137–41. On the political climate in the circum-Caribbean area in the post–World War II period, see Charles D. Ameringer, The Democratic Left in Exile: The Antidictatorial Struggle in the Caribbean, 1945–1959 (Coral Gables, Fla., 1974).

Asencio Menéndez who represented the Renovating Action party (Partido Acción Renovadora, PAR) which had originated in the civilian movement against Martínez. The PRUD and the PAR were El Salvador's first permanent electoral parties. The Revolutionary Council created the Central Council of Elections (Consejo Central de Elecciones, CCE), a permanent and theoretically independent three-man commission, in order to insure impartial enforcement of the electoral laws. The PAR challenge to Osorio and the *juventud militar* was a serious one. Although the PRUD won the election of March, 1950, Menéndez received nearly 45 percent of the vote and the PAR captured fourteen seats in the Constituent Assembly elected simultaneously.[33]

The assembly drafted a new constitution which, in addition to specifying the political regime, outlined the social and economic responsibilities of the state as well.[34] In the presidency, Osorio carried on the reformist policies of the Revolutionary Council. The government's two major concerns were economic development and social welfare. In the realm of the former—which admittedly received the bulk of his attention—Osorio emphasized public works, the promotion of industry and trade, the development of underutilized lands, and the diversification of agriculture. The most important projects begun during the PRUD era included the modern port works at Acajutla and the hydroelectric project on the Lempa River undertaken with an International Bank for Reconstruction and Develop-

33. Mauricio de la Selva, "El Salvador en 1960," *Cuadernos Americanos,* CXIII (November–December, 1960), 40; Elam, "Appeal to Arms," 143–45; Consejo Central de Elecciones, *Memoria de las elecciones de 1950* (San Salvador, 1951), 58–59, In a procedure that has now become traditional in El Salvador, the *paristas* immediately denounced the count as fraudulent. Many candidates who lost would have been unsuccessful with or without the presence of fraud, of course, but the persistence to this day of electoral abuses, especially in the rural, less developed areas of the republic, means that accusations of official imposition are never completely unfounded. There do appear to have been many irregularities in the election of 1950. One town, for example, with a population of 2,400 is reported to have cast 3,800 votes for Osorio. Joyce Elaine Gamble, "The Partido Acción Renovadora in the Elections of 1964, 1966, and 1967" (M.A. thesis, Tulane University, 1968), 70.

34. This document is analyzed at length in Ricardo Gallardo, *Las constituciones de El Salvador* (2 vols.; Madrid, 1961), II, 113–291. It was one of many Latin American social democratic constitutions, such as the Cuban Constitution of 1940 and the Guatemalan Constitution of 1945, that showed the influence of the Mexican Constitution of 1917 in rejecting the liberal concept of the economically passive state. The Constitution of 1962, under which El Salvador is governed today, is the 1950 document with a few minor changes.

ment loan for more than $12 million. In the area of social conditions, the regime claimed as its inspiration the ideas of Alberto Masferrer and sponsored programs in sanitation, health care, and housing construction. A new social security system made medical and hospitalization services available to a fortunate minority of workers which, over the next two decades, the government moved slowly to expand. The Revolutionary Council had restored the right of commercial employees to organize, and Osorio now recognized industrial unions as well as the right to bargain collectively. Of all these programs the prime beneficiaries were city-dwellers. The government was unprepared to antagonize the oligarchy by extending its protection to the *campesinos* although it did continue, "without demagoguery and without boasting," Martínez's policy of distributing parcels of land on government-owned *haciendas*.[35]

Osorio offered incentives to attract native capital home from abroad to participate in entrepreneurial endeavors both in agriculture and in industry. A close cooperative relationship soon developed between the traditional economic elite and the new, modernizing political elite. The fact that world coffee prices in this period were high and the Salvadoran crop bountiful encouraged this harmony. What is more, the oligarchs were sufficiently realistic to recognize that the officers and their middle-class civilian allies could not easily be displaced from power and, on the other hand, that they were hardly immune to the various forms of suasion available to the wealthy. The regime warned those who did oppose the PRUD's programs that El Salvador must accommodate itself systematically to a changing world if it hoped to prevent the spread of more radical approaches to social and economic transformation from nearby Guatemala.[36]

The December 14 Revolution's fulfillment of its promise of political reform was less impressive than its other achievements. Free-

35. Martz, *Central America*, 83–91; Raymond Charles Ashton, "El Salvador and the 'Controlled Revolution': An Analysis of Salvadorean Development, 1948–1965" (M.A. thesis, Tulane University, 1967); Secretaría de Información de la Presidencia de la República, *Por qué estamos con la revolución salvadoreña* (San Salvador, n.d.), for quotation; Secretaría de Información de la Presidencia de la República, *La Revolución salvadoreña: Folleto no. 1* (San Salvador, n.d.).

36. Elam, "Appeal to Arms," 145–48; Paul P. Kennedy, *The Middle Beat: A Correspondent's View of Mexico, Guatemala, and El Salvador*, ed. Stanley R. Ross (New York, 1971), 172.

dom of expression and the right to assemble were at first not much interfered with—as long as those expressing themselves and assembling kept their criticism within certain bounds—and political parties remained active throughout the period. But El Salvador had no real tradition of loyal opposition. Salvadoran leaders tended then, and many still do, to regard political activity not as a perfectly legitimate process through which various interests bargain the allocation of the resources and benefits of society, but as the base expression of selfish personal ambitions whose ultimate effect, if the state is not well insulated from it, is obstruction and corruption. Symptomatic of the idea of politics as a disruptive force has been a tendency to segregate "political" issues (questions of party, votes, and office) from "technical" issues (matters of public policy), as if policy should or even could be decided in a vacuum in which only technical considerations are relevant. One consequence of this has been the practice of Salvadoran governments, as early as that of Martínez, to enshrine major social reforms and public projects within semiautonomous agencies whose technical staffs could presumably conduct their business safe from political distractions.[37]

One technical agency whose mission could hardly long remain separated from politics was the Central Council of Elections. Established two years earlier as a guarantor of free and impartial elections, the CCE had effectively lost its independence by 1952. The Legislative Assembly selected, and continues to select, the three members of the council; it is recognized as routine that the party that controls the assembly will control the CCE as well. This control enabled the PRUD to drive the PAR out of the assembly in 1952, and thereafter the official party held every seat until its own disappearance in 1961.

The PRUD owed its status as the "official" party to the fact that it was organized by interests which had already achieved political power by other than electoral means. Once organized and in operation, it could draw upon official resources, such as the treasury or the

---

37. Important agencies of this sort established or reorganized during the PRUD era included the Salvadoran Social Security Institute (Instituto Salvadoreño de Seguridad Social, ISSS), the Urban Housing Institute (Instituto de Vivienda Urbana, IVU), the Rural Settlement Institute (Instituto de Colonización Rural, ICR), the Acajutla Port Authority (Comisión Ejecutiva del Puerto Acajutla, CEPA), and the Lempa Hydroelectric Authority (Comisión Ejecutiva Hidroeléctrica del Río Lempa, CEL).

agencies of social control, in order to attract support or discourage opposition. The fact that the men who came to power with the December 14 movement felt the need to organize themselves into a political party and legitimize their presence in power through frequent demonstrations of "power capability" derived from mass appeal testifies to the utility and durability of the constitutional myth in El Salvador.[38]

To say that the leaders of the PRUD valued the image of popular consent as manifested by the ballot, however, is not to say that they necessarily shared the traditional western democratic concept of elections as open competition for power among equally valid alternatives. It is the conceit of politicians anywhere to believe that the principles, ideals, and even interests they represent are those which in the long run will be most beneficial to society as a whole. Such a belief, with the consequent need to confirm and defend the principles themselves, tends to exaggeration in a society—such as El Salvador—with no appreciable ideological consensus. The lopsided electoral majorities of the PRUD era were meant to demonstrate to the doubtful and uncomprehending that the official party did, in fact, represent the real interests of the nation as a whole. At the same time, regular elections provided frequent opportunities for the ritual repudiation of deviant alternatives of the Right or Left.

In their appeals for support, prudistas made every attempt to confuse the concepts of party, government, and nation in the minds of

38. Charles W. Anderson, "Central American Political Parties: A Functional Approach," *Western Political Quarterly*, XV (1962), 125–39, suggests that in Central American politics the recognition of the capability to exercise power is "the equivalent of 'legitimacy' in advanced democracy." The power capability of the military establishment lies, of course, in its control of the institutional "means of violence." That of the urban "middle sectors," who provide most of the leadership for political parties in the Salvadoran system, lies in their capacity to mobilize mass support, which ideally will be expressed electorally but may also manifest itself through resistance or even open violence. Not surprisingly, individual power contenders seek to institutionalize the system that favors their particular power capability. Thus, civilian opposition parties demand strict enforcement of the electoral laws and rigid restrictions upon the political activities of the soldiers. Officers, on the other hand, resist these demands, although they obviously have no desire for a polity in which they would be constantly required to exercise their power capability in the form of naked force. The optimum solution is an alliance, such as the PRUD, between the ascendant faction within the army and the most cooperative civilian faction which combines recognition of the power capability of the former with the exercise of that of the latter through a system of regular elections managed to whatever extent necessary to compensate for the capabilities of rival alliances.

the electorate. To the extent that they worked from an established model at all, it was probably the Mexican Institutional Revolutionary party (Partido Revolucionario Institucional, PRI), also an "official" party, which claimed to be exclusive representative of the ideals of the Mexican Revolution and of the aspirations of the Mexican nation.[39] Although much less elaborately structured and firmly established than the PRI system, the PRUD resembled it in its attempts to organize support vertically within various sectors of society. The PRUD counted in its ranks leaders of business and industry, labor, professional groups, and the armed forces. The Salvadoran party differed fundamentally from the PRI, however, in the central and dominant role enjoyed within it by the military. Also unlike the PRI, the PRUD did not deal directly with the peasantry. The December 14 Revolution could in no way claim to be an agrarian movement. For support in the countryside, it counted upon the mobilizational capacity of its landholding allies, of local officials dependent for their positions upon the central government, and of the National Guard. The PRUD drew the majority of its national leaders from the capital where the nation's economic, political, and cultural elites were concentrated. In the provinces, by contrast, PRUD committees were virtually inactive in the periods between elections. A North American observer noted in 1955 that they were the object of little if any interest on the part of local residents.[40]

In practical terms, the PRUD system maintained its position by favoring its friends and punishing its enemies. Public works contracts were a common form of reward at the highest level, and other expressions of favor included patronage in the form of government employment. Manifestations of official displeasure included petty harassment, arbitrary arrest and detention, physical abuse, and even murder.[41] None of these practices has disappeared in El Salvador, although the incidence of serious physical harassment appears to be cyclical. During periods when levels of social and political tension are not high, official violence is more likely to be restricted to use against members of society with little standing, such as fractious or

39. White, El Salvador, 167.
40. Richard N. Adams, Cultural Surveys of Panama—Nicaragua—Guatemala—El Salvador—Honduras (Washington, D.C., 1957), 467, 472.
41. De la Selva, "El Salvador en 1960," 40–41.

uncooperative workers or peasants, rather than against individuals of high political or social visibility.[42] During times of crisis, on the other hand, governments have been known to turn the force of the repressive apparatus upon representatives of the urban political class. When this has happened in major proportions, as in the case of Hernández Martínez in 1944 or Lemus in 1960, it has generally been a sign of desperation and has contributed to temporary coalition against the existing regime on the part of otherwise incompatible interests.[43]

One of the difficulties in evaluating official violence in El Salvador lies in the need to identify its source. While it has not been the official policy of Salvadoran governments to murder or torture their citizens, it may be assumed that such actions have often been authorized at the presidential level. On the other hand, specific cases of violence have many times occurred on the initiative of personnel at much lower levels of command. This has been especially true in the countryside, where a symbiotic relationship has long existed between local landowners and National Guard commanders.[44] Cooperation with the oligarchy in the maintenance of "peace" in the countryside no doubt represents one of many ways in which Salvadoran military officers supplement their otherwise modest incomes. One of the names most commonly associated in rumor and popular repute with such activities throughout the 1950s and 1960s was that of General José Alberto Medrano, director-general of the National Guard until his sudden dismissal in November, 1970.[45]

Although there were obvious positive and negative incentives to support the PRUD, there were always individuals, especially in the

42. This has been one difficulty opposition parties have encountered since the early 1960s in their attempts to recruit leaders from the popular class. Urban professionals in the national leadership operate generally free of major governmental interference, but their local and less prestigious counterparts do not. Information from a leader of the Christian Democratic party, 1976.

43. White (El Salvador, 106), for instance, notes this tendency.

44. Legislation enacted under Martínez and still in force in the 1960s required National Guard agents "upon the first request of an hacendado or grower [to capture] any person or persons he may indicate as suspicious." Luna, "Dictadura fascista," 55.

45. White, El Salvador, 108. Much detail concerning repression in the years 1952–1954 came to light in a series of investigations in 1960 which were quite likely politically motivated by Osorio's break with Lemus the previous year. Among those implicated was Medrano, who had at the time been a major serving as chief of the investigations section of the National Police. Diario de Hoy (San Salvador), January 6, June 7, 1960.

capital with its more mobile and sophisticated style of life, who for reasons of principle or personal association opposed it. Such opposition generally took the outward form of political parties with such high-sounding names as the Authentic Constitutional party (Partido Auténtico Constitucional, PAC) or the Institutional Democratic party (Partido Institucional Democrático, PID). Since the rewards of electoral participation under the PRUD were few, there was little incentive for these parties to seek coherence or permanence and they consequently tended to be small, ephemeral, and conspiratorial. The only permanent opposition party throughout this period was the PAR.

The presidential election of 1956 provides an excellent example of the PRUD system in operation and simultaneously reveals some of its weaknesses. Osorio chose as his successor his minister of the interior, Lieutenant Colonel José María Lemus. This selection was not entirely popular within the army since many officers suspected Lemus of leftist tendencies and some had coveted the nomination for themselves. Many no doubt noted that Lemus had not been a member of the original conspiracy of 1948 and did not even join the PRUD until 1955. A number of Osorio's former associates emerged as presidential candidates representing ad hoc parties. Two of these, former inspector-general of the army Colonel Rafael Carranza Amaya of the PAC and former ambassador to Guatemala Colonel José Alberto Funes of the PID, were officers and as such enjoyed personal loyalties within the army that made them more than electoral threats. A third candidate, Roberto Edmundo Canessa, was a wealthy coffee planter who had served as Osorio's minister of justice and of foreign affairs.[46]

The candidate most dependent upon the electoral path and at the same time with the greatest potential for success in that direction was Canessa. Following his resignation from the foreign ministry, this suave, eloquent aristocrat had participated in the formation of the National Action party (Partido Acción Nacional, PAN), which, although it claimed to be a permanent, ideological party, resembled the other short-lived personalist organizations of the time. Canessa

46. Martz, Central America, 98; Parker, Central American Republics, 154–55; Elam, "Appeal to Arms," 150–53.

represented an essentially conservative position, but his rhetoric was populist and he called for social justice in a manner reminiscent of Alberto Masferrer. His primary criticism of the PRUD centered upon its authoritarianism, its militarism, and its fiscal corruption. The PAN also criticized Osorio and Lemus on the grounds that, since they were both Freemasons, they must therefore necessarily be anti-Catholic.[47]

Although Canessa financed his campaign out of his own fortune, he could hardly match the resources available to the government. Most of the press supported Lemus, not so much perhaps because of direct government control as because of political discretion. PRUD propaganda alternately described the PAN and its leaders as Fascists, Communists, and on occasion instruments of Yankee imperialism. More than once, the PRUD denounced the opposition candidates collectively as "leaders of the reaction." As the campaign progressed, Osorio, becoming less certain of a clear PRUD victory, brought more direct mechanisms of control into play. Barely a week before the election, the CCE disqualified Canessa on the basis of a technical error in his documentation, and at the same time suppressed the candidacy of Funes because of accusations of fiscal improprieties during his embassy to Guatemala. The two ex-candidates then joined Major José Alvaro Díaz of the Nationalist Democratic party (Partido Demócrata Nacionalista, PDN), whom the CCE had also stricken from the ballot, and united behind Colonel Carranza. When Canessa made a particularly strong radio speech attacking the government's electoral abuses, Osorio closed down the broadcast station and jailed his onetime foreign minister for "promoting public scandal." When Carranza himself then attempted to withdraw from the race, the authorities refused to permit it. The government ordered both him and PAR candidate Enrique Magaña Menéndez to continue campaigning. Immediately prior to the election, Osorio shuffled the military commands in order to isolate and neutralize units loyal to Carranza, Funes, or Díaz.[48]

47. Kennedy, *Middle Beat*, 176–77; José Salvador Guandique, *Roberto Edmundo Canessa: Directivo, fundador, ministro, candidato, víctima* (San Salvador, 1962), 111–51.
48. Martz, *Central America*, 99–102.

Colonel Lemus won the election with what a government publication modestly described as an "absolute majority" of 93 percent of the vote.[49] The opposition had already boycotted the elections of 1952 and 1954 because of government interference. This third experience with the PRUD machine served even more to lower respect for electoral politics. During his term in office, Lemus would attempt conciliation with members of the opposition but in the end he, like Osorio, would resort to repression, and in 1960 he and the PRUD would suffer the consequences of encouraging the opposition parties to operate outside the system. The official party that replaced the PRUD would retain many of its features but it would attempt to avoid this one error by promoting respect for the canons of representative democracy and the development of permanent, stable, establishment-oriented opposition parties.

The personality of José María Lemus was in some ways reminiscent of that of General Martínez. Of humble origins, Lemus had attended the National Military Academy with the aid of a financial grant and had graduated first in his class. He dabbled in poetry and scholarship and his pretensions as an intellectual partly accounted for some of the distrust of him among his fellow officers. As Martínez had done, Lemus placed heavy public emphasis upon fiscal integrity, compelling government officials to reveal their assets before the Supreme Court and campaigning in general against bribery and venality in government. Lemus continued Osorio's economic and social policies and revealed in his appeals for worker support a true gift for demagoguery.[50]

In the beginning, the new president was much more conciliatory in domestic political matters than his predecessor. Lemus did not condemn the opposition for its abstention as Osorio had done; he even invited representatives from the other parties to participate in

49. *Pensamiento político-revolucionario del teniente coronel José María Lemus* (San Salvador, 1956), 80. Government figures claimed that 712,000 Salvadorans voted in 1956. If this figure is accurate—the opposition charged it was too high by at least three times—it is perhaps a measure of the degree of apathy the PRUD system inspired that it was not until 1972, after eight years of relative electoral freedom and significant opposition party successes, that more than 700,000 voters would again participate in a Salvadoran election.

50. Kennedy, *Middle Beat*, 177–79. For a laudatory biography of Lemus that repeats the utterly fantastic official version of the 1956 election, see Eleodoro Ventocilla, *Lemus y la revolución salvadoreña* (Mexico, 1956).

his cabinet in order to form a truly "national" government. When his opponents spurned his offer, Lemus recruited among hitherto politically inactive members of the middle class and brought into public life for the first time a number of distinguished professionals. In order to emphasize the distinction between his regime and Osorio's, Lemus repealed the latter's antisedition "Defense of Democracy Law" and thus allowed political exiles to return to the country.[51] These attempts to govern wisely and liberally did not please everyone, of course. Military officers did not conceal their misgivings about the return of exiles, and the press largely abandoned the president when he opposed government subsidies to the newspapers and compelled them to print replies to stories and editorials. Finally, Lemus could never count upon support from politically active civilian democrats who refused to forgive the PRUD for the presidential election of 1956.[52]

Domestic conditions were not consistently propitious for the tolerant attitude Lemus sought to maintain. Osorio's retreat from his own avowed commitment to political democracy had been at least in part due to internal repercussions in El Salvador of contemporary events in Guatemala.[53] Concern over the possibility of infiltration had gradually lessened following the "pacification" of that country in 1954, but by mid-1959, a new source of subversion had appeared in the revolutionary regime led by Fidel Castro in Cuba. Primarily because of its antiimperialist content, the Castro movement found many sympathizers among the Salvadoran Left, concentrated as one might expect in the national university.

The republic's lone university had regained its juridicial autonomy with the Constitution of 1950 and become increasingly independent of the government, a trend which inevitably led to conflict. The powerful intellectual egos of Lemus and rector Romeo Fortín Magaña clashed in a heated debate over the issues of autonomy and

51. Martz, Central America, 103–107; Gallardo, Constituciones de El Salvador, I, 781.
52. Kennedy, Middle Beat, 177–78; Italo López Vallecillos, El periodismo en El Salvador (San Salvador, 1964), 437–39.
53. Although the PRUD government maintained scrupulously cordial relations with that of Colonel Jacobo Arbenz, Osorio exercised strict vigilance where the possibility of "Communist" subversion at home was concerned. Martz, Central America, 92–95; El Salvador, Secretaría de Información de la República, De la neutralidad vigilante a la mediación con Guatemala (San Salvador, 1954).

control of campus dissidents that appeared in the press in 1958. At the end of Fortín Magaña's term in 1959, the government blocked the election to succeed him of Arturo Romero, the hero of the struggle against Hernández Martínez and a long-time critic of military rule. The position, however, ultimately went to Napoleón Rodríguez Ruiz, who himself enjoyed extensive support from leftist students. University opposition to Lemus and enthusiasm for the Cuban Revolution increased throughout 1959 and into 1960. Government harassment was constant and the rolls of political prisoners routinely contained a large proportion of university students.[54]

Distrusted by the military, resented by the civilian population, and openly attacked by university leftists, Lemus had no need for economic difficulties. But they came, beginning in 1958 with a drop in coffee prices. By 1959, the Salvadoran economy, whose remarkable performance through the decade had done much to keep PRUD rule secure, was in a state of minor crisis. Lemus initiated government action to curtail production in hopes thereby of driving up prices, but this new state interference antagonized many growers. Meanwhile, rising costs and unemployment contributed to worker discontent. Disturbances broke out, and on the eleventh anniversary of the December 14 Revolution an angry crowd stoned the National Palace and tore down the flagpoles in Plaza Libertad, San Salvador's central square. Lemus blamed these troubles on Communist infiltrators, and arbitrary arrests and detentions were common throughout 1960.[55]

More difficulties appeared in connection with the municipal and assembly elections scheduled for April, 1960. Opposition to PRUD domination now began to unite in the National Civic Orientation Front (Frente Nacional de Orientación Cívica, FNOC), a loose coalition of political parties, student associations, and antigovernment labor organizations.[56] The most prestigious of the parties associated with the FNOC was the Renovating Action party (PAR). An outgrowth of the 1944 general strike that had brought down Martínez,

54. Mario Flores Macal, "Historia de la Universidad de El Salvador," *Anuario de Estudios Centroamericanos*, II (1976), 130–31; de la Selva, "El Salvador en 1960," 42–44; *Diario de Hoy*, January 8, 1960.

55. De la Selva, "El Salvador en 1960," 40–44; Martz, *Central America*, 107–108; Kennedy, *Middle Beat*, 179.

56. *Diario de Hoy*, January 23, 1960.

the PAR was the republic's oldest political party in continued existence and the preserve of a clique of liberal civilian politicians. Its program emphasized political reform and the only issue, not surprisingly, upon which the diverse membership of the FNOC could agree was that of political rights. In this sense, the front resembled any number of temporary coalitions of interest which have accomplished the destruction of arbitrary regimes throughout the modern history of Latin America only to find themselves unable to function in their place.

Much more youthful than the PAR and more disturbing to the authorities was the leftist April and May Revolutionary party (Partido Revolucionario Abril y Mayo, PRAM). Named for the two months of rebellion against Martínez in 1944, the PRAM was only beginning to organize in early 1960 and drew its leadership from the university community. The rhetoric of the party was frankly revolutionary and terrified the more conservative sectors of society. The government quickly denounced the boisterous young party as Communist and cited as proof its outspoken sympathy with the Cuban Revolution.[57]

Since the PAR was the only party belonging to the FNOC legally recognized by the CCE, it was the only one eligible to participate in the April elections. Although a brief attempt at formal coalition with the other parties failed, probably due to ideological antagonisms, the leaders of the PRAM nevertheless urged their members to support the PAR. The government, as usual, took no chances on the outcome of the election. PRUD candidates for the Legislative Assembly encountered no difficulty qualifying before the CCE for all fourteen departments, whereas PAR tickets won recognition in only seven. The regime also made use of intimidation. In the department of La Unión, for example, security agents arrested a PAR candidate while he was campaigning and held him eleven days without charge. Although the PRUD once again won every seat in the assembly, the PAR triumphed in six mayoralties including that of the capital where Gabriel Piloña Araujo, an economist and bank president, defeated the PRUD candidate, a local bakery owner. If the gov-

57. Parker, *Central American Republics*, 156; Unión Democrática Salvadoreña, "Barbudos comunistas invaden soberanía salvadoreña," *Diario de Hoy*, February 10, 1960. There were undoubtedly Communists in the PRAM but there were many non-Communists as well.

ernment's willingness to permit the PAR these token victories signified a desire for conciliation, it was a pathetic and ultimately vain attempt.[58]

President Lemus was quick to express his satisfaction with the "democratic" outcome of the voting and to offer the PAR officeholders his best wishes for success in their new positions. But the elections, in fact, resolved nothing. The PAR immediately filed a petition to overturn the results and ill feeling had in no way abated when the regime provided its opponents yet another cause célèbre. On July 14, the CCE announced its denial of the PRAM request for legal registration on the grounds that the party's ideology was Cuban-inspired and, therefore, a threat to the "democratic structure" of the country.[59] Following this decision, government agents subjected persons associated with the party to a wave of harassment, arrest, and detention.[60]

In an effort to marshal popular support for his embattled regime, Lemus announced on July 28 a massive program of reforms calling for the participation of both private and public sector capital and setting impressive goals in such areas as health, recreation, family income maintenance, and rural housing, diet, schooling, and credit. In his effort to enlist the masses in the campaign against the "Red menace," Lemus was able to count upon the support of the Roman Catholic church. On August 15, government trucks brought some twenty thousand campesinos to San Salvador to attend a church-sponsored rally and hear orators attack "Communist" parties such as the PRAM that wished to "abolish private property." The rally concluded with a mass offered by Archbishop Luis Chávez y González of San Salvador.[61] The importation of peasants to the city was significant; by this time Lemus could not have staged a show of popular support in the capital in any other manner. It has long been charac-

58. Parker, Central American Republics, 156; Diario de Hoy, March 6, 12, 27, April 1, 13, 21, 25, 1960. Although the PAR won the major municipal election in the department of San Salvador, the government had not permitted it to enter the assembly race there.

59. Consejo Central de Elecciones, "El Consejo . . . declara sin lugar solicitud de inscripción del 'P. R. A. M.' por tratarse de una agrupación antidemocrática," Diario de Hoy, July 16, 1960.

60. De la Selva, "El Salvador en 1960," 44; Diario de Hoy, August 7, 8, 9, 1960.

61. Diario de Hoy, July 29, August 16, 1960; De la Selva, "El Salvador en 1960," 44.

teristic of Salvadoran governments that, although their policies have been more beneficial to urbanites, they have made their ultimate appeal for support to the politically passive peasantry.

The evening following the great anti-Communist rally, a group of students took over Plaza Libertad and held a meeting of its own. Speakers praised the Cuban Revolution, attacked the government's actions against the PRAM, and loudly condemned the church hierarchy for interfering in politics. The regime responded immediately. Throughout the night of August 17 and into the next morning security forces rounded up and jailed the demonstrators and other members of the opposition. Despite efforts at mediation, the situation continued to deteriorate. On September 2, police dispersed a student demonstration with hoses and gas grenades. When the demonstrators sought refuge in the rectorate, security agents invaded the building and a young library employee caught in the ensuing violence was fatally injured. Many others, including the rector himself, were arrested, beaten, and jailed.[62] A fresh roundup of the regime's opponents began; among those taken and physically abused was Roberto Canessa. The government declared a thirty-day state of siege on September 5 and instituted press censorship. A plot to murder Lemus and his cabinet "discovered" by the police served as a pretext to maintain the suspension of guarantees throughout September and to renew it in October.[63]

In late 1960, sixteen years after the fall of the dictator Martínez, arbitrary violence and repression remained characteristic of Salvadoran politics. A single, official party ruled the country, and all other political organizations existed and operated under conditions subject to the caprice of its leaders. The government used a variety of means, both legal and extralegal, to render its opponents ineffectual.

62. De la Selva, "El Salvador en 1960," 44–45; Diario de Hoy, August 19, 25, September 1, 3, 4, 5, 1960; Parker, Central American Republics, 156; Flores Macal, "Historia de la Universidad," 131.

63. Prensa Gráfica (San Salvador), September 4, 6, 1960; Guandique, Canessa, 171–87; Diario de Hoy, September 6, 1960; Departamento de Relaciones Públicas, Casa Presidencial, "Es necesario que el Pueblo Salvadoreño conozca a algunos elementos extranjeros contratados expresamente por los líderes de la AGEUS, CGTS y comunistas para masacrar a las personas que honraban a la partria frente a la estatua de La Libertad," Diario de Hoy, September 22, 1960. From September 16–October 27, 1960, the only political coverage permitted San Salvador newspapers was in the form of presidential press releases such as that cited above. Their value is questionable.

Except in carefully regulated circumstances, it was impossible to oppose the regime through elections or in the courts. When its opponents became too vociferous, the ruling party denounced them as Communists or reactionaries and called upon the support of the church hierarchy in its campaign against them. When they took to the streets, it loosed the police upon them.

The primary weakness of this system, from the point of view of the PRUD, was its absolute dependence upon the army, whose creature, in the final analysis, it was. Lemus had never enjoyed the full confidence of the officer corps, but until now had been successful balancing his supporters against his opponents. As the political situation continued to worsen, however, more and more officers concluded that the president had lost control and they began to conspire against him. A key figure in the plan to depose Lemus was the president's old patron, Oscar Osorio himself. Dissatisfied with his successor's independence as well as his performance, the former president had split with the official party in 1959 to form his own organization, called initially the Authentic PRUD (PRUD Auténtico, PRUDA). He now saw in the regime's difficulties an opportunity to return to power.

Chapter II

The Early Days of the Christian Democratic Party

A North American newsmagazine described the military revolt that overthrew Lemus on the morning of October 26, 1960, as "one of the neatest, most peaceful coups d'état in Latin American history."[1] The actual victory salute was the only shooting heard in the capital. As the dust settled and the sleepy city gathered its senses, word spread that a six-man junta had assumed executive power. The new rulers dissolved the Legislative Assembly and the Supreme Court, lifted the state of siege, and within five hours of the initial call to rebellion threw open the doors of San Salvador's Central Penitentiary and released the prisoners of the Lemus regime into the welcoming arms of a cheering crowd. By nightfall a throng, estimated at more than eighty thousand, jammed into Plaza Libertad for an orderly celebration rally sponsored by the FNOC.[2]

Almost immediately, speculation spread regarding the ideological orientation of the new government. The osorista officers involved had recruited civilian participants among those sectors most disaffected with Lemus, the traditional liberal opposition and the university Left. The three civilian members of the new Governing Junta (Junta de Gobierno)—Fabio Castillo Figueroa, René Fortín Magaña, and Ricardo Falla Cáceres—were all young professionals with ties to the university. Castillo, at forty-two the oldest by a dozen years, was a a United States-trained pharmacologist of considerable intellectual reputation and an outspoken admirer of the Cuban Revolution. Falla Cáceres was an attorney, as was Fortín Magaña, the son of a former

1. "El Salvador: The Out—And the Ins," *Newsweek*, November 7, 1960, p. 66.
2. *Diario de Hoy*, October 27, 28, 1960.

rector. These men probably did not represent the views of the movement as a whole, but it was they whom critics identified when they warned of the possible emergence of a Castroite regime in El Salvador. Much to the members' annoyance, newsmen and critics frequently raised the issue of reputed Communists within the government. Although many countries quickly recognized the new regime in San Salvador, the United States, disturbed by these questions, declined to do so until December.[3]

The ideological heterogeneity within the movement that seized power from Lemus is apparent from the fact that it soon announced its sole mission to be the restoration of order and constitutionality and promised to conduct a free and open election as soon as possible. Substantial social and economic reforms were incompatible with the Junta's transitional role, its members concluded, and they would therefore attempt none. Fortín Magaña indicated the scope of political freedom the new government was prepared to allow when he announced that the hitherto proscribed April and May Revolutionary party (PRAM) would be allowed to participate in the scheduled election.[4]

The promise of free elections stimulated an increase in partisan activity. Already during the last two years of Lemus's rule, a number of new parties and organizations had emerged within the increasingly vocal opposition. Following the coup the proliferation continued until, by early 1961, there were nine political parties representing various positions, interests, and personalities.[5] Of all these new parties the most energetic, and ultimately the most long-lived, would prove to be the Christian Democratic party (Partido Demócrata Cristiano, PDC). The PDC grew out of a series of informal meetings in private homes where well-to-do and middle-class Salvadorans gathered to discuss national problems and politics. A regular topic at these meetings since about 1958 had been the ideas of Chris-

3. The military members of the Junta were Colonel César Yanes Urías, Lieutenant Colonel Miguel Angel Castillo, and Major Rubén Alonso Rosales. Parker, *Central American Republics*, 157; Kennedy, *Middle Beat*, 179–80; *Diario de Hoy*, November 17, 1960. Ironically, Havana delayed almost as long as Washington in recognizing the new Junta. Lemus, in spite of his charges of infiltration and subversion, had never broken relations with the Castro government. *Diario de Hoy*, September 30, December 4, 5, 1960.
4. *Diario de Hoy*, October 30, November 1, 1960.
5. Parker, *Central American Republics*, 155–58.

tian Democracy, an ideology which had come into its own in Europe after World War II and was, in the late fifties and early sixties, gaining currency in Latin America. Taking the lead in these discussions were two prominent San Salvador attorneys and law professors. Abraham Rodríguez and Roberto Lara Velado, the latter a writer or regional reputation on law, politics, and the philosophy of history.

The attendance at these sessions steadily grew larger and the ideas discussed more serious until, on November 21, 1960, more than one hundred persons gathered at the Hotel Internacional to organize themselves into a formal political party—a purely ideological party, they declared, whose programs would be based upon the principles of social Christianity. The eight-man organizing committee subsequently elected included Rodríguez and Lara Velado, along with León Cuéllar, Guillermo Ungo, Italo Giammattei, Juan Ricardo Ramírez Rauda, Julio Adolfo Rey Prendes, and José Napoleón Duarte.[6]

Duarte, although relatively new to the group, was a vocal participant in the proceedings and would become increasingly important within the movement as it developed. Born in San Salvador in 1926, he was the second of three sons of José Jesús Duarte, a minor industrialist. Although the family owned a prosperous confections business, Duarte made much in his subsequent political career of his humble origins, describing his father as a self-made man and his mother variously as a domestic servant, a seamstress, and a market vendor. Educated at the Liceo Salvadoreño, a Catholic secondary school, Duarte graduated in 1944, the year of the general strike against Hernández Martínez in which he participated as a member of the secondary students' strike committee. After Aguirre seized power, young Duarte made two unsuccessful attempts to join Arturo Romero's government-in-exile in Guatemala. The authorities captured him at the frontier and returned him to his father, who apparently decided to keep him from further mischief by sending him to study in the United States at the University of Notre Dame where his older brother Rolando was already a student. After receiving his degree in civil engineering in 1948, Duarte returned to El Salvador,

6. *Diario de Hoy*, November 23, 1960; José Napoleón Duarte Fuentes, "Intipucá" (unpublished manuscript, copy in possession of Professor Roland H. Ebel).

married the daughter of the owner of a large construction firm, and went into business with his father-in-law. He devoted his spare time to such service organizations as the Boy Scouts and the Red Cross, and to teaching courses in engineering at the national university and at the military academy. By his own account, Duarte took little interest in politics until 1960 when he accepted an invitation from a business associate to attend one of the Christian Democratic study groups. Following the formation of the party, when the organizing committee divided itself into functional subcommittees devoted to doctrine, propaganda, legal affairs, administration, and organization, Duarte assumed leadership of the organization branch—among the least controversial positions and at the same time among the most active, important, and powerful.[7]

The internal affairs of the Christian Democratic party in its early days reflected the uncertainties of the political situation in the country itself. By the time the nascent party met a second time, doctrinal differences had already begun to appear. The movement's ideological orientation was in general affirmative, but it had certain negative aspects as well. The decision to organize as a formal political party had come largely in response to the "Communist" threat represented by the Junta's sanction of the PRAM; the PDC had therefore attracted a number of conservatives who had been disaffected with the PRUD but had no sympathy for the new government either.[8] There was also a well-founded concern among the younger and more ideologically motivated participants—many of whom were students or professors at the national university—that discredited prudista politicians hoping to return to power would infiltrate the new party.

Upon learning of the formation of a Christian Democratic party in El Salvador, the Junta sent its secretary, Enrique Borgo Bustamante, to interview the organization's leadership. According to Duarte's account, Borgo assured the party committee of the Junta's blessing. The only exception to its general enthusiasm, he claimed, was the leftist Fabio Castillo. Privately, Borgo confessed himself troubled by

---

7. Duarte, "Intipucá"; José Napoleón Duarte Fuentes, taped interviews conducted by Professors Roland H. Ebel, Ralph Lee Woodward, Jr., et al., New Orleans, Louisiana, January 22–February 2, 1973 (Howard-Tilton Library, Tulane University), reels no. 1, 2.

8. "Democracia Cristiana salvadoreña en acción," Información Democrática Cristiana, IX (June, 1961), 4–5.

the fractiousness of Castillo and the growing restiveness of the "comunistas." He was afraid, he concluded, that increased leftist agitation might be causing anti-Junta sentiment to spread within the army.[9]

The Junta was well aware that it never enjoyed the full confidence of the armed forces. Soon after the coup, its members had made a tour of military installations to canvass reaction within the officer corps. A number of commanders were privy to the original plot, but there were many who were not and they were anxious to question the new leaders. The concerns shown in their questions gave no reason to believe the Junta's avowed commitment to democratization could expect their unqualified support. Would the military lose its accustomed ascendancy in national affairs? Would there be transfers or changes of command without consultation? What would be done to contain the Communists and Cuba-oriented leftist groups? The almost entirely civilian composition of the Junta's new cabinet did nothing to assuage the officers' fears.[10]

As if the suspicion of the army were not enough, the Junta de Gobierno also met pressure from the Left. The university, closed down during Lemus's brutal attempt to suppress dissidence, now reopened and the academic community began once again to call for reform. In an interview published early in November, rector Napoleón Rodríguez Ruiz, barely two weeks out of prison, called for sweeping changes to include agrarian and tax reform, new labor legislation, and a minimum wage. The FNOC meanwhile called for a purge of reactionary elements from the armed forces and the government, and labor and student groups demanded proof that the Junta was, in fact, moving toward civil supremacy. Rightist elements, both military and civilian, quickly came to fear that the Junta would ultimately succumb to so much subversive rhetoric and pressure. The genuine participation in the government of the three universitarios was, to conservative minds, particularly frightening.[11]

Amid rumors of an impending countercoup, the eight-man permanent committee of the Christian Democratic party met to discuss

9. Duarte, "Intipucá."
10. Elam, "Appeal to Arms," 156–57.
11. Diario de Hoy, October 27, November 9, 1960; Parker, Central American Republics, 157; Elam, "Appeal to Arms," 157–60.

the political situation. Military conspirators had already attempted to contact key members of the movement and party leaders worried that the officers planned to appropriate the party structure of the PDC as an instrument of legitimacy once they seized power. Having considered the alternatives and weighed the possible benefits and adverse consequences of PDC participation in a new government, the committee reached a decision which came to be known in party lore as "El Pacto de los Ocho"—the Agreement of the Eight. The individual officers believed to be involved in the plot were considered antidemocratic and authoritarian and the Christian Democratic movement could not hope to maintain its identity and integrity in a coalition with such forces. Therefore, the Eight decided, the party would under no circumstances accept participation in any government which might come to power by extraconstitutional means. Rather, it would automatically take up the opposition. With this question apparently settled, Duarte left El Salvador on a business trip to the United States.[12]

The Junta de Gobierno discovered and broke one conspiracy against it, but its reprieve was a short one. In the early morning hours of January 25, 1961, a group of young army officers rose against the government at the San Carlos barracks in downtown San Salvador. Other officers soon joined the insurrection and began to concentrate their troops at San Carlos while units loyal to the Junta marshalled at the Zapote, a fortress across town near the presidential palace. The insurgents surrounded the loyalist stronghold with tanks and artillery and demanded its surrender. Zapote offered no resistance. Fortín Magaña and Falla Cáceres fled to Guatemala, while rebel troops placed the remaining members of the Junta under arrest. The new government imposed martial law and brutally put down, at the cost of several lives, a popular rising in San Salvador.[13]

The coup, a manifesto circulated on the twenty-fifth explained,

12. Duarte, "Intipucá"; Duarte, taped interviews, reel no. 2. It is possible that the imprisonment in Nicaragua of Christian Democratic leaders Reinaldo Antonio Téfel Vélez and Pedro Joaquín Chamorro after an unsuccessful attempt to overthrow the Somozas by force in 1959 may have had a restraining effect upon their Salvadoran coreligionaries in 1961. Thomas W. Walker, *The Christian Democratic Movement in Nicaragua* (Tucson, 1970), 27.

13. Duarte, "Intipucá"; *Diario de Hoy*, January 26, 1961; Parker, *Central American Republics*, 158.

was a necessary reaction to the dangerous political tensions that had built up as a consequence of the Junta's having allowed extremist forces to run wild in the country. The rebels made no pretense that this was anything but a military undertaking. By late morning, officers from all the armed services gathered in a general meeting at San Carlos and chose Lieutenant Colonel Julio Adalberto Rivera and Colonel Aníbal Portillo to form a new junta. Rivera, who did all the talking, immediately declared the orientation of the rebellion to be primarily anti-Communist, anti-Castro, and anti-Cuba. Speaking to a group of medical students who sought him out in the afternoon, Rivera assured them that the coup's leaders were not reactionaries. But, he added significantly, the new regime would fight communism wherever and however it appeared, and, if necessary, it would abrogate the constitution and rule by decree to do so.[14] The United States, which had only hesitantly and belatedly recognized its predecessor, came immediately to the support of the new junta. Governments such as this, President John F. Kennedy later insisted, were very effective allies in the fight against communism.[15]

The officers who overthrew the "leftist" Junta de Gobierno were probably more militarist and more authoritarian than the men they replaced, but they were not because of this necessarily representatives of the oligarchy. They acted as much out of opposition to the possibility of a return by Osorio as to the threat of communism. There is no ideological homogeneity within the Salvadoran officer corps, but there is a virtual consensus on the need to defend the corporate interest of the military and on the role of the armed forces as the premier guardian of a narrowly interpreted constitutional order. Whenever a regime's actions or omissions have aroused sufficient popular opposition to make that order or those interests appear threatened, the officers have moved. Once in power, however, the direction a regime takes has always depended upon the personalities of the individual conspirators rather than upon the political orientation of the army as a whole; and the new regime's ability to remain in power has depended upon the manner in which it has balanced not

14. *Diario de Hoy,* January 26, 1961; Elam, "Appeal to Arms," 160–62; Kennedy, *Middle Beat,* 180–83.
15. Mauricio de la Selva, "El Salvador: Trés décadas de lucha," *Cuadernos Americanos,* CXX (January–February, 1962), 217.

only interests in the nation at large but also ideological differences within the officer corps.

Although they intended to maintain the army's control of the situation, the men who now ruled El Salvador moved quickly to bring civilians into the government. In the early morning hours of January 25, with the coup barely underway, rebel elements made an attempt to recruit the leadership of the PDC into a new junta. An officer fetched Abraham Rodríguez from his home and brought him to San Carlos. After he arrived, the insurgents told the party leader of the coup and urged him to join their projected Civil-Military Directorate (Directorio Cívico-Militar) and to assist in the immediate selection of a cabinet. Rodríguez, however, stood by the Agreement of the Eight and refused.[16] Undaunted, the golpistas eventually found three men willing to participate in a military government, although not necessarily identified with the reformist image it would later attempt to project. Of the civilians who thus joined Colonels Rivera and Portillo to form the new Directorio, San Salvador physician José Francisco Valiente and the lawyers Feliciano Avelar and José Antonio Rodríguez Porth, perhaps the best known was Rodríguez Porth. A strict laissez-faire liberal, he was a long-time defender and apologist for the country's most powerful economic interests. Long recognized as an implacable foe of corruption and imposition in government, and just as implacable a defender of the privileges of the rich, he was active in opposition movements throughout the period. Rodríguez Porth's reputation for personal integrity and political courage outweighed for certain purposes his social insensitivity to the extent that, although he was never a member of their party, the Christian Democrats had chosen him to represent them at the meetings the recently deposed Junta had called to rewrite the electoral law. The presence of Rodríguez Porth on the Directorio made a neat contrast to the abuse and peculation popularly identified with prudismo as well as the irresponsible radicalism said to characterize

16. Duarte, "Intipucá." Other civilians were not so reluctant. Of five lawyers listed in the press as having been consulted by the coup leaders, four received government positions. José Antonio Rodríguez Porth became a member of the ruling Directorio. Ricardo Avila Moreira and Carlos Guerra became minister and subsecretary of justice respectively. Rodolfo Cordón eventually became provisional president of the republic. Only Rodríguez of the PDC remained outside the regime. Diario de Hoy, January 26, 27, 1961.

the Junta de Gobierno, but it would prove to be inconsistent with the reformist pretensions of the new government. Although civilians outnumbered officers on the Directorio, their participation was apparently nominal and by April both Valiente and Rodríguez Porth had resigned.[17]

Duarte returned from the United States in the first week of February and found that the events of the previous few days had aggravated the internal differences in the PDC. A struggle had developed between those who believed the party should cooperate with the Directorio and those, mostly younger, who wished to continue adherence to the principle of the Agreement of the Eight. Party leaders, after discussing the situation, agreed that someone should speak with the members of the Directorio in an effort to assess the sincerity of their intentions. In his political memoir, Duarte, the chosen emissary, tells of his subsequent visit to the Casa Presidencial. Upon arriving at the palace, he found that the military members of the junta had segregated themselves from the civilians, taking up quarters in the opposite end of the building. Shown to the east wing, Duarte met with the civilian members for more than two hours. According to his account, Avelar complained that the PDC's refusal to support the Directorio jeopardized the establishment of democracy. Taking a sheaf of documents from his desk drawer, Avelar announced, "We have a rural welfare law, a rent reduction act, a labor code, and several economic measures to [obscenity] the rich." Duarte recalls that he left the Casa Presidencial with the unsettling impression that the Directorio planned to resort to demagoguery and embark upon a series of ill-conceived and unprogrammed economic and social changes.[18]

The Directorio in fact identified itself with the Alliance for Progress, and everywhere there was talk of "reform." Speaking in June at the inauguration of an urban housing project begun under a previous administration, Rivera declared that "in El Salvador, the exploitation of man by man has ended." He called this a warning to

17. Duarte, "Intipucá"; Duarte, taped interviews, reel no. 2; *Diario de Hoy*, April 7, 1961; Elam, "Appeal to Arms," 162.
18. Duarte, "Intipucá" (censorship in original). Although the progressive members of the PDC endorsed the professed social and economic aims of the new government, they explained their continued opposition in terms of the alleged lack of sincerity of Rivera and the colonels and the fact that the Directorio had assumed power unconstitutionally. "Democracia Christiana salvadoreña en acción," 4–5.

reactionaries, but he also had words for the extreme Left. "Our people," he announced, "do not want the blood money with which [the Communists] plan to consummate, here as they have elsewhere, their campaigns of agitation and demagoguery." On another occasion, he echoed the underlying premise of the Alliance for Progress: "If we do not make the reforms, the Communists will make them for us." [19]

In reality, Rivera merely continued the policies of the PRUD, adding a few innovations of his own, including a rural labor protection law that, among other things, required employers to give their workers one paid day of rest a week. The Directorio also nationalized the Central Reserve Bank and the national Mortgage Bank and imposed new restrictions on the export of currency. In an effort to bring relief to urban workers, the regime decreed a reduction in rents. And, of course, there were safely vague references to changes in the agrarian sector. Leftist critics were quick to belittle these efforts. They charged that large landowners would sooner dismiss extra workers than pay them more, that the fiscal and monetary decrees were in fact merely emergency measures designed to bail out the economically pressed oligarchy, and that the projected agrarian reform was strictly "made in U.S.A."—a program of soil conservation and reforestation that would not alter the existing system of land tenure.[20]

Although the regime's program completely failed to satisfy the Left, it infuriated the Right. Particularly objectionable to the oligarchs were measures designed to ease the burdens of the rural poor, especially a decree establishing a minimum dietary requirement for rural workers. Landowners angrily denounced "Bolsheviks" such as John Kennedy for presuming to interfere in the way they fed their workers. Under the spell of the Alliance for Progress, conservatives charged, Rivera and the Directorio were leading El Salvador "down the Fidel Castro road." While the new regime won few friends either among the radicals or among the oligarchy, it was not unpopular among the masses, and it found much support in

19. *Diario de Hoy*, June 20, 1961; "El Salvador: Vote for Reform," *Newsweek*, January 1, 1962, p. 25.
20. De la Selva, "El Salvador: Trés décadas de lucha," 218–19.

Washington. During 1961, El Salvador received more than $25 million in U.S. loans, with promises of more.[21]

The old Junta de Gobierno had declined to pursue social and economic reforms ostensibly because of its transitional nature. If the members of the Directorio showed no such reluctance, it was perhaps because they did not see themselves as transitional. As the weeks became months, at least two of the Directorio's members, Rivera and Portillo, began to exhibit presidential ambitions.[22]

The pressure upon the Christian Democrats to abandon their noncooperationist stand increased as the various presidential aspirants went about in search of support. Colonel Portillo, acting through the good offices of a mutual friend, Bishop Pedro Arnoldo Aparicio y Quintanilla of San Vicente, summoned Napoleón Duarte one day to the Casa Presidencial. According to Duarte, the colonel was prepared to offer the PDC a political alliance in which the party, in return for supporting his candidacy, could receive every ministry and every seat in the Legislative Assembly. Feliciano Avelar, Duarte's account continues, made a number of personal visits to Duarte's home to press the question of support for Portillo. On one of these occasions, with Roberto Lara Velado and Abraham Rodríguez also present, Avelar's entreaties became menacing. "If you do not go along," Duarte quotes him as saying, "you will be responsible for the dictatorship we will be forced to set up." As far as Duarte, Lara Velado, and Rodríguez were concerned, however, the Agreement of the Eight should prevail, dictatorship or no.[23]

Colonel Rivera's search for political support carried him on a fruitless mission to the veteran Renovating Action party (PAR) before he began contacting prominent members of the PDC. He showed up at Duarte's house one evening after dark, accompanied by a number of ranking government officials and carrying an offer much the same as Portillo's. The PDC could fill all the ministries and deputies' seats in return for its backing. Rivera, according to Duarte, expressed the fear that the Directorio's reforms were in danger from

21. "El Salvador: Fury," Newsweek, November 20, 1961, pp. 60–61; "El Salvador: Vote for Reform," 25.
22. Duarte, "Intipucá."
23. Ibid.; Duarte, taped interviews, reel no. 2.

vaguely defined "Communist" and "reactionary" elements and that only his continued leadership with PDC support could preserve them. The PDC leaders present that night took Rivera's fear of sinister antireform forces lightly. They reminded him that, if the wrong people ever did come to power, the army could always stage another coup d'état. In the end, Rivera received no support from the Christian Democrats.[24]

The Agreement of the Eight itself, however, was beginning to show the deteriorating effects of constant temptation. The general party membership had never ratified the doctrine and it was not at all certain that it reflected the view of the majority. Even one of the Eight, Italo Giammattei, had abandoned the position and become the center of a collaborationist clique which included Benjamín Interiano, Vicente Vilanova, and Miguel Muyshondt. Opposing this group were the leading ideologists of the party, Roberto Lara Velado and Abraham Rodríguez, who counted upon the support of a large segment of the youthful membership of the party.

These two factions were clearly drawn as the PDC went into its first national convention in May, 1961. At stake in a bitter struggle for leadership of the party were the secretary-generalship and a host of lesser national offices. The cooperationist candidate for secretary-general was Interiano, a physician from Santa Ana, while the purist choice was Lara Velado. Long before the issue came to a vote on the floor, the debate between the two factions degenerated into name-calling. The impasse between the two forces was the signal for a move prearranged between Napoleón Duarte and some of the junior members of the purist element. A young man took the floor and entered Duarte's name in nomination. The new nominee, having remained aloof from factional and ideological disputes while devoting his energies and talents to party organization, entered the contest without major enemies. The purists especially were inclined to support him because of his youth, but not before Adolfo Rey Prendes, Roberto Lara Velado (who was willing to defer to a more effective candidate), Abraham Rodríguez, and several members of the party's youth movement had subjected him to a grueling ideological catechism. All doubts resolved, the question went to a vote and

24. *Ibid.*

Duarte easily won election as the party's first permanent secretary-general. Purists carried most of the other offices as well. In the wake of the convention's overwhelming repudiation of their position, a number of major collaborationists left the party.[25]

Almost simultaneously with the purist triumph in the PDC convention, rumors began to circulate in San Salvador to the effect that the Directorio would form a party of its own to support its programs and the presidential candidacy of Rivera. As late as September 1, Interior Minister Colonel Francisco José Sol still denied knowledge of any such plan. He did admit, however, that there were efforts to form a party "with the same philosophy as the Directorio." Asked if such an organization could count upon official support, Sol replied that, naturally, it would enjoy "moral support." The following day, the capital learned of the formation of the National Conciliation party (Partido de Conciliación Nacional, PCN), a party composed of "elements representative of the various national sectors" and supporters of the Directorio.[26]

The PCN was the product of a meeting held in late August at the Quinta Santa Teresita, a government retreat in the resort community of Los Planes de Renderos. Among the more than one hundred Rivera supporters attending could be found a number of prominent PDC apostates. The eight-man provisional committee chosen to lead the new party included two former Christian Democrats, Vicente Vilanova and Italo Giammattei. Vilanova would become very important in the PCN and eventually serve as party secretary-general, president of the Supreme Court, and president of the Central Council of Elections. Another dissident, Benjamín Interiano, resigned the PDC later amid rumors the new official party would offer him its vice-presidential nomination. The nomination offer never materialized, but Interiano eventually became president of the PCN-dominated Legislative Assembly.[27]

Soon after the party's foundation, the Directorio announced elections to be held December 17, 1961, to choose a constituent assembly. The established parties not unexpectedly greeted the news of

25. The above account of the power struggle within the PDC is based upon Duarte, "Intipucá"; Duarte, taped interviews, reel no. 2.

26. *Diario de Hoy*, May 24, September 1, 3, 1961.

27. Duarte, taped interviews, reel no. 2; *Diario de Hoy*, September 3, 1961.

the PCN's formation and the precipitous call for elections with great indignation. Speakers from every conceivable political position harangued a large crowd gathered in Plaza Libertad to protest the new party. Representing the Christian Democrats, Abraham Rodríguez warned of the threat to democracy posed by an official party and, in his debut as a political speaker, Napoleón Duarte read a manifesto entitled "Treason Against the Salvadoran People!"[28]

In an interview in October, 1961, Rivera, who had resigned the government to assume leadership of the PCN, denied the charge that the new movement was a government party. He did admit, however, that it enjoyed the support of the Directorio. Furthermore, he announced that he would accept the presidential nomination should the party offer it. That it would, no one doubted. The colonel, in fact, planned to base his campaign on the Directorio's record of reform in a populist appeal to the lower and middle classes. With the complete support of the military and his own substantial popularity, there was no chance he would lose.[29]

Lack of organization among the opposition greatly enhanced Rivera's prospects. Recognizing their fundamental weakness against the *oficialistas*, the three major legal opposition groups—the PAR, the PDC, and Osorio's Social Democratic party (Partido Social Demócrata, PSD)—formed themselves into a united front, the Union of Democratic Parties (Unión de Partidos Democráticos, UPD). As in the case of the ill-fated opposition coalition of 1960, this union enjoyed no programmatic unity. The PAR was an experienced but ideologically bankrupt party of the moderate Right, while the PDC was a youthful and idealistic reform movement. The rightest PSD—because of Osorio's exile by the Directorio, now led by Agustín Alfaro, a liberal veteran of the struggle against Hernández Martínez—had little faith in the electoral process and, according to Duarte, thought more in terms of instigating a coup d'état than of running a coherent campaign. Throughout the campaign for the constituent assembly in late 1961, the UPD was never able to group itself solidly around a single

28. *Diario de Hoy*, September 12, 1961; Duarte, "Intipucá"; Duarte, taped interviews, reel no. 2; Partido Demócrata Cristiano, "¡¡Tración al pueblo salvadoreño!!" *Diario de Hoy*, September 4, 1961.
29. Kennedy, *Middle Beat*, 182.

valid issue. It accused the government party of demagoguery, but the PCN answered effectively with charges of reaction. The PCN reminded the voters of the Directorio's reforms and promised more, while the UPD was unable to list one thing it truly stood for as a whole. Having access to the resources of the entire government and military establishment, the official party was able to carry its message to every corner of the republic, while the UPD had to restrict its campaign to a small area around the capital. Not surprisingly, the PCN easily triumphed over its opposition, winning every single seat in the constituent assembly.[30]

When the assembly convened in January, 1962, it unanimously elected Eusebio Rodolfo Cordón Cea, a sixty-two-year-old lawyer, to serve as provisional president of the republic until Rivera could arrange his own legal election and installation. For the first time in thirty-one years, El Salvador had a civilian president, a fact Cordón exploited in his public appearances. At a press conference with the visiting president of Honduras, civilian Ramón Villeda Morales, Cordón declared his belief that every country in Latin America should have a civilian president. "Of course," he hastened to add, "that is just my personal opinion. The Salvadoran people will elect whom they choose."[31] Everyone knew who really ran the country.

The constituent assembly set aside the Constitution of 1950, then reenacted it with only minor changes. It also legalized the actions of the Junta de Gobierno and the Directorio, declared a general amnesty for everyone active in politics since 1960, and scheduled a presidential election for April 29, 1962. At a televised convention in early February, the PCN quickly nominated Colonel Rivera as its candidate for the presidency. As his vice-presidential candidate, Rivera chose Francisco Roberto Lima, El Salvador's ambassador to the United States. The choice of Lima was significant. In addition to being an economist with close ties to Washington and the Alliance for Progress, he was also an attorney who represented some of the wealthiest families in the country and was related to the oligarchy by marriage. If anyone could smooth over the natural antagonisms be-

30. Duarte, "Intipucá"; Duarte, taped interviews, reel no. 2; Diario de Hoy, December 20, 1961; Kennedy, Middle Beat, 186.
31. Diario de Hoy, January 9, February 27 (quotation), 1962.

tween the economic elite and the reformist regime, it was thought Lima could.[32]

The opposition, meanwhile, still hurt from the December election which many claimed the government had stolen for the official party.[33] The PAR now announced it would not participate in the April elections unless the regime met certain conditions. These included changes of command in the National Guard and National Police, a purge of those agencies thought to have cooperated with the PCN, reorganization of the CCE, and OAS supervision of the voting. The PAR also demanded immediate promulgation of the Civil Service Law, a project delayed since the Lemus years. When the government ignored these admittedly difficult demands, the PAR dropped out of the campaign.[34]

As for the Christian Democrats, they were currently engaged in an unedifying feud with the PRAM. During the December campaign for the constituent assembly, the PRAM had denounced the PDC for its personal ties to members of the regime, charging it with complicity in the coup which established the Directorio in January, 1961.[35] The PDC, in response, attacked the PRAM as a tool of Cuban communism and, for good measure, charged there were Communists within the official party as well. This brought an angry reply from the PCN to which the Christian Democrats responded by "revealing" the participation of the PRAM and the PCN in a Communist conspiracy to destroy El Salvador. Such irrational and unfounded accusations testify to the anger and confusion that pervaded the PDC in the wake of December's bitter electoral experience. In March, explaining they had no confidence in the intentions or good faith of the authorities, the Christian Democrats joined the PAR in declaring their

32. *Ibid.*, January 4, February 7, 8, 1962; Kennedy, *Middle Beat*, 186.

33. Unión de Partidos Democráticos, "Un golpe más a la democracia," *Diario de Hoy*, December 20, 1961; Guillermo Ungo, "La Guardia Nacional ganó las elecciones," *Diario de Hoy*, January 7, 1962. Ungo was administrative secretary of the PDC.

34. *Diario de Hoy*, March 5, 1962; Partido Acción Renovadora, "Ciudadanos," *Diario de Hoy*, February 10, 1962.

35. Duarte's brother Rolando served as minister of economy in the Directorio's cabinet. *Diario de Hoy*, February 9, 1961. The PDC explained to its sister parties of the world that the charges were understandable because it shared with the new regime its anticommunism, its opposition to Osorio, and its social and economic reformism. But, it concluded, other differences, presumably on the issue of political democracy, were too great to justify cooperation. "Democracia Cristiana salvadoreña en acción," 4–5.

resolve to abstain from the election.[36] The old pattern of *prudista* politics seemed to be reestablishing itself.

As the deadline for filing candidacies approached, it became apparent that none of the opposition parties intended to offer a nominee. The CCE asked the Legislative Assembly for a twenty-day extension but this too passed without the appearance of a candidate. Rivera remained unopposed except for a donkey the university students nominated as the "only candidate worthy to compete against officialism."[37]

Determined that his forthcoming victory by default should not be entirely meaningless, Rivera campaigned as hard as, or perhaps harder than, he would have had he been opposed. The success or failure of his presidency would depend largely upon his ability to carry out his commitment to bring El Salvador forward within the framework of the Alliance for Progress. This would mean persuading or forcing the oligarchy to accept some reforms, a task difficult enough in itself. In addition, it would mean inspiring confidence on the part of the opposition in the democratic process in El Salvador.

How Rivera would accomplish the latter was far from clear. Genuine electoral democracy seemed a long way from realization. To all appearances, El Salvador had come full circle in the less than two years since the fall of Lemus. Once again a government party ruled and a president had come to office unopposed. Meanwhile, the opposition was weak and in disarray. The young Christian Democratic party had suffered an acrimonious internal power struggle and seen the losers abandon its ranks to participate in the formation of the official party. The PDC's first electoral experience was a disaster, and in the wake of this defeat, the party had expended valuable time and energy in a futile polemic with another antigovernment organi-

36. Partido Demócrata Cristiano, "Frente al paredón comunista," *Diario de Hoy,* January 24, 1962; Partido Demócrata Cristiano, "Demócrata Cristiano contesta al Conciliación Nacional," *Diario de Hoy,* February 9, 1962; Partido Demócrata Cristiano, "¿Por qué el PRAM rehuye el debate periodístico?" *Diario de Hoy,* February 20, 1962; Partido de Conciliación Nacional, "Con relación a los conceptos," *Diario de Hoy,* February 6, 1962; Partido Demócrata Cristiano, "El Partido Demócrata Cristiano frente a las próximas elecciones," *Diario de Hoy,* March 5, 1962.

37. Asociación General de Estudiantes Universitarios Salvadoreños, "El pueblo tiene una cita," *Diario de Hoy,* April 16, 1962. The students chose Ambassador Lima as the donkey's running mate. Lima, a man with a limited sense of humor, spent the rest of the campaign denying he had solicited or accepted the nomination. *Diario de Hoy,* March 9, April 14, 16, 18, 1962.

zation. Professing a lack of faith in the democratic pretensions of Rivera and his party, the opposition now abstained entirely from a second round of elections. Finally, recent coups d'état had twice reaffirmed the crucial importance to any regime of retaining the confidence of the officer corps in its ability to maintain political tensions at a manageable level and to protect the military's corporate interests.

If Rivera wished to avoid the fate of Lemus, he must discover a way to keep his opponents out of the streets. As shall be seen, he ultimately did find such a device in the liberalization of the electoral system. Reforms promoted by Rivera made it possible for opposition parties beginning in 1964 to win seats in the Legislative Assembly and to expand beyond the token victories in municipal elections the PRUD had allowed in 1960. This electoral solution, by providing a permanent institutional forum for the expression of dissent as well as access, however limited, to decision-making and patronage, promoted the growth of the relatively well-organized and ideologically coherent Christian Democratic party. At the same time it mitigated against the traditional alphabetical proliferation of mini-parties. The electoral solution also enhanced the prestige of Rivera and El Salvador in the estimation of influential North Americans in government, journalism, and academe, whose approval is not an inconsequential factor in the formula for regime survival in Central America.

Chapter III

Christian Democracy in El Salvador

The period of democratic experimentation in El Salvador in the 1960s coincided with a time of apparent electoral stability in many Latin American countries and thus served to confirm the beliefs of those who argued that the process of political development was linear and cumulative and would inevitably lead to a golden era of civil supremacy and parliamentary democracy. Somehow the collapse in 1964 of the boisterous Brazilian democracy went unappreciated amidst the general optimism. Few people would have guessed that the authoritarianism of the Brazilian colonels and not such enthusiastically welcomed democratic regimes as that of Rómulo Betancourt in Venezuela would come to characterize Latin America in the 1970s or that even such countries of long democratic tradition as Chile and Uruguay would ultimately produce repressive regimes.

What non-Communist progressives sought in Latin America in the years immediately following the Cuban Revolution was a safe reformist alternative to the threat of a proliferation of Castroist revolutions in the area. The most substantial tradition for such a movement was that provided by the Peruvian APRA and such other "social democratic" parties as Acción Democrática in Venezuela and Liberación Nacional in Costa Rica. Although these movements enjoyed impeccable democratic credentials forged in the struggle against dictatorship that passed for revolutionary activity in most of Latin America before the triumph of Fidel Castro, they had over the years grown staid and conservative. Another possible model, although one peculiar to a single country, was the Mexican PRI. Sal-

49

vadorans were familiar enough with this alternative; it was the one imperfectly emulated first by the PRUD and then by the PCN. North American liberals called the Mexican system the "preferred revolution" when they compared it with the Cuban experience,[1] but it was not an ideal solution. The single-party model was deficient in terms of political democracy, and the system itself seemed too much the singular outcome of a unique evolutionary process to have general applicability.

A third alternative, which must have seemed to come virtually from nowhere in the late 1950s and early 1960s, was Christian Democracy. The expansion of this movement was remarkable. By 1964, the year of the first Christian Democratic victories in El Salvador, there were similar parties in sixteen of the twenty Latin American republics. Only Honduras, Paraguay, Haiti, and Cuba lacked them. For the most part, Christian Democracy in Latin America was a relatively recent phenomenon. Although the oldest parties, those of Uruguay and Chile, were of much earlier origin, most of the parties were founded in the period following World War II. Their leaders were inspired by the role European Christian Democratic parties had played in the postwar recovery of West Germany, Italy, and France.[2]

The early 1960s were important years for Christian Democracy in all of Latin America. In 1963, the Peruvian Christian Democrats joined the government in coalition with Fernando Belaúnde Terry's Acción Popular and, by the end of the year, elected one of their own leaders mayor of Lima. In Venezuela, Rafael Caldera's Social Christian COPEI placed second in the 1963 presidential race and was the only party that actually gained in voter support over the previous

1. Stanley R. Ross, "Mexico: The Preferred Revolution," in Joseph Maier and Richard W. Weatherhead (eds.), Politics of Change in Latin America (New York, 1964), 140–51.

2. "The Rising Force," Time, September 18, 1964, pp. 48, 53; "Socialistas que rezan," Visión, July 26, 1963, pp. 24–25. The best comprehensive work in English on Latin American Christian Democracy in general is Edward J. Williams, Latin American Christian Democratic Parties (Knoxville, Tenn., 1967). Of particular interest also are Frederick C. Turner, Catholicism and Political Development in Latin America (Chapel Hill, N.C., 1971), especially Chap. 1; Robert J. Alexander, The Venezuelan Democratic Revolution (New Brunswick, N.J., 1964); Rafael Caldera, The Growth of Christian Democracy and its Influence on the Social Reality of Latin America (New York, 1965); Franklin Tugwell, "The Christian Democrats of Venezuela," Journal of Inter-American Studies, VII (1965), 245–68; and Giles Wayland-Smith, The Christian Democratic Party in Chile: A Study of Political Organization and Activity with Primary Emphasis on the Local Level (Cuernavaca, Mex., 1969).

elections. By far the most successful of all the Latin American Christian Democratic parties in 1964, however, was the Chilean PDC. In the municipal elections in 1963 the Christian Democrats had suddenly replaced the Radicals as Chile's leading political party. Then in 1964 Eduardo Frei Montalva's triumph in the presidential race made Chile the first Latin American republic to come under a modern Christian Democratic administration.[3]

Many observers hailed Frei's victory as the coming of a new era in Latin America—an era in which social injustice would fall beneath the onslaught of humane and Christian government operating in an open atmosphere of democracy and liberty. To reformers, progressives, even revolutionaries who found communism distasteful, Christian Democracy seemed to offer an excellent alternative. Frei's defeat of a Communist-backed coalition led by Salvador Allende Gossens offered encouragement to those who feared that all of Latin America was in imminent danger of Communist takeover. The Communists themselves recognized the potential significance of this setback. Although Radio Havana attributed the Frei victory to fraud, intimidation, and bribery, Cuban Prime Minister Fidel Castro candidly admitted that "sometimes our opponents surpass us in ability."[4]

By the end of the decade, it would become abundantly clear that Christian Democracy was no more a panacea or a wave of the future than had been the APRA movement or even the guerrilla socialism practiced by Castro in Cuba. In particular, observers tended to overlook the importance of the fact that Frei owed his victory to a coalition with Chile's intransigent right. Still, in 1964 when Frei's triumph was fresh, all was euphoria and optimism.

Latin American Christian Democrats state with pride that theirs is an ideological movement, a claim significant in a region where political parties have seldom been more than vehicles for personal ambition, with little goal other than the conquest and enjoyment of high political office. From the beginning, the leaders of the Salvado-

3. Rafael Caldera, "Democratic Revolutions," *Commonweal*, October 29, 1965, p. 122.
4. "The Rising Force," 53. This article is an excellent example of the enthusiastic and optimistic reception given the Latin American Christian Democrats by foreign observers. See also Leonard Gross, *The Last, Best Hope: Eduardo Frei and Chilean Democracy* (New York, 1967).

ran PDC emphasized this major difference between their party and the crowd of ephemeral, personalist parties that continued to characterize Salvadoran politics. Their party, they declared upon announcing its formation, would be "permanent [and] purely ideological in character, . . . something new in our country."[5]

The most important single source of inspiration for the Christian Democratic movement has been the social doctrine of the Roman Catholic church, especially as set forth in Pope Leo XIII's encyclical *Rerum Novarum* (1891). Leo attacked both Marxist socialism and classical liberalism. He admitted the similarity between many socialist tenets and the teachings of the Gospel, but he condemned the notions of economic materialism and determinism as denials of the spiritual nature of man. He defended private property as a natural right but cautioned that it must be held and used in a socially just manner. He upheld the rights of labor against capitalist exploitation and called for state intervention on behalf of workers. He urged trade unionization, collective bargaining, experiments in agricultural cooperatives, cooperation among the classes (whose natural enmity he denied), and the preservation and strengthening of such traditional social institutions as church and family. In short, his was a call for Christians to work together to build a better society based upon traditional spiritual values and founded in the teachings of the Catholic church. Forty years later, Pope Pius XI echoed Leo's ideas in his *Quadraggesimo Anno* (1931), a condemnation of laissez-faire liberalism and defense of proletarian organization. More recently, two encyclicals of Pope John XXIII, *Mater et Magistra* and *Pacem in Terris*, have provided further reinforcement for the Social Christian position as has the important *Populorum Progressio* (1967) of Paul VI.[6]

Perhaps the most important lay spokesman for Christian Democracy in the post-World War II period has been the French philosopher Jacques Maritain, whose writings urging a Christian, pluralistic, democratic social order have been widely read in Latin America as well as in Europe. Latin America itself has produced a number of highly able spokesmen for Social Christianity, not the least of whom

5. *Diario de Hoy*, November 23, 1960.
6. Carlton J. H. Hayes, *A Generation of Materialism, 1871–1900* (New York, 1963), 144; Williams, *Latin American Christian Democratic Parties*, 26.

have been Eduardo Frei (president of Chile, 1964–1970) and Rafael Caldera (president of Venezuela, 1969–1974).[7] The Christian Democratic party of El Salvador emerged from a series of meetings dedicated to the study of the writings of these men and others. The men who participated in these discussions were mostly lawyers who had studied political theory at the National University. They were also Catholics attracted by the spiritual foundation of Christian Democracy. Roberto Lara Velado, Abraham Rodríguez, and such younger men as the student leaders Héctor Dada Hirezi, José Ovidio Hernández, and Carlos Herrera Rebollo, were all familiar with the works of Maritain, Caldera, and Frei. On the other hand, some were not so well read. Party leader Napoleón Duarte, an engineer by training and profession, freely admits the deficiency of his own ideological preparation. In the early days of the movement, he devoted his time and talent almost exclusively to the mechanical aspects of party organization, leaving theory to the lawyers and humanists. Whenever he did speak on ideology or program, Rodríguez and Lara Velado would carefully coach him in advance.[8]

Not surprisingly, the Catholic background of Christian Democracy at times caused the movement to be identified in the public mind with the church itself. In Latin America, where passivism and obscurantism rather than progressivism traditionally characterized the social attitude of the ecclesiastical establishment, this was potentially a source of great misunderstanding and embarrassment. The radical and Marxist Left often criticized the Christian Democrats for their supposed "clericalism."[9] The truth was, however, that, despite the religious inspiration and symbolism evident in the movement, there were no formal and very few informal ties between it and the church. In fact, in most cases neither the parties nor the church was willing to accept or encourage any such connection. Christian Democracy is not a religion. It is a social and political movement concerned with worldly rather than heavenly kingdoms. The founders

7. Williams, *Latin American Christian Democratic Parties*, 26; Georgie Anne Geyer, "Latin America: The Rise of a New Non-Communist Left," *Saturday Review*, July 22, 1967, p. 23.
8. Duarte, taped interviews, reel no. 2.
9. For example, Carlos M. Rama, "La religión en América Latina," *Casa de las Américas*, VI (March–April, 1966), 11–26.

of the Salvadoran party made their position as clear as possible when they declared that the PDC "categorically denies that it is in any way directed by the Catholic Church or any other religious body, believing that politics and religion should not be mixed." [10]

In spite of the lack of formal ecclesiastical connections, most PDC members in El Salvador have been Catholics, either nominal or devout. This is only natural, Lara Velado once replied sarcastically to a critic, since the majority of Salvadorans are Catholics. The Duarte family is demonstratively Catholic. Napoleón and his brother Rolando are both graduates of the University of Notre Dame. Another brother, José Alejandro, is a progressive priest who endorsed the goals of the PDC and later became involved in more direct clerical social activism. As a youth, Abraham Rodríguez was a leader of the University Catholic Action movement (Acción Católica Universitaria Salvadoreña, ACUS), and a number of other party members have belonged to it as well. But there have also been Protestants in the party and, as Lara Velado has maintained, even Jews, agnostics, and atheists would be welcome assuming they subscribed to the socioeconomic and political philosophy of Christian Democracy. [11]

While the Left has attacked the Christian Democrats for their "clericalism," the Catholic Right has generally disowned them for their progressivism. There are some issues upon which the PDC and conservative churchmen and laity have found agreement, such as support for religious education and opposition to birth control, [12] but there are many others on which they have remained antagonists.

10. "Foundation of the Christian Democratic Party of Salvador," Christian Democratic Review, II (May, 1961), 10, cited in Williams, Latin American Christian Democratic Parties, 73.

11. Roberto Lara Velado, "La Democracia Cristiana salvadoreña y sus detractores, II: El partido y la iglesia," Prensa Gráfica, October 24, 1966; Duarte, taped interviews, reel no. 3; Partido Demócrata Cristiano, "Sexto aniversario celebra el P. D. C.," Prensa Gráfica, November 25, 1966.

12. The PDC delegation in the Legislative Assembly, for instance, supported the legislation which permitted the establishment of the Roman Catholic José Simeón Cañas University in San Salvador. Paul R. Hoopes, "El Salvador," in Ben G. Burnett and Kenneth F. Johnson (eds.), Political Forces in Latin America: Dimensions of the Quest for Stability (Belmont, Calif., 1970), 107. On birth control, see Roberto Lara Velado, "Aspecto socio-económico del control de la natalidad," La Universidad, XCII (January–February, 1967), 57–69. Lara Velado's objections to any policy of controlling population growth are based upon utilitarian rather than moral grounds, although he feels strongly about the latter as well. He asserts that a growing population is ultimately necessary to the development of a dynamic economy and that overpopulation is a symptom of underdevelopment, not a cause.

In addition to the accusation of clericalism, another charge frequently leveled at the Christian Democrats was that they were an international party. They denied this, but Christian Democracy was in fact an international movement and the individual parties always stressed their ties with one another. Since 1947 there has been a hemispherewide confederation of Social Christian parties, the Christian Democratic Organization of America (Organización Demócrata Cristiana de América, ODCA), which, while it cannot compel adherence to its polities, does exercise a great deal of influence over its member organizations. A constitutional provision designed to disable the Communist party by prohibiting political organizations with international affiliations prevented the Salvadoran PDC from formally associating itself with the other Latin American parties. Because the law made an exception for associations limited to Central America, however, the Salvadoran Christian Democrats were able in 1966 to participate in the founding of a Central American Christian Democratic Union (Unión Demócrata Cristiana Centro-Americana, UDCCA), of which Abraham Rodríguez served as executive secretary.[13]

In the eyes of nationalists both right and left, the international character of the Christian Democratic movement was only slightly more suspect than its emphasis upon a foreign policy of international cooperation. The Salvadoran PDC was as concerned with national autonomy and rights as any nationalist group, but—with the notable exception of its wholehearted support of the government's position in the 1969 war with Honduras—it generally translated this concern into a call for cooperation, regional integration, and international social justice, instead of an irrational isolationism. Of particular interest to El Salvador's Christian Democrats was the strengthening of the Latin position in the Organization of American States, the defense of the rights of smaller countries in the United Nations and of producer nations in world markets, and the economic integration of Central America.[14]

The PDC, in fact, favored an international order from which im-

13. Williams, Latin American Christian Democratic Parties, 134; El Salvador Election Factbook, March 5, 1967 (Washington, D.C., 1967), 17; Partido Demócrata Cristiano, "Sexto aniversario celebra el P. D. C."

14. See the foreign affairs plank of the PDC's 1967 presidential platform, Prensa Gráfica, October 26, 1966.

perialism and colonialism of all types were absent. To critics who charged that Christian Democrats took their orders from Rome, Caracas, or Santiago de Chile, Roberto Lara Velado replied not only that this was not true but also that, even if it were, these were hardly sinister imperial powers on a level with Washington, Moscow, or Peking, from whom the official party and the Marxists derived their inspiration.[15] Christian Democracy, Lara Velado explained, differed from the two major alternatives in that it was not an imperial ideology. According to him, liberalism and communism both required the subordination of smaller states to larger ones in order to function properly. Thus, while the liberal and Communist systems achieved their highest expression in the world's three great imperial states— the United States, Russia, and China—Christian Democracy was more suited to the small national or territorial state that wished only to safeguard its own rights and autonomy.[16]

The Salvadoran PDC repeatedly condemned colonialism and was as critical of the Soviet version as of the North American, citing Cuba as a victim of both forms. The party's first national convention in San Salvador in 1961 condemned the Cuban Revolution as a betrayal of the Cuban people's struggle for liberation and warned of the threat it posed of Soviet domination in the Caribbean. Equally conscious of a threat from the North, the Christian Democrat minority in the Salvadoran Legislative Assembly successfully urged the passage in 1965 of a resolution condemning the United States military intervention in the Dominican Republic.[17] On the issue of economic penetration, Lara Velado opposed the establishment of a local branch of the First National City Bank of New York as "another spearhead of foreign imperialism," and Abraham Rodríguez, in his 1967 presidential campaign, condemned the Rivera government's policy of floating large foreign loans for public works projects, then using the money to buy foreign materials and hire imported workers and technicians.[18] In 1969, José Napoleón Duarte, then serving as mayor of San

15. Roberto Lara Velado, "En resumidas cuentas," Prensa Gráfica, November 5, 1966.

16. Roberto Lara Velado, "La Democracia Cristiana salvadoreña y sus detractores, III: Los partidos internacionales," Prensa Gráfica, October 26, 1966.

17. Diario de Hoy, May 19, 1961. The Casa Presidencial quickly disassociated itself from the legislature's declaration. Lara Velado, "La Democracia Cristiana salvadoreña y sus detractores, III."

18. Prensa Gráfica, February 18, 1964; Diario de Hoy, February 10, 1967.

Salvador, shocked a gathering of Central American municipal officials in Vera Cruz, Mexico, by condemning United States policy in Latin America as designed to "maintain the Iberoamerican countries in a condition of direct dependence upon the international political decisions most beneficial to the United States, both at the hemispheric and world levels. Thus [the North Americans] preach to us of democracy while everywhere they support dictatorships."[19]

Continentwide, Christian Democrats resist location within the simplistic typology of Right-versus-Left. A Nicaraguan Social Christian leader has made perhaps the most precise statement of this problem:

> If by left we understand the struggle for social justice, the great battle for the social and economic redemption of the people, the incorporation of workers and peasants into the mainstream of culture and civilization, then undoubtedly we are leftists. If, however, by left is understood historical materialism, communist totalitarianism, and the suppression of liberty, then in no way are we leftists. If by right is understood the conservation of the spiritual values of civilization, the historical legacy of humanity, and the dignity and liberty of man, then there can be no doubt that we are rightists. But if by right we understand the conservation of an economic order based on the exploitation of man by man, on social injustice, we energetically refuse the name of rightists.[20]

Roberto Lara Velado insisted from the beginning that Christian Democracy could not be classified in the same system with liberalism and socialism, both of which Christian Democrats rejected for their materialism and determinism. Rather, the PDC, by the addition of a spiritual, humane element alien to the established materialist ideologies, transcended them and became a third, autonomous position.[21]

Adhering to Catholic teaching, Christian Democrats rejected the belief in the ultimate perfectability of man and the determinism therefore inherent in laissez-faire liberalism and Marxist socialism. But the movement itself drew fire from critics for the "determinism"

19. Manuel Mejido, "Hablan cuatro alcaldes centroamericanos: Pesimismo sobre un cambio en las relaciones con EU," Excélsior, May 19, 1969, pp. 1, 19, 23; Diario de Hoy, June 9, 1969.
20. Reinaldo Antonio Téfel Vélez, "Izquierdas y derechas en Latinoamérica y el movimiento socialcristiano," Revista Conservadora del Pensamiento Centroamericano, IV (August, 1962), 18.
21. Roberto Lara Velado, "Ni liberalismo, ni socialismo, sino Democracia Cristiana," Diario de Hoy, June 5, 1961.

supposedly implicit in its own belief in the inevitability of revolution in Latin America. Christian Democrats believed that the inequities in Latin American society must eventually lead to violence if they were not corrected. Since they did not believe that most of these inequities could be remedied short of drastic structural change, they called in reality for a "revolution" of their own, a peaceful, Christian revolution to prevent a violent, materialist one.[22]

The word "revolution" often appeared in the polemics of the Salvadoran party. A revolution, the party declared in 1966, was unavoidable. But, spokesmen hastened to add, the Christian Democratic revolution would not be violent or destructive of national institutions. Rather it would be a scientifically and technically planned process designed to effect, within the limits of liberty and national reality, a peaceful and rapid change in political, economic, and social structures.[23] In his political memoirs, Napoleón Duarte rejects the Marxian notion that the clash of thesis and antithesis must necessarily lead to a constructive synthesis. It is just as likely to lead to the reinforcement of the thesis or to an orgy of wasteful violence. Change is necessary, Duarte is in effect saying, but it cannot be undertaken lightly or without careful preparation. He likens the revolution contemplated by the Christian Democrats to a controlled chain reaction produced in a nuclear reactor.[24]

The Christian Democratic call for "revolution in liberty" aroused suspicion among observers of all political persuasions. One Uruguayan leftist saw it as an attempt on the part of the Catholic bourgeoisie to "short-circuit" the aspirations of the workers by bringing about minor social change, preserving capitalism, and restoring the temporal authority of the church.[25] In El Salvador, a right-wing clerical polemicist who often faulted the Salvadoran PDC for the thoughts and actions of its Chilean counterpart accused the Christian Democrats of adopting Marxist theory and giving the concept of revolution priority over that of liberty. The notion of the inevitability of such a revolution he condemned as Hegelian and, therefore, presumably determinist, Marxist, and heretical. Finally, he charged that

22. Caldera, "Democratic Revolutions," 121.
23. Partido Demócrata Cristiano, "Sexto aniversario celebra el P. D. C."
24. Duarte, "Intipucá."
25. Rama, "Religión en América Latina," 25.

Christian Democrats prefaced democracy with the word "Christian" for the same reason Communists used "people's"—to deceive the masses.[26]

The Christian Democrats had quite definite ideas about the kind of world they hoped to build as a result of their "revolution." The new regime would above all be one of democracy and social justice. From the beginning the Salvadoran party declared these popular aspirations to be its overriding goals. The PDC used the word democracy in the classic political sense—open elections, respect for the dignity of the individual, the guarantee of human and constitutional rights, and an end to persecution and imposition. By social justice the Christian Democrats meant the just payment of labor, the economic and cultural redemption of the peasantry, and a more equitable distribution of property and the fruits of production. Party leaders here placed the greatest stress on the right of the individual Salvadoran to gain a decent living from his work. Above and beyond any moral basis for this position, both Duarte and Lara Velado argued that a more just diffusion of Salvadoran wealth would be beneficial to the nation as a whole, as the increased number of consumers would serve as a stimulus to industrial growth and the widened propertied class would contribute to political stability.[27]

The minimum acceptable standard of living in El Salvador, as defined by party leaders at a round table discussion in 1962, would be one in which every citizen would be guaranteed: (1) a nutritious and filling diet; (2) sanitary, comfortable housing; (3) adequate shoes and clothing; (4) access to medicine and health care; (5) the basic skills of literacy and sufficient vocational preparation to contribute in a productive fashion to the economy; (6) protection in his or her old age. This program was reminiscent of Alberto Masferrer's *Mínimum vital* but, as the PDC recognized in its first presidential platform, if what Masferrer urged was difficult in the economic and

26. Ricardo Fuentes Castellanos, "Democracia cristiana y revolución," *Diario de Hoy*, March 4, 1967; "La democracia cristiana y el marxismo," *Diario de Hoy*, March 13, 1967. Fuentes Castellanos was an extremely conservative priest who vehemently opposed liturgical innovation as well as social and political change.

27. Partido Demócrata Cristiano, "La Democracia Cristiana ante el problema social," *Diario de Hoy*, March 2, 1961; José Napoleón Duarte, "Democracia cristiana y justicia social," *Diario de Hoy*, March 28, 1961; Roberto Lara Velado, "Los pronunciamientos sociales de la Democracia Cristiana," *Diario de Hoy*, March 22, 1961.

social context of the 1920s and 1930s, it was more so in the 1960s given the large increase in population in the intervening years. Hence, the Christian Democrats' insistence on the necessity of serious structural reform.[28]

The key to social justice, according to the PDC, was structural reform designed to remove the obstacles the old order posed to the economic development of the country. It first set forth its plans to accomplish this on a national level in the presidential campaign of 1966–1967. In their platform of that year, the Christian Democrats declared their primary goal to be full employment at dignified wage levels. Since El Salvador had a large corps of unemployed or underemployed citizens, the necessity of a high rate of economic growth was obvious—especially since the rapid increase in population meant that more than 30,000 new workers joined the labor force each year. As more than 60 percent of the existing labor force was already competing for a limited amount of work in the agricultural sector, the PDC hoped to incorporate the increment into nonagricultural pursuits by fostering industrial development and national productivity in general. How this prodigious feat was to be accomplished was never clear, but party leaders constantly invoked the sacred precepts of economic planning and state direction as the answer to the nation's ills.[29]

While they called for industrialization, the Christian Democrats placed virtually equal emphasis upon increasing productivity in the agricultural sphere. They urged a program to increase crop yields, but warned against the ruthless exploitation of the nation's soil resources without attention to the problem of conservation—a particularly important consideration in a country as small as El Salvador. The agricultural problem had a troublesome social aspect as well. Something must be done to insure a decent living for the vast numbers of landless or nearly landless peasants who lived by selling

28. *Diario de Hoy*, May 17, 1962; *Prensa Gráfica*, October 14, 1966.
29. *Prensa Gráfica*, October 14, 1966. For the continuing emphasis upon planning, see also particularly three early essays by José Napoleón Duarte: "Democracia Cristiana y justicia social"; "Estudios sobre objetivos del Partido Demócrata Cristiano, I: Unidad de gobierno," *Diario de Hoy*, May 25, 1961; and "Estudios sobre objetivos del Partido Demócrata Cristiano, IV: Aumento de la producción nacional," *Diario de Hoy*, June 3, 4, 1961. For the approach to industrialization, economic planning, and state intervention on the part of Latin American Christian Democratic parties in general, see Williams, *Latin American Christian Democratic Parties*, 123–27.

their labor to the large operators. The demand for itinerant farm workers was seasonal. The PDC estimated in 1967 that the average laboring *campesino* worked only 120 days out of the year and guessed the productive income lost each year due to this situation to be more than 80 million colones. The government could employ some of these workers on housing and transportation infrastructure projects, the party declared, but the only lasting solution would be some sort of alteration of the prevailing pattern of land use and ownership.[30]

In the early years, the Christian Democrats never made clear the details of their orientation toward agrarian reform, but it was apparent that their approach was essentially moderate. In 1961, the party gave land redistribution fifth place in a field of seven proposals to ease the lot of the rural worker.[31] By 1967, the PDC gave land reform a higher priority, but the program envisaged was to be a gradual one geared to the development of markets and infrastructure and to the raising of sufficient capital to compensate the expropriated landholders. Far from a radical proposal, this was in accord with the government's own proposed irrigation and drainage law which the PDC supported in the Legislative Assembly. The Christian Democrats distinguished themselves from the government's position principally by questioning the sincerity of Rivera and the PCN. When the president declared that, in spite of the clearly pressing need, no program of agrarian reform could be attempted without the support of *ciertos sectores*, the PDC delegates led a movement in the assembly which demanded and received a resolution of inquiry to the executive branch as to the identity of these "certain sectors." Observers could recall no precedent in Salvadoran constitutional history for such a challenge from the legislature to the Casa Presidencial.[32]

The Christian Democrats' moderate proposals received little

30. *Prensa Gráfica*, October 14, 1966.

31. Partido Demócrata Cristiano, "La Democracia Cristiana y el problema campesino," *Diario de Hoy*, March 7, 1961. The seven proposals were: (1) job security, just compensation, and paid rest days; (2) an attack on rural cultural isolation; (3) profit sharing; (4) the regularization of the landlord-tenant relationship; (5) an effort through the Rural Settlement Institute to increase the small holder population by distributing public, unexploited, and underexploited land; (6) the encouragement of cooperative action among small holders; (7) a program of agricultural credit. In addition to social justice, the party declared the goal of its agrarian policy to be public tranquillity.

32. *Prensa Gráfica*, October 4, 6, 14, 1966; *Diario de Hoy*, December 2, 7, 1966.

criticism from the Left in El Salvador, largely because the government was a more prominent target. Certain facets of the PDC program, however, scandalized traditional liberals on the right who chose to regard the party's approach to the problems of urban and rural labor as an attack upon private property. Very early, party leaders made it clear that they did not consider labor to be a commodity subject to the caprice of the law of supply and demand. When the editorial staff of *El Diario de Hoy* uncritically attacked this position as Marxism, Roberto Lara Velado replied that workers were as much investors as were stockholders and, as such, deserved a share of the company's profits as well as a guarantee of a decent living. He went on to distinguish the Christian Democratic position, based upon the human dignity of the individual worker, from the alternative positions of liberalism and communism. Whereas in a liberal system the means of production remained in the hands of private capital and in a Communist system in the hands of the state, Lara Velado argued, in an ideal Christian Democratic community production would be a free and dignified collaboration between capital and labor.[33] The concept of free collaboration of capital and labor along with the related concept of "communitarian" ownership of the means of production were popular themes in abstract discussions, but party ideologues rarely approached the question of practical implementation.

Although conservatives, usually arguing weakly from the Chilean experience, charged that Christian Democrats favored the destruction of private property as an institution,[34] the position of the Salvadoran PDC on this issue was essentially conservative. In an early declaration the party maintained its belief that property was a natural right justified in that it constituted a fair reward for work and provided for the satisfaction of the individual's present and future material needs. The Christian Democrats, however, also believed that social justice required property-holding to be broadly diffused throughout society. To effect this, they urged just compensation for labor and easily accessible credit to encourage savings and consumption on the part of wage-earners. They also demanded state protection for small proprietors in agriculture, industry, and com-

33. Roberto Lara Velado, "La Democracia Cristiana y la remuneración del trabajo," *Diario de Hoy*, April 25, 1961.
34. For example, Ricardo Fuentes Castellanos, "La democracia cristiana y la propiedad," *Diario de Hoy*, March 9, 1967.

merce. The stated economic and social aim of the PDC was the growth of a large, comfortable middle class. Such a class, it believed, would provide the backbone for a stable economy and a durable democracy. As party leaders declared on many occasions, the solution of El Salvador's social problems did not lie in pulling down the oligarchy, but in elevating the oppressed.[35]

Closely linked in liberal minds with the question of property was that of liberty. In fact, Roberto Lara Velado charged, they often tended to confuse the two, thinking it perfectly proper the masses should live in misery so that a few could enjoy economic "liberty." To the criticism that the PDC's social programs threatened liberty, Lara Velado replied that liberty was above all an expression of individual dignity. Any attempt to use a single manifestation of liberty, such as the right to hold property, in order to depreciate another man's dignity was not only unjust but also a contradiction in terms.[36] Along the same line, Lara Velado on another occasion charged both liberals and Communists with divorcing economics from all other human considerations. In the Christian Democratic view, he declared, economic activity was merely a single facet of human endeavor and should therefore be subject to the same standards of morality and justice as every other social activity.[37]

Of special concern to Christian Democrats in general and of the Salvadoran party in particular was the position in society of the family and, closely related to this, the position of women. The PDC saw the family as the basic unit of society and repeatedly expressed a determination to strengthen it. According to the party, the family was the primary nucleus of socialization, education, moral formation, and economic activity, and a strong family could provide the vanguard in every struggle from that against hunger to that against juvenile delinquency.[38]

A major obstacle to the achievement of family strength and stabil-

35. Partido Demócrata Cristiano, "La Democracia Cristiana y la propiedad privada," Diario de Hoy, March 8, 1961.
36. Roberto Lara Velado, "Aclarando posiciones, III: Libertad y justicia," Prensa Gráfica, October 10, 1966.
37. Roberto Lara Velado, "La economía no es independiente de la ética," Diario de Hoy, June 30, 1961.
38. Partido Demócrata Cristiano, "La Democracia Cristiana y la familia," Diario de Hoy, March 9, 1961. The strong family also plays a key role in the Christian Democratic scheme for a pluralistic, decentralized polity. See Williams, Latin American Christian Democratic Parties, 59, 64.

ity in El Salvador has been the large number (about 50 percent) of households formed from "free unions" instead of legal marriages. This has particular implications for the position of women in society. In the lower classes where the entire family must function as a productive unit in order to stay ahead of starvation, the needs of the family have forced the Salvadoran woman to serve as breadwinner as well as mother. Working-class men, repeatedly bested in the uphill struggle to maintain a hovel full of hungry children, often leave home in search of work, or simply out of frustration. Many never return, abandoning their families entirely.[39] In the city of San Salvador, the vast majority of the market vendors are women, many of whom must provide for families without any assistance from men. In recognition of this situation, the PDC called early for legislation to protect the economic rights of wives and mothers and to require fathers and husbands to meet their domestic responsibilities. Only with her economic interests thus protected, the party declared in its Mother's Day message for 1961, could the Salvadoran woman be free "to accomplish her grand mission as queen of the home and educator of her children."[40]

PDC concern for women's rights and interests was not completely altruistic, of course. Since 1945, women have become increasingly important as voters and political leaders in Latin America. Politicians, Christian Democrats not the least among them, have been quick to recognize this. Women have been particularly receptive to the message of Christian Democracy because of its religious inspiration and because of its emphasis upon social stability and family security. The Salvadoran party was quick to organize feminine groups whose pronouncements to their sister Salvadorans sought to link the party's rejection of caudillismo (strong man rule) to a rejection of machismo (the strong man ethos) in general, and called upon them to become active in public affairs and to fight "on a plane of equality with men."[41] In the light of this emphasis and con-

39. Adams, Cultural Surveys, 454–61.
40. Sector Femenino del Partido Demócrata Cristiano de San Salvador, "Mensaje a las madres de Cuscatlán," Diario de Hoy, May 9, 1961.
41. "Manifiesto del Sector Femenino del Partido Demócrata Cristiano en San Salvador," Diario de Hoy, January 19, 1961. See also "Mensaje del Comité Femenino Santaneco del Partido Demócrata Cristiano a la mujer salvadoreña," Diario de Hoy, February 19, 1961.

cern, it is not surprising that the PDC eventually found an important source of support in San Salvador among the women of the markets.

From a broad examination of party pronouncements on various issues it soon becomes apparent that, although the rhetoric of the PDC may at times have been radical or even revolutionary, the ends and means it actually proposed in El Salvador were generally moderate and at times socially conservative. The PDC's interest in political reform and espousal of traditional Western democratic values are reminiscent of the program of the moderate rightist "Old Guard" PAR which it displaced in 1964 as the dominant opposition party. The movement's scriptural inspiration and its emphasis upon Christian morality appealed particularly to traditionalist sentiment in society as did its claim to be an ideology compatible with El Salvador's Hispanic heritage. The PDC's call for regional (that is, Hispanic) solidarity to be accompanied by the rejection of "alien" ideologies, such as communism and liberalism, represented an attachment to the fundamentals of Salvadoran culture and society. Similarly conservative was the party's desire to maintain an ordered society along established lines through the strengthening of traditional social institutions, such as the family and the church. The PDC's concern for the position of women in Salvadoran society is noteworthy in this respect. Its program envisioned freeing the Salvadoran woman from economic responsibilities in order that she might return to her traditional, "proper" role of wife and mother and, as such, the bulwark of the family as a social institution. This position, of course, is opposed to the modern Western concept of women's liberation. The party's philosophy also reflected a general fear of the expansion of centralized, all-powerful, impersonal government (whether democratic or authoritarian) in its emphasis upon social pluralism and the diffusion of political power to the local level through community organizations, religious societies, service groups, labor unions, and producers' associations.[42]

42. On the political role community groups and service organizations would play under a PDC administration, see Partido Demócrata Cristiano, "Reforma Metropolitana," *Prensa Gráfica*, February 27, 1964. With regard to labor unions, the PDC has always championed the right of all workers to unionize and expects that these unions would be effective political units in a Christian society. The Christian syndical movement, however, although prominent elsewhere in Latin America, has never achieved much importance in El Salvador.

The economic programs of the Christian Democratic party may appear at first examination to have been more radical than its social goals. But one should remember that the economic changes the party proposed were designed specifically to achieve the restoration of its vision of an ideal social order. Party theorists were thoroughly committed to the concept of private property which they did not believe to be mutually exclusive with social justice. While they did recognize the need for more broadly distributed property-holding (and, therefore, a large middle class) in order to achieve social justice and political stability, they spoke more of diffusion than of redistribution. The goal was to create new wealth through industrial growth and increased productivity in general and to insure its fair distribution in society, rather than to divide up existing property. In the one area of Salvadoran economic life where this course was clearly impossible, that of land ownership, Christian Democrats agreed, however reluctantly, to the necessity of expropriation and redistribution. But, even here, the PDC opposed precipitous action. The process of redistribution must be keyed to the development of markets, roads, and technical education, in order to guarantee that the peasants would be able to exploit their new holdings in the most efficient manner. Above all, the Christian Democrats insisted that the expropriated landowners be compensated for their lost property.

Salvadoran Christian Democracy was in many ways an ideology well suited to the middle-class lawyers and other professionals who founded and led the party. While it adopted a moral orientation toward the question of social justice, it did not question the concept of class advantage itself. It retained private property as the foundation of economic life and assumed individual inequities in its distribution, condemning such inequities only when they were so gross as to threaten social order and development. It sought the support and cooperation of disadvantaged members of society in order to promote changes that it believed would contribute to the orderly expansion of a propertied middle class, and saw the growth of such a class as the best guarantee of political democracy and a tranquil social order. To manage social tensions from below, the PDC urged the organization of the masses into associations (syndicates, cooperatives, neighborhood organizations) similar to those interest and professional guilds (gremios) the elites had always employed to articulate and defend their class positions. The party also advocated measures designed to ease access to the middle class from below and welfarist programs designed to ameliorate the lot of those who inevitably would remain at the bottom. The Christian Democrats hoped through education not only to promote social stability but to inculcate the masses with middle-class values. Thus the PDC stressed wholesomeness and respectability in family life and campaigned against nonmarital unions, irresponsible fathers, alcoholism, and other such socially dissolutive practices as gambling and prostitution.

In spite of the protestations and denials of Christian Democratic leaders, not only in El Salvador but all over Latin America, it is hard to avoid the judgment of one North American scholar that Christian Democratic social theory is "essentially traditional, Catholic corporatism."[43] Christian Democracy is not forward-looking; it is backward-looking: back past the dehumanizing rise of liberalism and nationalism, past the centralizing age of political absolutism, past the secularizing world of the Renaissance, back to the medieval ideal of unity and order, to a world where all Christendom was theoretically a community and where the moral laws that guided man's spiritual and personal life supposedly guided his political and economic activities as well. The applicability of this charming vision to modern industrial society is, of course, highly questionable.

Prescribing against the possibility of social violence from below was a simple matter when compared to the necessity to manage elite attitudes. The PDC's vision of an ideal society, while moderate, required significant concessions on the part of an established oligarchy that had developed an elaborate moral vision of its own to justify the existing order. While the goal of a revolution accomplished solely through Christian suasion and moral education is an attractive one to those who abhor bloodshed, one must be skeptical about its chances for success in any society, much less one such as El Salvador's where the privileged have routinely demonstrated their will-

---

43. Williams, *Latin American Christian Democratic Parties*, 234. The attraction of Latin American Christian Democracy to the middle class is discussed in Joseph M. Macrum, *Themes and Appeals of Christian Democracy in Latin America* (Washington, D.C., 1967).

ingness to employ any means whatsoever to preserve intact their advantages by stifling all but the most innocuous attempts at change. One must particularly doubt the wisdom of advocating the diffusion of power and decision-making responsibility in a region where a major difficulty for governments (whatever their form) has always been that they have generally not been powerful enough to enforce compliance with policies other than those most favorable to established interests. The fact that in El Salvador the government party tended to favor programs similar to those of the PDC served to increase the oligarchy's sense of isolation and defensiveness. The PCN dealt with this situation through accommodation. How the Democrats intended to do so, outside of reliance upon the ultimate triumph of Christian good will, was never clear. Christian Democratic parties that have come to power have tended to subordinate theory to practical political considerations. To what extent the Salvadoran PDC would do so were it to achieve national political power is difficult to say, but there is little reason to think it would be an exception.

Chapter IV

Years of
Optimism

More than that of any other man the name of Colonel Julio Adalberto Rivera is associated with the "liberalization" of Salvadoran politics in the mid-1960s. There is as yet no thorough, critical study of the Rivera regime and it is consequently difficult to separate reality from appearance. Certainly, the president himself was a complex figure. Chosen by his fellow officers to head a government which had overthrown a supposedly progressive junta, Colonel Rivera seemed at first to represent the hard-line authoritarian group within the military. He made no secret of his staunch anticommunism and firmly expressed his willingness to rule by decree, if necessary, to keep leftist forces under control. In spite of his rigidity on this issue, however, Rivera appeared to recognize that force alone could never defeat communism. Seeking to cultivate popularity among the peasants and urban masses, the colonel advertised himself as a man of the people, and often dressed in workman's clothes on ceremonial occasions. Rivera generously expended public resources to give his newly formed political party, the PCN, complete control of the Legislative Assembly and himself ran unopposed in 1962 to enter the Casa Presidencial for a full five-year term. Although he appeared more concerned with the form than the substance of democracy, Rivera numbered among his personal heroes Abraham Lincoln and John F. Kennedy, whose portraits adorned his office wall.[1]

In keeping with his populist political style, Rivera had as head of

1. Ramón Chez, "Al museo todos los disfraces del cnel. Rivera," *Diario de Hoy*, March 10, 1967; Henry Giniger, "Salvador is Calm for Voting Today," *New York Times*, March 13, 1966, p. 27. Kennedy returned the compliment, proposing to in-

the provisional Directorio championed a number of economic reforms which, although moderate by most standards, tended to alienate members of the economic elite. Once president in his own right,
he sought to reach an accommodation with the upper class. A policy
of "readjustment" between the government and the oligarchy
characterized the second half of 1962. This alliance was never an
easy one, but at least some of the wealthy saw in Rivera's tendency
toward moderation and compromise perhaps the last realistic hope
of the privileged in their struggle to survive in a changing world. As
one wealthy Salvadoran commented, "If [Rivera] goes down we all
go down."[2]

The "readjustment" decreased tension between those who held
economic power and those who held political power at the expense
of a slowdown in the campaign for reform. Nothing ever came of the
much heralded rural diet law; the measure was as unenforceable as it
was necessary. The Rivera regime attempted to overcome this failure
by promulgating a rural minimum wage in 1965. This law struck at
the core of the meal slavery system by forbidding payment in food in
lieu of cash. The measure was a visible sign of the regime's concern
for the common man but it did in fact very little to effect a more just
distribution of income from agricultural production. Growers
dodged it with a number of fraudulent devices and continued to appropriate as clear profit the largest portion of gross earnings, while
many workers now had to purchase their own food out of meager
daily wages.[3]

An income tax passed in 1963 actually favored the higher brackets at the same time it exempted the coffee industry. This exemp-
tion was itself prejudicial to smaller coffee producers since they remained liable to the export tax which, in contrast to the income tax,

---

clude Rivera in a "club" of democratic presidents he once thought of forming. Arthur
M. Schlesinger, Jr., A Thousand Days: John F. Kennedy in the White House (Boston,
1965), 768.
2. Kennedy, Middle Beat, 190–91.
3. Paul P. Kennedy, "Salvador Assays Red Labor Drive," New York Times, June
13, 1965, p. 25; Kennedy, Middle Beat, 193–94; White, El Salvador, 118–22; Daniel
and Ester Slutzky, "El Salvador: Estructura de la explotación cafetalera," Estudios Sociales Centroamericanos, I (May–August, 1971), 107–109. The Christian Democratic
minority (after 1964 a substantial bloc in the Legislative Assembly) proposed a
mininum wage with meals but to no avail. Partido Demócrata Cristiano, "Sexto
aniversario celebra el P. D. C."

was not graduated. While the tax affected seriously only the middle class, all comfortable sectors opposed it because it attacked certain traditional institutions of the wealthy, such as interlocking family corporations, and because the government indicated its intention actually to collect the levy. Powerful economic interests demanded that the regime redraft the law, but the relative prosperity of the Rivera years probably served to minimize these expressions of discontent. Enforcement was uneven and efforts to make major changes in the law regularly failed.[4]

The Rivera government never offered a direct challenge to the established social and economic structures critics identified as the major obstacles to Salvadoran development. The president needed the electoral support of the masses but could not afford to abandon the economically powerful. He therefore tended to favor measures that would have an immediate and visible effect on the quality of life, such as the minimum wage or housing construction projects, but would represent little threat to the privileges of the rich. Rivera himself, in assessing his five years in office, seemed most impressed with the material achievements of his regime—the increase in housing and school construction; the extension of electrification, potable water, and telephone service; and technical reform in agriculture. Perhaps one can best describe the social policy of the National Conciliation government as an attempt through increased government intervention, regulation, and provision of services to widen the distribution of benefits in Salvadoran society without unduly disturbing the traditional distribution of property.[5]

Contributing to optimism about Rivera's chances of successfully guiding El Salvador through a bloodless transition to political democracy and social justice was the country's remarkable economic

---

4. "Central America: The Seven Presidents," Newsweek, March 25, 1963, p. 59; Kennedy, Middle Beat, 194; White, El Salvador, 124–25; Francisco Roberto Lima, "La Ley del Impuesto sobre la Renta de 1963," La Universidad, XCV (May–June, 1970), 5–24; Oliver Oldman, "Tax Reform in El Salvador," Inter-American Law Review, VI (1964), 379–420. The repeated demands on the part of coffee growers that they be made subject to the income tax rather than the export tax suggests that the latter was much more effectively collected. Slutzky and Slutzky, "Explotación cafetalera," 122.

5. Guillermo Peñate Zambrano, "Rivera satisfecho de labor de gobno.," Diario de Hoy, January 1, 1967. The government cites its accomplishments and further plans in Consejo Nacional de Planificación y Coordinación Económica, El Salvador: Su desarrollo económico y su progreso social (San Salvador, 1966).

growth in the early 1960s. The almost two years of political uncertainty which preceded Rivera's assumption of the presidency had little effect on the republic's economy. By the close of 1962 El Salvador showed a substantial budgetary surplus and an increasingly favorable balance of international payments. Characteristic of this period was a tendency toward greater diversification of Salvadoran exports. Coffee, while remaining the nation's most important product, had already begun to decline in importance due to overabundant harvests and low international quotas and prices. Whereas coffee accounted for 90 percent of El Salvador's exports in 1957, it fell to 52 percent by 1964. Cotton and sugar production grew to fill the gap left by its decline. More important perhaps for the confidence it inspired in El Salvador's future, a new type of production and export activity, manufacturing, became important in the early 1960s with the activation of the Central American Common Market (CACM). Most Salvadoran manufacturing was light industry—processed foods, paint and paper products, batteries, wire, light bulbs, assembly of prefabricated items. It was generally highly mechanized, employed few workers, and was dependent upon foreign technology, capital, and raw materials. But it was enough to establish El Salvador as the "Ruhr of Central America."[6]

More realistic observers, while they acknowledged the country's dramatic economic expansion, also noted obstacles to the goal of consistent, self-sustained growth. Cotton and sugar were subject to the same fluctuations of world price and market access as coffee, while El Salvador's manufactured goods were not highly competitive. The only profitable outlet for these products was among the other members of the CACM. Outside the region, Salvadoran goods were not as attractive in price or quality as those produced in the more developed industrial nations. What is more, the return from exports of manufactures was insufficient to match the drain on cash

6. Henry Lepidus, "Salvador Cheered by Better Balance of Payments," New York Times, April 8, 1963, p. 74; Henry Giniger, "Salvador Seeks to Push Industry," New York Times, November 6, 1965, p. 34; New York Times, September 22, 1963, sec. V, p. 17; White, El Salvador, 151–52. Nicholas Wollaston, Red Rumba: A Journey through the Caribbean and Central America (London, 1962), 107, employs the Ruhr analogy. See also David R. Raynolds, Rapid Development in Small Economies: The Example of El Salvador (New York, 1967), 36–58.

reserves caused by the necessity to import raw materials and spare parts.[7]

Perhaps the greatest obstacle to Salvadoran development was the nation's rapidly increasing population. According to estimates, Rivera's masive drive to create jobs would result at the end of his term in a real decrease of only nine thousand out of the hundreds of thousands in the ranks of the unemployed. Neither schools nor housing could keep up with the expanding population. In spite of the effort the government put into construction, the urban and rural housing deficits grew during the Rivera period rather than shrank. Inadequate or completely absent facilities for vocational training were partly responsible for some of the unemployment in urban areas, but basically the productive sector of the economy was simply not large enough to accommodate the available labor force. In the cities, a disproportionately large service sector provided menial employment, while in the countryside subsistence farming absorbed surplus workers in the period between harvests. Many rural laborers migrated each year into towns and cities, displaced by the unavailability of land or attracted by the promise of work or public services. Since the 1920s, the traditional Salvadoran solution to the population dilemma had been to export people. In an interview, Rivera once described El Salvador as a labor pool for the rest of the Common Market. A great deal of emigration did occur, especially to the neighboring republic of Honduras. But the isthmian partners in the final analysis all had social and economic problems of their own, and the hostility engendered by the movement into Honduras finally led to war in 1969, an event which retarded the process of regional integration and had domestic political consequences as well.[8]

Thus, although the Rivera regime committed itself to a program of social and economic modernization, it worked against major internal and external constraints and its efforts at reform were often the products of delicate compromise—when, that is, they did not

7. Giniger, "Salvador Seeks to Push Industry"; Henry Lepidus, "Salvador is Confident About Future," New York Times, January 28, 1966, p. 66.

8. Henry Giniger, "Salvador Fears Population Rise," New York Times, April 3, 1966, p. 24; Kennedy, Middle Beat, 195; White, El Salvador, 223–28; Wilson, "Crisis of Integration," 128. For the war between El Salvador and Honduras and its consequences, see Chapter V, herein.

represent mere rhetorical excess. If there was any ideological basis to Rivera's proposals at all, it could probably be found in his demonstrative (and perhaps sincere) adherence to the ideals of the Alliance for Progress. From the beginning, Rivera enjoyed the confidence and favor of the United States government, and El Salvador received generous funding throughout his administration. United States approval was due in part to Washington's recognition that Rivera wished to promote Salvadoran development within a framework that was safely non-Communist, capitalist, and gradualist. In addition to his willingness to side with the Kennedy administration against Cuba and to pursue recommended social and economic reforms, Rivera delighted the United States by restoring constitutional norms and encouraging broader participation in politics. To some North Americans he seemed to be disproving daily the idea that only violence and authoritarianism could achieve development or control the spread of communism.[9]

Rivera's approach to the "democratization" of Salvadoran politics was confined almost exclusively to the realm of electoral competition among formal political parties. Even within this limited scope, Salvadoran history provided little enough tradition to build upon. The only election in which a candidate not associated with the existing regime had come to power was that of 1931 when Arturo Araujo won the presidency. Araujo's overthrow only months later introduced an era of domination by official parties of which the National Conciliation party was only the latest. The basic ideal underlying the PCN was that of a single national party which could "conciliate" the various interests in Salvadoran society, a party in which planters and peasants, capitalists and workers, soldiers and civilians could all find a home.[10] As unrealistic as this ideal may seem, it may have

9. Robert A. Packenham in *Liberal America and the Third World: Political Development Ideas in Foreign Aid and Social Science* (Princeton, N.J., 1973), 59–110, identifies three basic doctrines regarding the utility of foreign aid in the 1960s: the beliefs that aid could be used to encourage (a) long-term economic development, (b) cold war loyalty, or (c) adherence to democratic norms. Usually it was a matter of choice which goal Washington must give priority in its relationship with any particular regime. The case of Rivera must have seemed proof that the three need not be mutually exclusive.

10. The place of the single-party ideal in Spanish American political thought is discussed by Glen Dealy, "The Tradition of Monistic Democracy in Latin America," in Howard J. Wiarda (ed.), *Politics and Social Change in Latin America: The Distinct*

and physical support upon military officers, for financial support upon powerful capitalists (as well as the national fisc), and for electoral support upon the rural masses.

No party, of course, could hope to represent everyone. The events that precipitated the collapse of the Martínez regime in 1944 and the Lemus regime in 1960 demonstrated the political strength of the expanding urban middle sectors. Rivera's goal was to insure the order and stability thought necessary for continued sound economic development. The experience of the past seemed to indicate that authoritarian excess and the monopolization of political power tended ultimately to provoke crises rather than prevent them. Aside from pleasing the United States and fulfilling any sincere democratic inclinations of his own, Rivera probably hoped that his "liberalization" would, through the provision of opportunities for patronage and institutional avenues for the expression of discontent, domesticate his opponents sufficiently to obviate the need for future violence and extraconstitutional ventures on the part of the military.

Many Salvadorans who opposed the National Conciliation party did so simply because it was the official party. As such it recalled memories of the corruption and imposition that accompanied the Pro-Patria of Martínez and the PRUD of Osorio and Lemus. The Renovating Action party (PAR), for example, had opposed *oficialismo* since 1944. PAR's politics was a good example of what the aging radical Abel Cuenca called "oppositionism," a program based upon negativism.[11] The PAR's function as a party was simply to oppose whatever the government did. Under the early leadership of Colonel José Asencio Menéndez, the PAR defended democratic norms against the official party's tendency toward authoritarianism. But the defense of political democracy and constitutional freedoms provided a useful vehicle to legitimize upper-class opposition to reform measures, and the PAR with its uninspired program maintained until the mid-1960s a basically conservative constituency. Outside approached reality in the early days. The PCN drew its national leadership from middle-class professionals and counted for moral

---

Tradition (Amherst, Mass., 1974), 71–103. The Mexican PRI is the most notable example of a reasonably successful attempt to comprehend widely varying interests in a single party.

11. Abel Cuenca, *El Salvador: Una democracia cafetalera* (Mexico, 1962), 71.

the PAR a similar pattern was evident. Men like Roberto Canessa and José Antonio Rodríguez Porth, whose courage in opposition to tyranny was quite edifying, were at the same time rigid social conservatives. And few Salvadorans have been more vocal in the defense of individual liberty, especially freedom of expression, and less sympathetic to the needs of the masses than has Napoleón Viera Altamirano, the influential editor of El Diario de Hoy.[12]

There were, of course, also opposition parties to the left of the PCN. The university-linked April and May Revolutionary party (PRAM) and the Salvadoran Communist party (PCS) dominated the radical Left, but their extralegal status kept them in enforced inactivity. More moderate was the Christian Democratic party (PDC), whose social and economic programs were in practical terms often difficult to distinguish from those of the official party. By 1963, the Christian Democrats had overcome the defeatism that led to their boycott of the previous year's elections and were beginning to expand their organizational effort from San Salvador into the provinces.

A major question in the early 1960s was what role these opposition parties (especially the legal PDC and PAR) would play in Salvadoran politics. Opinion on this issue within the PCN was apparently divided between hardliners, who tended to think of opposition as treasonous, and moderates, more in sympathy with Rivera's declarations in favor of open electoral democracy. The president himself had been embarrassed by the opposition's 1962 abstention. The PDC now announced to the government that it would continue to abstain unless significant reforms were made in the electoral system. Most important among the party's demands was the establishment of a system of proportional representation in the Legislative Assembly. At that time, El Salvador elected its assembly deputies from multimember districts on the principle of majority representation; that is, whichever party won a plurality in a particular department would receive all the seats for that department. Since opposition parties rarely enjoyed sufficient concentrated voter strength to carry a department, this measure insured the maintenance of the *oficialista* monopoly over the Legislative Assembly. Under proportional representation, however, minority parties would gain seats in proportion to their showing at the polls. Advocates of electoral reform had urged this innovation since the 1930s without success. Rivera, however, agreed to the change in spite of the fact that it would weaken his party's formal position. In doing so, he insured that the opposition would not boycott the assembly and municipal elections in 1964; and he reinforced his own reputation as a democrat as well.[13]

In 1964, only three Salvadoran parties possessed anything resembling a national organization—the official PCN, the veteran PAR, and the emerging PDC. As the March elections approached, rumors abounded that two of the parties might ally against the third. Speculation matched the Christian Democrats first with the *oficialistas*, then with the *paristas*, but all parties loudly denied any such intentions. Coalition had been an unfortunate experience for the PDC in 1961 and, although Secretary-General Roberto Lara Velado conceded there had been talks with the PAR, it would be another seven years before Christian Democrats would once again seriously consider teaming themselves with other forces.[14]

PDC strategists intended to concentrate their campaign efforts upon the capital city and the surrounding department of San Salvador. Here their organization was most substantial and they believed that a strong candidate for mayor, while most likely not himself a winner, would attract enough voters to put two or three deputies into the assembly. Party leaders assigned Guillermo Ungo and Adolfo Rey Prendes to the first and second spots on the San Salvador assembly ticket. The task of insuring their victory fell to José Napoleón Duarte who received the mayoral nomination. Duarte was already one of the best known Christian Democrats in the country and had been extremely active in party organization. The party also fielded candidates for the deputies' seats from the other 13 departments and for some 60 of the republic's 261 municipal councils. Many of these candidates, especially in provincial areas, were not in

13. Duarte, "Intipucá"; Duarte, taped interviews, reel no. 2; New York *Times*, August 18, 1963, p. 55; V. Emmanuel O., "Problemas legislativos: Asamblea unipartidista o proporcional," *Diario de Hoy*, May 12, 1970. For a discussion of the importance of proportional representation in Latin America as a whole, see Ronald H. McDonald, "Electoral System, Party Representation, and Political Change in Latin America," *Western Political Quarterly*, XX (1967), 694–708.

14. Partido de Conciliación Nacional, "El Partido de Conciliación Nacional aclara," *Diario de Hoy*, January 25, 1964; *Diario de Hoy*, February 4, 1964.

fact members of the PDC. They were sympathizers or independents who allowed the party to use their names in order to fill its ticket.[15]

In keeping with its general strategy, the PDC emphasized its mayoral campaign in San Salvador. Duarte, his campaign director Fidel Chávez Mena, and a group of advisors made a study of the problems of urban administration and drafted a municipal government program they called the "Metropolitan Reform." In addition to identifying the city's most pressing problems and recommending solutions, the Metropolitan Reform also outlined the doctrinal basis for a new municipal administration code which, assuming acceptance by the central government, would grant municipalities greater autonomy in their own administrative and financial affairs. Among specific proposals of the reform were the construction of modern, sanitary markets, youth centers, and urban housing projects. The reform also called for the decentralization of administrative functions to make them more easily accessible to the working citizenry, and the reorganization of both the municipal police and the municipal revenue structure. Finally, the Metropolitan Reform promised a vaguely defined "moralizing crusade" aimed at "making the city a true community."[16]

In promising administrative efficiency and improved public services, the Christian Democrats appealed to professionals and businessmen; to the capital's poor they promised better conditions of life and greater participation in civic affairs. The PDC's open appeal to the masses alarmed conservatives. When one of these objected to a radio broadcast calling for "the revolution of the poor," a call he claimed amounted to advocacy of class warfare, Secretary-General Lara Velado replied with the standard explanation that the Christian Democratic "revolution" would be peaceful and a matter not of destroying the upper class but of elevating the lower classes to a just and humane standard of living.[17] As often as party leaders would repeat this rationale in the future, the idea that a PDC victory would

15. *Diario de Hoy,* January 13, 16, 1964; Duarte, "Intipucá"; Duarte, taped interviews, reel no. 2.

16. Duarte, "Intipucá"; Partido Demócrata Cristiano, "Reforma Metropolitana." Although neither as thorough nor as well-organized, the PAR program made many of the same suggestions. *Diario de Hoy,* February 18, 1964.

17. Arturo Morales Zavaleta, "Peligrosa incitación a la lucha de clases," *Diario de Hoy,* January 25, 1964; Roberto Lara Velado, "Qué es la revolución de los pobres,"

result in violence and social disintegration remained a favorite conservative accusation.

While the official party's campaign offered such attractions as bands, clowns, and door prizes, and thus gathered large crowds at its rallies, opposition candidates at first received little attention. In San Salvador, Duarte used a loudspeaker as he drove from *barrio* to *barrio* in order to deliver his message whether the inhabitants chose to assemble to hear it or not. As the campaign progressed, the Christian Democrats seized opportunities to profit from the overconfidence of the other two mayoral candidates, Oscar Eusebio Argueta of the PCN whose father had once been mayor and Gabriel Piloña Araujo of the PAR who had defeated the old PRUD in San Salvador in 1960. Duarte's campaign managers devoted extreme care to the development of their candidate's image. Noting, for example, the official party's particularly unfortunate choice of a publicity photograph of Argueta, the PDC leaders rejected more than 150 shots of Duarte before choosing one that made him look especially young, handsome, and sincere. The purpose, the candidate later admitted, was "to give the image of a good-looking fellow against an ugly fellow."[18]

During the course of the campaign, the PDC learned to exploit the fact that Duarte possessed considerable charisma. This was particularly evident when, just two weeks before the election, the party took its candidate to the city's markets. Because of the market's role as the natural center of community life, Salvadoran politicians considered the support of the vendors extremely important. The official candidate had already begun to campaign among them when Duarte made his first appearance before the women of the Mirian market. The Christian Democrat's speech on that occasion received such favorable comment that he soon began to receive invitations from other markets. The antigovernment vendors, who had traditionally supported the PAR, now began to adhere to the PDC. On the last day of the campaign some ten thousand capital residents, many from the

Diario de Hoy, January 31, 1964; Roland H. Ebel, "The Decision-Making Process in San Salvador," in F. F. Rabinovitz and F. M. Trueblood (eds.), *Latin American Urban Research,* I (Beverly Hills, Calif., 1971), 198–99.

18. Duarte, taped interviews, reel no. 3; *Diario de Hoy,* February 15, 1964; Carmen Delia de Suárez, "Peces en el pavimento y conciliación en el aire," *Diario de Hoy,* February 15, 1964. Piloña resigned the mayoralty shortly after taking office in 1960 to become economy minister to the short-lived Junta de Gobierno that displaced Lemus.

markets, gathered in Plaza Libertad in an enthusiastic rally in support of Duarte.[19]

Although the government continually reiterated its pledge that it would maintain the electoral process "free of fraud and violations of the law," the two opposition parties made no secret of their willingness to abandon the race should such assurances prove worthless. The PDC and the PAR both drew criticism from more committed oppositionists for their decision to participate in the elections at all; but, despite the woeful predictions of cynics and pessimists, the government appeared true to its word. The Defense Ministry posted notices in headquarters, barracks, and public places, reminding officers and men of the army's "apolitical and obedient" status. The executive removed the mayors of Guatajiagua (Morazán department) and Panchimalco (San Salvador) from their posts when the Christian Democrats accused them of partisan harassment and intimidation. When the official party violated the election law by distributing literature weeks before the legal opening of the campaign, the Central Council of Elections sternly reprimanded it.[20]

The highly publicized vigilance of national authorities, however, did not entirely prevent abuses. A semiofficial smear campaign sought to identify the opposition as Communist. Appearing on the television program "Ante la Prensa," a PCN assembly candidate charged that Moscow had infiltrated both the PDC and the PAR. Meanwhile, at least according to accusations by Christian Democrats, members of the National Guard went from town to town in rural areas telling the inhabitants the PDC was in reality the Communist party. The National Guard, because of its role as the principal instrument of public order in the countryside and the consequent long tradition of alliances between local commanders and landowners, was both a natural vehicle for intimidation of the peasant vote and a perfect villain for the pronouncements of opposition propagandists. At least two reported incidents of abuse seem to have ample foundation—one in mid-February in Soyapango, near San Salvador, where guardsmen in civilian clothes supposedly beat and

19. Duarte, "Intipucá"; Duarte, taped interviews, reel no. 3; Diario de Hoy, March 4, 1964.

20. Diario de Hoy, January 11, 12, 14, 18, 1964; Carlos Arturo Imendia, "El conflicto de la oposición," Diario de Hoy, March 5, 1964; Prensa Gráfica, February 19, 1964.

arrested three PDC workers; and another similar occurrence less than two weeks later in San Pedro Perulapán (Cuscatlán). In both cases, higher authorities quickly ordered the release of the victims. Another incident of violence of which there are widely conflicting accounts was a brawl that erupted at official party headquarters in early March between supporters of the PCN and the PDC. Among those reportedly injured was Christian Democrat assembly candidate Adolfo Rey Prendes.[21]

Despite a serious effort by the government to produce a large popular participation on election day, only about one-fourth of the electorate turned out. Early, unofficial returns surprised all observers. Napoleón Duarte actually won in the capital by a narrow plurality, and the PDC picked up deputies' seats not only in the department of San Salvador but also from nine others. In the end, the Christian Democrats emerged with thirty-seven municipalities, including the capital, and fourteen deputies in the Legislative Assembly. The PCN, of course, retained a healthy majority in the legislature and swept the remainder of the municipalities; but the significance of this election was that the opposition had broken the official party's monopoly and had done it with the government's encouragement and support. Also significant was the fact that the PDC now eclipsed the PAR as the dominant party within the opposition. Rumors that the PCN would not accept the results concerned the other parties, but the regime offered assurances through the person of Interior Minister Fidel Sánchez Hernández who presided over the negotiation of a "gentlemen's agreement" among them. Leaders of the Christian Democratic party, pleased and perhaps somewhat surprised not only by their strong showing but by the government's acceptance of it, were quick to praise the president and his cabinet for keeping faith with the people. Now, a party declaration announced, El Salvador could finally proceed down the road to democracy and social justice.[22]

---

21. *Prensa Gráfica*, February 14, 1964; *Diario de Hoy*, February 15, 24, March 5, 1964.

22. Partido Demócrata Cristiano, "El pueblo nos dió la razón," *Diario de Hoy*, March 20, 1964; *Diario de Hoy*, March 7, 8, 14, 15, 17, 20, 1964. See also statements by Deputy-elect Guillermo Ungo, *Diario de Hoy*, March 16, 1964, and Mayor-elect Napoleón Duarte, *Diario de Hoy*, March 10, 1964. The composition of the new assembly was: PCN, 32; PDC, 14; PAR, 6.

While the 1964 elections greatly strengthened the position of the Christian Democrats, they did not fundamentally weaken that of the official party. The government's majority in the assembly was entirely adequate to insure safe passage for PCN legislation and policies. In addition, the *oficialistas* retained the crucial support of the officer corps, the force most capable of completely bypassing the formal political system in order to impose its desires.

The mayoralty of San Salvador, which the Christian Democrats in the person of Napoleón Duarte now controlled, was a highly visible position but not a particularly powerful one. Prior to Duarte's victory, it had generally been held by allies or representatives of the central government. Under this arrangement many municipal functions and prerogatives passed from the mayor and council to the national executive. The concept of municipal autonomy had very little meaning. The city administration was forced to meet public expenditures out of scarce revenues raised from an antiquated and wholly inadequate municipal tax structure which only the Legislative Assembly had the constitutional power to alter. The city budget was subject to review by the Interior Ministry which interpreted its power as a veto. Authority over all sorts of urban problems was widely dispersed among local, national, and semiautonomous agencies. With the PDC in control, the potential for discord between authorities at the municipal and the national level was even greater than that already built into the system. The capital was not merely a city; it was the center of Salvadoran political life. City issues were national issues and in dealing with them the regime must consider their significance in terms not only of the principles of sound public administration, but also of party prestige and the desires of the PCN's economic backers. The PDC for its part never concealed its intent to build upon its control of San Salvador in order to expand its organization and appeal throughout the republic.[23]

In spite of the congenital weakness of the municipality and the obstructionism of the central government, both of which served to limit the ability of any city administration to effect significant change, the Christian Democrats during the period of their control

23. Duarte, taped interviews, reel no. 3; Ebel, "Decision-Making in San Salvador," *passim.*

from 1964 to 1976 did manage to accomplish some important administrative and material improvements. Upon assuming office on May 1, 1964, Duarte inherited a plethora of urban problems. These problems were in part the consequence of San Salvador's rapid growth since the 1920s, when the improvement of transportation and communications as well as the expansion of the national economic and administrative structure had combined to promote the city's expansion and the relative decline of local centers and elites. From a population of less than 100,000 in 1930, the municipality of San Salvador had grown to more than 250,000 by 1960. Many of these new capitalites were recently arrived poor migrants who drew heavily upon already inadequate public services while offering no compensatory increase in tax revenues, and existed under primitive conditions, often in shanty towns erected on unoccupied public or private land.[24]

Neither the physical nor the administrative structure of San Salvador was adequate to accommodate the city's growing population. The PDC attributed the municipality's inability to meet new demands to its institutional relationship to the central government. To correct what they saw as an excessive concentration of authority at the center, the Christian Democrats proposed a new municipal code which, reflecting the party's ideological commitment to decentralization, proposed to expand the effective autonomy of all municipalities in El Salvador. While it vainly pursued this broad reform at the national level, the PDC also proposed more immediate solutions to specific problems. Among these, one of the most significant was the outdated municipal tax system in the capital.[25]

Upon taking office in San Salvador, Duarte encountered a large accumulated debt. The mayor and his advisors blamed this situation

24. On the growth of San Salvador, see Raynolds, *Rapid Development*, 3–4; Wilson, "Crisis of Integration," 143–44; El Salvador, Dirección General de Estadística, *Anuario estadístico correspondiente al año 1930* (San Salvador, n.d.), 21; El Salvador, Dirección General de Estadística y Censos, *Tercer censo nacional de población, 1961* (San Salvador, 1965), 3. On the city's lower class, see White, *El Salvador,* 144–48; Louis J. Ducoff, "Población migratoria en un área metropolitana de un país en proceso de desarrollo: Informe preliminar sobre un estudio experimental efectuado en El Salvador," *Estadística,* XX (1962), 131–39; Robert C. Williamson, "Some Variables of Middle and Lower Class in Two Central American Cities," *Social Forces,* XLI (1962), 195–207.

25. Duarte, taped interviews, reel no. 6.

on the indifferent collection of authorized municipal taxes, which were in themselves insufficient. After spending six months putting the city's accounts in order, Duarte sought to reduce the deficit by collecting back taxes from wealthy individuals notoriously in arrears. This expedient, which at times required personal visits to delinquents on the part of the mayor, ultimately resulted in the collection of some two million colones, but by 1967 it had exhausted its possibilities. In that year, Duarte estimated the amount still outstanding at four times that collected and expressed the fear that it was largely uncollectible, being owed by people who were now dead or whose whereabouts were unknown. Current municipal revenues, the mayor complained, barely covered the essential costs of administration. An agreement with the Canadian-owned Electric Lighting Company of San Salvador (Compañía de Alumbrado Eléctrico de San Salvador, CAESS) required the dedication of scarce surplus funds to the retirement of the city's fifteen-year-old light and power debt which by itself amounted to one million colones each year. In the end, very little was left for new public projects. Previous city administrations had balanced their accounts with subsidies from the central government, but this aid ceased when the opposition captured the mayoralty. The Christian Democrats would not have preferred a subsidy in any event since it implied a subordinate relationship to the regime. The only satisfactory approach would be a reform of San Salvador's revenue structure.[26]

The municipality of San Salvador had no independent authority to levy taxes. For operating revenues it depended upon its right to collect certain duties and fees conceded it by the central government. The current codified statement of these rights, the tarifa de arbitrios, which dated from 1947 although individual taxes contained in it had a much longer history, was completely unsystematic. Compiled in alphabetical order, the tarifa included categories of revenue from capital investment taxes to entertainment taxes, from taxes on construction and the use of market stalls to fines and charges for municipal services. The law was so confusing that it was often impossible for businessmen to determine which charges applied to them. What is more, the schedules tended to benefit the wealthy; although some of the taxes on commercial and industrial activities

26. Ibid., reel no. 3; Diario de Hoy, March 19, 1967; Ebel, "Decision-Making in San Salvador," 204.

were graduated, the highest brackets were set at absurdly low levels. Only the Legislative Assembly had the authority to amend or replace the *tarifa*, and here the fact that San Salvador was the republic's capital and most important city was of critical importance. While the assembly could easily raise taxes in a municipality of low visibility, such as neighboring Mejicanos where taxes were in fact higher than in the capital, it could not do so in San Salvador where local issues tended to blur with national issues.[27]

Duarte and the Christian Democrats began lobbying for a thoroughgoing reform of municipal taxation as early as 1964. Their proposal sought the establishment of uniform, graduated schedules and the simultaneous transfer of the burden to those most able to pay. While the PDC's primary goal was to increase city revenues, thereby increasing municipal autonomy as well as providing the funds for material improvement projects that would enhance party prestige, the reform had other goals as well. Among these, the Christian Democrats' ideal of distributive justice was of obvious importance as was their commitment to administrative rationalization. Also, Duarte and his advisors hoped that a major increase in the tax liability of manufacturing industries would discourage their location in the capital. Duarte did not concede the claim of capitalist interests that these plants were a major source of urban employment; instead, he argued that low taxes by benefiting industry led to urban congestion, internal migration of the unemployed, and the unnatural overexpansion of the capital in comparison with other cities and towns. A final goal of the PDC municipal tax reform, one which prompted some ridicule from critics, was in connection with the party's *cruzada moralizadora*; by taxing night clubs, pool halls, and houses of assignation out of business, the new municipal council hoped to make San Salvador a more wholesome place in which to live.[28]

The Christian Democrats sought the collaboration of major eco-

27. Duarte, taped interviews, reel no. 4; Ebel, "Decision-Making in San Salvador," 204–205; Municipalidad de San Salvador, "La municipalidad de San Salvador aclara y explica al pueblo," *Prensa Gráfica*, April 30, 1970; Jane Campbell, "The Chamber of Commerce and Industry of El Salvador: A Latin American Interest Group" (M.A. thesis, Tulane University, 1969), 37–41.

28. Duarte, taped interviews, reel no. 4; Ebel, "Decision-Making in San Salvador," 206; Campbell, "Chamber of Commerce and Industry," 41–44; interview with Duarte, *Prensa Gráfica*, April 23, 1970. Opponents claimed a special tax on brothels proposed by the PDC would amount to municipal licensing of prostitution.

nomic interest groups in their campaign for tax reform, but from the time they first introduced their proposal before the Legislative Assembly they experienced little but opposition. The primary opponent was the Salvadoran Chamber of Commerce and Industry (Cámara de Comercio e Industria de El Salvador) which charged that business already suffered from overtaxation, that the municipality did not collect its existing taxes with efficiency or exercise proper thrift in its expenditures, and that Duarte had submitted no plans for the future sufficiently concrete to justify an increase in municipal revenue. The essence of the accusations was that the tax reform was a scheme on the part of an irresponsible minority to bleed the city's hardworking businessmen in order to finance its political ambitions. Duarte repeated that current revenues barely sufficed to meet the city's existing obligations. In response to the chamber's claim that private enterprise would suffer irreparably from heavier taxes, he asserted that under the proposed schedule 85 percent of San Salvador's businesses would actually find their liabilities lowered. The municipality proved unreceptive to changes suggested by the Chamber of Commerce and Industry and declined to supply the specific information on city finances it requested. Joined in its opposition by the National Private Enterprise Association (Asociación Nacional de Empresa Privada, ANEP), the chamber made full use of the press as well as its connections with the leadership of the PCN. The influence of its opponents with the executive and the leadership of the assembly kept the bill stalled in committee from 1965 to 1970. Special circumstances following the war with Honduras momentarily gave the PDC dominance in the assembly and party leaders were able to push the tax reform through in late April, 1970. President Fidel Sánchez Hernández, however, vetoed the measure in the closing days of the session and the PDC lost its advantage when the new assembly convened.[29]

While the tax reform campaign ultimately failed, Duarte and the PDC did enjoy some successes in San Salvador. Chief among these

29. Duarte, taped interviews, reel no. 4; Duarte, "Intipucá"; Campbell, "Chamber of Commerce and Industry," 44–59; Prensa Gráfica, April 20, 22, 25, 1970; interview with Duarte, Prensa Gráfica, April 23, 1970; Diario de Hoy, May 11, 14, 15, 1970; Asociación Nacional de la Empresa Privada, "Declaraciones . . . en relación a la nueva Tarifa de Arbitrios Municipales," Diario de Hoy, May 7, 1970; Ebel, "Decision-Making in San Salvador," 206–207.

was the municipality's proposal to build a new system of public markets. Crowded, unhygienic, and disorderly, San Salvador's existing markets were inadequate either to handle the quantity of goods demanded by an expanding population or to provide space for the increasing number of urbanites seeking to earn their livings in petty commerce, Most migrants who arrived in the capital in search of work found little opportunity other than trafficking in high volume, inexpensive, and often inconsequential items such as lottery tickets, pocket combs, and fresh fruit. Only the most fortunate found space in the public market; the rest operated on the streets, often living as well as working there. The fact that many of these vendors were women with fatherless families complicated the situation. The authorities considered such sellers an aesthetic and public order nuisance and campaigns against them were almost as old as the problem itself. But although the municipality many times ordered them off the streets, there was nowhere for them to go and the problem persisted.[30]

The PDC's market plan called for the construction of two new central markets, one wholesale and one retail, as well as four new satellite facilities. Although the municipality wished to avoid regime involvement, it ultimately found the government's collaboration indispensible in its efforts to obtain the extensive funding such a project obviously required. In July, 1969, after four years of negotiations, the city finally signed a $6.3 million credit agreement with the Inter-American Development Bank. This loan, guaranteed by the central government, accounted for slightly more than one-half the expected cost of the project, with the remainder to be raised by sale of municipal lands and a tax on market users. By November, the municipality was preparing to let contracts for planning and construction. With the PDC briefly dominant in the Legislative Assembly, a generous appropriation for the first two years' work easily passed. A joint commission manned by three representatives from the municipality and three from the central government undertook

30. Duarte, taped interviews, reel no. 5; Henry Giniger, "San Salvador's Chaotic Market Reflects the Nation's Problems," New York Times, June 26, 1968, p. 12; Ebel, "Decision-Making in San Salvador," 205. On the life of a San Salvador street peddler and her children, see Cornell Capa and J. Mayone Stycos, Margin of Life: Population and Poverty in the Americas (New York, 1974), 101–103.

supervision of the project. The uneasy cooperation between the regime and the municipality reflected the political importance of the undertaking. Neither the PDC nor the PCN cared to risk losing support among the capital's market vendors. Political wisdom in El Salvador held that "he who controls the market runs the nation." Certainly the Christian Democrats based every one of their electoral campaigns between 1964 and 1972 upon their faith in this adage.[31]

In addition to the markets, the PDC municipal council in San Salvador was responsible for a number of material improvements ranging from such long needed projects as a new street lighting system, completed and in operation by the summer of 1967, to such essentially frivolous contributions as the giant floral clock on Paseo Independencia dedicated by Duarte in his final days in office. The Christian Democrats also took pride in their efforts to increase the availability and general quality of city services. New equipment purchased in 1969 permitted the municipality to collect 300,000 tons of garbage and trash daily; Duarte hoped to raise this figure by 50 percent in 1970. The opening of mobile city offices in various locations permitted citizens to conduct their municipal business, such as paying taxes or securing documents, without the inconvenience of a time-consuming trip downtown. Also in the interest of reducing congestion at the municipal hall, the Christian Democrats rationalized and mechanized the city's record-keeping procedures, installing modern business machines and computerizing accounts. In 1968, Duarte announced that more than 500,000 birth certificates were available on microfilm and that copies could now be produced instantaneously. Such technical reforms appealed to a certain type of middle-class voter who admired efficiency and businesslike methods, but they must also have been popular among workers who found themselves standing in shorter lines to complete their dealings with officialdom.[32]

31. Duarte, taped interviews, reel no. 5; Giniger, "San Salvador's Chaotic Market"; Diario de Hoy, March 15, 1967, June 24, 1969; Prensa Gráfica, July 9, September 4, 19, October 1, November 7, 1969; "Sitios definitivos para mercados capitalinos," Prensa Gráfica, September 22, 1969; Inter-American Development Bank, Tenth Annual Report, 1969 (Washington, D.C., 1970), 83, 111. Aphorism quoted in Ebel, "Decision-Making in San Salvador," 195.

32. Ebel, "Decision-Making in San Salvador," 199, 207–209; Duarte, taped interviews, reels no. 3, 4; Duarte, "Intipucá"; Prensa Gráfica, March 28, 1968, April 30, 1970; interview with Duarte, Prensa Gráfica, January 5, 1970; Diario de Hoy, January 13, 1964.

The Communitarian Action (Acción Comunitaria) program was perhaps the Duarte administration's most far-reaching attempt to put Christian Democratic social thought into practice in San Salvador. The idea of organizing community groups at the neighborhood level to work with the municipality as well as on their own initiative in solving the city's problems was a natural extension of the value the PDC placed on the decentralization of authority and responsibility as well as the encouragement of "communitarian" as opposed to individualist values. In El Salvador, however, any attempt to organize anyone other than elites outside the patronage of the central government has traditionally been suspect.

Apparently in the not entirely unfounded belief that the motives behind the Christian Democrats' proposal were partisan, the Interior Ministry at first used its power of budgetary review to prevent the appropriation of municipal funds for the program, but later relented in order to avoid a constitutional confrontation. Numbering eventually between sixty and eighty, the Communitarian Action groups met weekly in their neighborhoods and contributed labor to the building of schools, bridges and retaining walls, community centers, parks and gardens, and other civic projects. Special civil defense units raised from the Communitarian Action organizations rendered valuable service both in the aftermath of the earthquake which struck San Salvador in May, 1965, leaving more than one hundred dead and thousands homeless, and again during the Honduran War. If, as the regime originally suspected, the PDC intended the groups to evolve into political cadres, their effectiveness in that role is open to question. Although Communitarian Action was already well established in San Salvador by 1967, the Christian Democrat candidate for president that year, Abraham Rodríguez, ran only third in the city. According to Duarte, the neighborhood organizations, being in closer touch with the people than were the mayor or municipal council, became interest groups in their own right, often disagreeing openly with the authorities over questions of budget and policy. Assuming the accuracy of this assertion of the movement's independence, one of the contributing factors was probably the employment of professional organizers (social workers, sociologists, psychologists) as promoters and advisors.[33]

33. Duarte, taped interviews, reels no. 4, 5; Duarte, "Intipucá"; *Prensa Gráfica*, January 5, 1970.

In the context of Latin American politics, where such transcendent issues as colonialism and underdevelopment tend to dominate the literature, it is easy to overlook the importance of something as mundane as street lighting or garbage collection. But in attacking these problems the Christian Democrat municipal administration concentrated its efforts upon the possible, and in achieving it accomplished improvements in city life that were both immediate and visible. While the PDC was in no position to produce the mobile health units, telephone systems, and electrification projects for which the official party claimed credit nationwide, the philosophy behind its approach was the same. The structural roots of the problems that plagued El Salvador and its capital were not only invisible and inconceivable to the majority of voters, they were not susceptible to treatment by short-term, painless measures. By demonstrating their respective capacities to effect with as little inconvenience as possible tangible solutions to tangible problems, each party hoped to build and retain an electoral following.[34]

The PDC's performance in San Salvador enabled it to build a hard core of voter support in the republic's largest city. The mayoralty of the capital was the most visible elective post outside the presidency. During his six-year tenure, Duarte not only developed a strong personal following in the city itself but also emerged as a national political figure of considerable importance and appeal. When he ran for reelection for the first time in 1966 he did so with widespread backing, including that of the normally conservative newspaper *El Diario de Hoy*, and won overwhelmingly. PDC gains elsewhere were more modest, but the party did increase its delegation in the Legislative Assembly to fifteen and it also picked up a large number of minor

34. This is obviously not the exclusive explanation for electoral support of Salvadoran parties. The PCN, in particular, has never depended for its power entirely upon the voluntary adherence of voters. But while fraud and intimidation, both explicit and implicit, undoubtedly account for a sizable portion of the official party's strength, especially in the countryside, one should bear in mind that the PCN has not been as unpopular among the masses as its critics claim and that its identity with the central government has probably served to link it in the public mind with the source of largesse and problem-solving capacity. See, for example, the discussion, in terms of "mediators," of support for the official PRI in the less advanced areas of Mexico in Pablo González Casanova, *Democracy in Mexico*, trans. Danielle Salti (New York, 1970), 125–34. In El Salvador as in Mexico, or elsewhere, the most effective "mediator" is likely to be the one with the closest ties to the party in power. White, *El Salvador*, 206.

municipalities. Although occasional underhandedness and even violence had marred the campaign, many observers both Salvadoran and foreign chose to interpret the election as the harbinger of a glorious age of political maturity and stable democracy. The Guatemalan voting of the previous week in which civilian Julio César Méndez Montenegro defeated two military candidates for the presidency gave further encouragement to optimists who professed to foresee the end of the military's accustomed ascendancy in Central American politics. In March, 1966, Christian Democrats were asking, "If Guatemala can elect a civilian President, why not El Salvador?"[35]

The assembly and municipal elections of 1964 and 1966, although not entirely free of abuse, conferred a new dignity upon the electoral process in El Salvador. At the same time, by promising the major opposition parties a permanent share in the distribution of power and patronage, they went a long way toward institutionalizing the expression of discontent and directing it into peaceful, rather than violent, channels. The elections demonstrated that sympathy for opposition parties, especially in the capital city and especially for the Christian Democrats, was considerable and that it was growing. But while the PDC made gains in 1966, it did not yet threaten the official party's control of the Legislative Assembly nor had it yet had the opportunity to contest the republic's highest office. Such an opportunity was due in 1967, when Rivera's term would end. The success of the electoral experiment to this point as well as the election of Méndez Montenegro in Guatemala and that of the Christian Democrat Frei in Chile in 1964 all tended to encourage the Salvadoran PDC as it prepared for its participation in what promised to be the first meaningful presidential election in El Salvador since 1950.

The PCN in this period was already demonstrating some of the weaknesses of the national party model. Its attempt to accommodate a wide variety of ideological orientations led early to internal disunity. In 1964, Vice-President Francisco Roberto Lima resigned his appointive posts as ambassador to the United States, Canada, and the

35. "The Hemisphere: Two Forward, One Back," Newsweek, March 28, 1966, p. 58; Prensa Gráfica, March 15, 23, 1966; Duarte, taped interviews, reel no. 6. For a foreign journalist's assessment of the 1966 election, see three dispatches by Henry Giniger: "Street Art Stirs Salvador Voters," New York Times, January 21, 1966, p. 12; "Salvador is Calm for Voting Today"; "Opposition Gains in Salvador Vote," New York Times, March 15, 1966, p. 15.

Organization of American States, charging the Rivera government with insensitivity to the plight of the poor. Lima retained his elective office, but although he expressed a desire to remain within the PCN as a member of its "left wing," the party reacted to his announcement by expelling both him and his brother Ramón who had resigned his own post as minister of public health. Following his expulsion from the party, Lima became an itinerant nuisance, living in the United States but from time to time issuing attacks on the Rivera government. On one occasion, he even challenged the president to a live televised debate.[36]

While the Lima episode emphasized ideological differences within the PCN, there were also antagonisms arising from the personal and corporate ambitions of the most prominent military members of the party. The inclusion of the army within the fold of the official party and the reservation of the presidency of the republic to a military officer were Salvadoran political traditions sanctified by usage since the ascendancy of General Martínez. The revolutions of 1944 and 1948, and especially the system that emerged under the PRUD in the 1950s, altered that system fundamentally only in the restoration of the principle of single-term presidencies. Rivera further altered the system by introducing "open" elections complete with relatively uninhibited campaigns and genuine opposition victories. It was apparent that 1967 would be a testing year for the new order. No one knew how Rivera's "liberalization" would affect the PCN's role in the presidential election. In particular, no one knew if the army, the party, or the president himself would choose the "official" nominee.

Leaving aside a number of civilians whom it soon became apparent were not under serious consideration, the most likely aspirants to the nomination were all colonels. Under-Secretary of Defense Mauricio Rivas Rodríguez in particular had reason to believe he was the favorite of the officer corps as well as of a large proportion of the PCN's legislative delegation. Mario Guerrero, head of the state telecommunications network and widely considered a man of authoritarian tendencies, was no less sanguine about his own chances. When,

36. New York *Times*, November 20, 1964, p. 12, December 13, 1964, p. 135; White, *El Salvador*, 205; Francisco Roberto Lima, "Al pueblo salvadoreño," *Prensa Gráfica*, March 4, 1966.

therefore, Rivera surprised them both by dictating to the party's national convention his choice of Interior Minister Fidel Sánchez Hernández, an unremarkable political moderate, neither was prepared to accept his defeat with resignation. Rivas declared publicly that the PCN had ceased to exist and hinted darkly that "events" would "have the last word."[37] This was not the last intimation that elements of the military might intervene to prevent a constitutional transfer of power in 1967.

The PCN's size, the vagueness and flexibility of its ideals, and the certainty that few adherents would lightly abandon the access to influence and power it guaranteed mitigated the effects of the divisions within it. Such was not the case with the internal difficulties in the PAR. Once the republic's oldest and proudest opposition party, the Renovating Action party suffered a bitter power struggle in the wake of the 1964 elections in which the Christian Democrats displaced it as the strongest opposition group. This struggle, from which a radical leftist faction including many former *pramistas* and led by university rector Fabio Castillo Figueroa emerged victorious, precipitated a split in the party's ranks. The leftists, calling themselves the "New Line" (*nueva línea*), retained the *parista* name and banner while the party's conservatives, the "Old Guard" (*vieja guardia*), gradually drifted away and into a new organization, the Salvadoran Popular party (Partido Popular Salvadoreño, PPS). Among the founders of the PPS, which soon became the focus of right-wing opposition to the government, was Agustín Alvarenga, onetime chairman of the pre–New Line PAR. Also active in the PPS were conservative deserters from the official party.[38]

The problems of the PCN and PAR had no parallels among the Christian Democrats. The PDC's national convention in October, 1966, accepted the decision of Napoleón Duarte not to sacrifice certain reelection in San Salvador in 1968 for a gamble on the presidency and turned overwhelmingly to its secretary-general, Abraham Rodríguez, a thirty-eight-year-old lawyer and university professor.

37. Henry Giniger, "Salvador Fears a Pre-Vote Coup," New York *Times*, December 10, 1966, p. 18; White, *El Salvador*, 197; Pablo Conde Salazar, "El Salvador en 1967," *Cuadernos Americanos*, CLV (November–December, 1967), 27.

38. *Diario de Hoy*, December 24, 1966, January 4, 1967; *El Salvador Election Factbook*, 17; Gamble, "Partido Acción Renovadora," Chap. 3.

Rodríguez had been leader of the Catholic student group at the university and active in the party since its founding. He had a reputation as an orthodox Christian Democrat, but his personal views on national problems were not well known. He would probably not make as effective a candidate as Duarte, but the PDC strategists did not consider victory a serious likelihood and were interested primarily in publicizing the party's message through the campaign. As its vice-presidential candidate, the convention chose Mario Pacheco, an engineer educated in Mexico and, like Rodríguez, a founding member of the PDC.[39]

In addition to Sánchez Hernández of the PCN and Rodríguez of the PDC, there were two other candidates for the presidency in 1967. The nominee of the New Line PAR was Fabio Castillo, whom conservatives considered a Communist. A member of the "leftist" junta deposed when the current government came to power in 1961, Castillo later became rector of the national university and annoyed the regime when he traveled illegally to Moscow to negotiate the hiring of Soviet professors to teach mathematics and physics. Already the most popular leftist politician in El Salvador, Castillo had gained national exposure—although not necessarily beneficial exposure—from this incident and even appeared on television to debate the issue with Interior Minister Sánchez Hernández.[40]

The conservative PPS chose as its candidate a retired army major named Alvaro Martínez. Martínez was a finance and trade specialist trained in the United States and Europe. He had taught economics at El Salvador's Command and General Staff School and had served as manager of the Salvadoran Coffee Company. A coffee grower himself, Martínez's connections with the landed oligarchy and the officer corps potentially threatened two major elements in the PCN coalition. In addition to Martínez and his vice-presidential candidate, the former parista Alvarenga, the PPS also nominated two al-

39. Prensa Gráfica, October 10, 1966; Jorge Larde y Larín, "El próximo debate electoral," Prensa Gráfica, November 15, 1966; Partido Demócrata Cristiano, "Sexto aniversario celebra el P. D. C."; Giniger, "Salvador Fears Coup." On Duarte's decision not to run in 1967, he claims that to have acted otherwise would have cost him the confidence of the people who elected him mayor. Taped interviews, reel no. 6.
40. Giniger, "Salvador Fears Coup"; White, El Salvador, 202–203; New York Times, August 9, 1964, p. 9, August 22, 1965, p. 53. The government refused to allow the Russians to come; a year later it arrested and expelled two Chilean economics professors before they even cleared customs.

ternates, explaining that this was an innovation designed to guard against any government attempt to disqualify the ticket.[41]

In a country with El Salvador's social and economic problems, there should have been no shortage of valid issues in the presidential campaign of 1966–1967. To be certain, each party had its program and there were important differences among them. Even so, the programmatic gap between the two major parties, the PCN and the PDC, was not so great as one might imagine.[42] Both parties agreed upon the importance of industrial development, and they both favored to some degree government direction of and participation in the economy. The two parties also agreed upon the value of continued cooperation with the United States, although the Christian Democrats rejected the tendency to think of world politics in terms of competing blocs. On the issue perhaps most important to the future of El Salvador, that of agrarian reform, there was virtually no difference between the two positions. Both supported a gradual program of compensated redistribution, accompanied by diffusion of technical training and infrastructural improvement. What distinguished the position of the Christian Democrats was their insistence that their adherence to these goals was more sincere than that of the PCN and that a PDC government would be more likely to implement them successfully. One distinctive feature of the PDC program was the disproportionate emphasis it gave issues related to its own interpretation of the moral basis of society, such as the family, individual human development, administrative capacity and honesty, and similar matters. Also, the Christian Democrats differed from the official party on the question of civilian control of the military. Here, of course, the PCN denied there was an issue since the army was "apolitical" under the constitution and soldiers who engaged in politics did so only in their role as responsible citizens.

Outside what might be called the centrist consensus of the official party and the Christian Democrats were the fringe parties of the

41. *Diario de Hoy*, December 12, 1966; Henry Giniger, "Salvador Elects President Today," New York *Times*, March 5, 1967, p. 27.

42. The synthesis that follows is based upon material contained in various party pronouncements and statements appearing in the daily press in the course of the campaign. A brief analysis can be found in *El Salvador Election Factbook*, 25–26. The formal PDC program was serialized by *La Prensa Gráfica*, beginning October 13, 1966; the PCN program was also serialized, beginning November 11, 1966.

Right and Left. The PPS and PAR shared with the larger parties the belief that industrialization was the only appropriate avenue to economic development; but, while the former advocated a return to laissez-faire capitalism, the latter championed state control of major industries. In world affairs, both parties urged a more nationalist foreign policy and in particular rejected further close cooperation with the United States, the conservatives because of resentment of the Alliance for Progress, the leftists because of opposition to "imperialism." An important sector within the PAR favored restoring relations with Castro's Cuba and closer ties with the Communist bloc. The PPS, of course, rejected the notion of agrarian reform entirely. The PAR, however, proposed a radical scheme to limit all holdings to 260 acres and to divide the remaining land among the propertyless peasants. Both the PDC and the PCN joined Alvaro Martínez in denouncing the PAR's land program as "demagoguery," although they presumably stopped short of endorsing his impassioned televised defense of the beleaguered Salvadoran landlord class now threatened with despoliation in spite of its long record of contributions to society in the form of employment and protection for its workers.[43]

In reality, the great issue upon which the campaign ultimately hinged was not, except in the most tangential sense, the nation's problems or the various solutions the parties proposed for them, but the alleged "communism" of the PAR. The emotion-charged accusation of Communist subversion used by Salvadoran presidents against their opponents since the days of Martínez and the 1932 revolt had lost none of its effectiveness by 1967. In fact, the issue had become even more potent in the 1960s as a result of the revolution in Cuba and the subsequent efforts by the Castro government to export its ideas and methods to other Latin American countries. So established a part of the nation's political tradition was the image of a tiny El Salvador balancing unsteadily on the brink of a Communist abyss of bloodshed and disorder, that it seemed no party could long refrain from invoking it against its rivals. The PDC and PCN blithely charged each other with Communist infiltration while the right-wing PPS accused them both of insufficient vigilance against the

43. *Diario de Hoy,* January 14, 1967.

Red threat.[44] But this was mere ritualistic skirmishing. The objects of the real crusade, undertaken in deadly seriousness by the government and the PCN, were Fabio Castillo and the New Line PAR.

Characterizing the 1967 election as a choice between communism and liberty, Sánchez Hernández ignored the other two parties and concentrated his attacks almost exclusively upon Castillo and the PAR. As a United Nations military observer in Korea, the PCN candidate declared, he had witnessed firsthand the ends and means of communism and he could not rest while such a malign force threatened his beloved republic.[45] The *oficialistas* spared no effort in their campaign of innuendo, direct accusation, and harassment. Police raided several printing establishments and arrested a number of PAR adherents on charges of producing Communist propaganda. Governor Constantino Hernández of Cabañas department declared the party to be saturated with Red agents and forbade it to meet publicly in his jurisdiction. The Central Council of Elections pronounced the PAR's promise "to give six *manzanas* of land to each peasant family" illegal propaganda and proscribed its use in the campaign.[46] Castillo found access to the media increasingly difficult. In January, radio station YSEB (owned by CCE member Gerardo Ramos) cancelled the PAR-sponsored program "Bienestar Campesino" because, Ramos explained, it was in "open violation of the laws of the republic" which prohibited antidemocratic propaganda. In solidarity with Ramos, the member stations of the Salvadoran Association of Broadcasters agreed not to sell further time to the PAR on the grounds that it was a "subversive, dangerous, and undesirable entity."[47]

As the campaign intensified, conservative elements demanded even sterner measures against Castillo and his supporters. In his Christmas message to his diocese, Bishop Pedro Arnoldo Aparicio y Quintanilla of San Vicente condemned the New Line PAR and threatened with excommunication any member of his flock who

---

44. *Ibid.*, December 17, 1966; *El Salvador Election Factbook*, 24.
45. Luis Rivas Cerros, "La filiación democrática del cnel. Sánchez Hernández," *Diario de Hoy*, January 12, 1967; Giniger, "Salvador Elects President Today."
46. *Diario de Hoy*, February 3, 13, 22, March 1, 4, 1967. One *manzana* equals 1.73 acres.
47. Ricardo Mejía, "Inoficiosa prevención del Consejo Central de Elecciones," *Diario de Hoy*, January 16, 1967; *Diario de Hoy*, January 23, 1967.

dared to associate himself with it. Meanwhile, a right-wing columnist attacked President Rivera himself for his decision to allow the *paristas* to participate in the election in spite of a constitutional ban on Communist political activity. National prosecutor Francisco Arturo Samayoa pursued this issue when he appeared before the CCE to demand unsuccessfully the revocation of the PAR's legal inscription as a political party. Samayoa submitted as evidence of the party's subversive character Bishop Aparicio's message, the statement of the broadcasters' association, and a collection of editorials from the local press.[48]

El Diario de Hoy, San Salvador's largest daily newspaper, contributed to the campaign as well. The *Diario* praised Bishop Aparicio as a defender of the constitution, lauded the radio station owners for their patriotism, and reported with horror that Fidel Castro had endorsed the PAR as the hope of Latin America. When in the closing weeks of the campaign Cuban exile leader Luis Conte Agüero arrived in El Salvador to speak on the dangers of communism, the *Diario* accorded his visit extensive publicity. Finally, no doubt as a reminder to the short of memory, the paper began running a feature series on the bloody Communist rising of 1932.[49]

Not surprisingly, the rapid polarization of the campaign along lines that avoided intelligent discussion of all issues greatly annoyed Abraham Rodríguez and the Christian Democrats. Rodríguez angrily accused the Rivera government of attempting to subvert the democratic process by spreading a "psychosis of fear" among the populace and thereby creating an atmosphere sufficiently explosive to justify a pre-emptive coup. The PDC candidate called upon the people and armed forces not to be deceived by the "phantasm" or "false image of Communism." Although Rodríguez himself accused the PAR of demagoguery, he defended Castillo and his supporters

48. Joaquín Meléndez, "Lo irremisible del mañana evitémoslo con la previsión hoy," *Diario de Hoy,* January 13, 1967; *Diario de Hoy,* January 5, February 1, 1967. The text of Aparicio's message is in *Diario de Hoy,* January 15, 1967. All the nation's bishops joined together in February to remind voters of the church's condemnation of communism. "Declaración conjunta del episcopado salvadoreño ante la situación política," *Diario de Hoy,* February 22, 1967.

49. *Diario de Hoy,* February 9, 24, 1967; "Otra vez la amonestación de monseñor Aparicio y Quintanilla," *Diario de Hoy,* January 23, 1967; "El boicot radial a la propaganda marxista," *Diario de Hoy,* January 24, 1967; Gustavo Pineda, "La tragedia comunista de 1932: Hablando de un ex-dictador," *Diario de Hoy,* January 15, 1967.

against the communism charge. In spite of the distance between the PDC's proposals and those of the *paristas*, therefore, some conservatives began to attach the Red stigma to the Christian Democrats as well as the PAR and denounce both Rodríguez and Castillo.[50]

Neither the Christian Democrats nor the PAR had the financial resources for a sustained nationwide campaign. The first 50,000 colones the PDC collected went to settle debts left from the 1966 election. By contrast, the PCN was able to mobilize government resources as well as large contributions from frightened oligarchs. The wealthier sectors of Salvadoran society needed no propaganda-induced "psychosis" to understand that the radical proposals of Castillo and his supporters posed a threat to the established order. Especially feared were the crowds of peasants that attended the PAR's rallies, which themselves took on increased importance because of the media ban on *parista* messages. On the day of Castillo's final mass meeting in San Salvador, residents of the capital's most affluent sections blockaded their neighborhoods and posted armed guards in anticipation of an invasion that never materialized. Meanwhile, rumors swept the city that army officers were plotting a coup to stop the election. Whatever the origin of the rumors, no one doubted that the military would move should Castillo prove the winner.[51]

The most certain indication that the regime in no way anticipated a PAR victory was the fact that it resisted all appeals to disqualify Castillo and cancel the party's inscription. In allowing the *paristas* to finish the race, Rivera may simply have been indulging his image as a democrat. More likely still, he considered that the suspense of an "open" election heightened the value of the Red scare issue to the PCN. He may also have wished to gauge the extent and location of leftist sentiment before moving to suppress the party. Probably,

50. *Diario de Hoy*, December 2, 7, 1966; Giniger, "Salvador Elects President Today." Conservative attacks on the PDC included Julio Escamilla Saavedra, "La 'falsa imagen del comunismo,' Dr. A. Rodríguez?" *Diario de Hoy*, November 9, 1966; and Francisco E. Nuila V., "La patria está en peligro: Partido Acción Renovadora y Partido Demócrata Cristiano," *Diario de Hoy*, March 1, 1967. For a rare leftist criticism of the PDC, see Luis Alonso Posada, "Las declaraciones del Dr. Abraham Rodríguez," *Diario de Hoy*, March 14, 1967.

51. Duarte, "Intipucá"; Giniger, "Salvador Elects President Today"; Henry Giniger, "Two Leftist Parties Rebuffed in Salvador as Army Colonel Wins Presidency," *New York Times*, March 7, 1967, p. 4. After the election, Rivera dismissed talk of a coup conspiracy as "mere speculation."

however, the best explanation is one suggested by Alastair White, that Rivera wished to arrange a public humiliation of the PAR in order to dispel any idea that it might enjoy extensive support. Also Rivera was probably aware that the suppression of left-wing parties in Guatemala prior to 1966 had produced the center-left coalition that brought Méndez Montenegro and the opposition Revolutionary party to power in that year.[52] In fact, since the far-right PPS failed to gain a significant following, it became more and more apparent that disaffected voters would split their ballots between the PDC and the PAR. A much greater number, satisfied with the government's performance or anxious about the possibility of disorder, would vote for the official party. As one observer noted, the PCN regime had established and maintained domestic peace while an opposition victory promised only disruption.[53]

As expected, the *oficialista* candidate Sánchez Hernández easily won an absolute majority at the polls on March 5. The opposition parties neither offered congratulations nor conceded defeat. Their sole gesture of acceptance was their failure to contest the results. While Fabio Castillo expressed his pleasure with the PAR's showing and concluded that the fact a significant number of people were not afraid to support a leftist party was victory enough, Abraham Rodríguez of the PDC was more bitter. At a press conference, Rodríguez announced the "psychosis" had triumphed but only temporarily. The danger of communism, he warned, would not pass as long as there were hunger and misery in El Salvador. Social and economic changes would come whether they were welcome or not and the only choice the country had was how.[54]

On the eve of the presidential election a group of North American analysts, although impressed by the PDC's growth to date, predicted that if the party failed to win 35 percent of the vote in 1967 it might "soon be relegated to the alphabetical graveyard of misfounded parties in El Salvador."[55] At 22 percent the Christian Democrats fell considerably below this hypothetical survival plateau, but party

52. White, *El Salvador*, 202.

53. Isidro Martínez Vargas, "¿El partido oficial ganará las elecciones?" *Diario de Hoy*, January 3, 1967.

54. *Diario de Hoy*, March 6, 1967; Maximiliano Rodríguez Mojica, "Triunfa psicosis dice A. Rodríguez," *Diario de Hoy*, March 7, 1967.

55. *El Salvador Election Factbook*, 18.

leaders did not foresee disaster. In spite of its poor showing, the PDC had still run second overall. Christian Democrats had never anticipated victory, and although the PAR's strong performance in urban areas (especially the capital) gave them some cause for concern, they could derive solace from the fact that the PDC had held its own in rural areas in spite of the *paristas'* more explicit appeal to the peasantry. Fabio Castillo was a much better known and more charismatic candidate than Abraham Rodíguez, but his appeal was narrowly concentrated. While the PAR displaced the PDC in the emerging opposition strongholds of San Salvador and Santa Ana, Rodríguez easily outdistanced Castillo in every rural department except Ahuachapán.[56]

Christian Democrats attributed their difficulties in 1967 in part to the campaign style of the PCN which exploited anti-Communist hysteria to block intelligent discussion of more genuine issues. Also, while they preferred not to admit the extent to which personal rather than programmatic appeals accounted for voter adherence to their cause, they surely recognized that their loss of San Salvador was largely due to the absence of Napoleón Duarte from the ticket. The presidential election was different from prior electoral experiences of the PDC as well. It involved a countrywide race by a single candidate and thereby tested party strength and appeal throughout the republic independently of the popularity of local candidates or the importance of local issues. While PDC strength in the provinces in 1967 should not be exaggerated—the PCN carried all fourteen departments, nine by absolute majorities—it was clear that the Christian Democrats, in contrast to other opposition parties, were slowly developing a truly national following. With proper steps to increase support in rural areas and prevent future defections on the part of the capital, the PDC could look forward, always assuming the survival of the electoral system itself, to major victories.

The municipal and assembly election of 1968 appeared fully to confirm such an optimistic view. Napoleón Duarte was once again the mayoral candidate in San Salvador and that department overwhelmingly returned to the PDC column with nearly 60 percent of the vote. The Christian Democrats also won the municipalities of

56. *Prensa Gráfica*, March 10, 1967.

Santa Ana and San Miguel, El Salvador's second and third largest cities. In all, the PDC held or gained control of 78 of the republic's 261 municipalities (a net decline of 5 from the previous period, but a decline compensated by the importance of the cities won). Much more significant, however, was the increase in the party's Legislative Assembly representation from 15 to 19. Counting 6 deputies elected from smaller parties, the opposition now controlled 25 seats to the government's 27.[57]

A number of factors may account for the PDC's dramatic gains in 1968. Besides improved organization and the increasing credibility of electoral opposition in general, the Christian Democrats may have profited from economic reverses the country had begun to experience by mid-1967. The administration faced declines in coffee and cotton prices as well as an increase in labor unrest. Particularly difficult was a strike on the part of the nation's schoolteachers that began with a dispute with the Education Ministry over dismissals and transfers and remained unsettled at the time of the 1968 election. The PDC had devoted considerable attention to the occupational anxieties of teachers in its presidential program of 1967, and its concern with education in general is believed to have paid off in extensive support within this group.[58] The Christian Democrats also benefited from the regime's decision finally to outlaw the PAR. This measure, an early sign that government faith in the electoral solution might be waning, created a vacuum to the left of the PDC which permitted the emergence to prominence of a small group called the National Revolutionary Movement (Movimiento Nacional Revolucionario, MNR). Founded in 1965, the MNR represented a highly intellectualized democratic socialism whose adherents valued ideological purity over broad political appeal.[59] It never achieved the prominence of the PAR and steadily lost ground to the Christian Democrats to the point that, after 1970, it no longer participated independently in elections.

57. *Ibid.*, March 16, 1968; Duarte, "Intipucá"; Duarte, taped interviews, reel no. 6; Henry Giniger, "Left in Salvador Scores Big Gains," New York *Times*, March 12, 1968, p. 55; Henry Giniger, "Salvador's Left Widens Pressure," New York *Times*, June 21, 1968, p. 9; Roberto Lara Velado, "Las elecciones de 1968," *Prensa Gráfica*, March 29, 1968.
58. Mario Monteforte Toledo, et al., *Centro América: Subdesarrollo y dependencia* (Mexico, 1972), II, 43.
59. White, *El Salvador*, 203.

By 1968 a clear pattern had developed regarding the location of voter support of the government and opposition parties.[60] The opposition enjoyed its greatest strength in San Salvador department, which includes the capital, and such immediately adjacent departments as Cuscatlán, La Paz, La Libertad, and Chalatenango. The PDC and, before 1968, the PAR were also particularly successful in outlying cities, such as Santa Ana. The official party was strongest in remote, predominantly rural departments such as Ahuachapán, Cabañas, San Miguel, La Unión, and Morazán. This greater strength shown by the PCN in less advanced regions reflects a pattern found in other developing countries. None of the Salvadoran parties in the 1960s was truly a mass party, but the government party, for various reasons, regularly won a large peasant vote while the PDC was able to mobilize a considerable following among the working class in the capital city.[61]

There was also emerging by 1968 a possible trend toward a two-party system in El Salvador. The greatest gains made by the Chris-

60. These considerations are based upon simple calculations from official returns and upon the general description of gross trends given by Ronald H. McDonald, "Electoral Behavior and Political Development in El Salvador," *Journal of Politics*, XXXI (1969), 397–419. Salvadoran electoral returns can be found in the daily press and in such government publications as Consejo Central de Elecciones, *Memoria de las labores realizadas por el Consejo Central de Elecciones durante el año 1964* (San Salvador, n.d.); and Consejo Central de Elecciones, *Memoria de las labores realizadas por el Consejo Central de Elecciones durante el período comprendido entre abril de 1965 y marzo de 1968* (San Salvador, n.d.). The author is aware of no attempt at detailed ecological analysis of Salvadoran voting behavior. Indeed, there are several obstacles to such a study. First, in provincial areas it is impossible to be certain of the reliability of voting returns as indications of public sentiment. Second, in the capital, where free elections seem to have been the rule in the 1960s, there are no territorial voting districts. What is more, events since 1968 cast doubt upon McDonald's assertion that "with increasing party activity and competition [El] Salvador also experienced a growth of impartial electoral institutions" (407). A Salvadoran political scientist, who is also a leader of the PDC, insisted in a conversation with the author that electoral analyses in the Salvadoran context would be pointless, and that students of politics should examine instead the mechanisms of fraud. Those techniques used in El Salvador with which the author is familiar do not in general differ much from the ones described by John W. Sloan, "Electoral Fraud and Social Change: The Guatemalan Example," *Science and Society*, XXXIV (1970), 78–91.

61. PDC mobilization of the market vendors has already been noted. Duarte (taped interviews, reel no. 3) explains that the vendors seldom vote themselves, since the market is busy on election day, but spread the party's word to their customers. Monteforte Toledo, et al., *Centro América*, II, 43, argue that the magnitude of PDC victories in San Salvador would be inconceivable without the votes of large numbers of workers affiliated with government-dominated unions as well as unions supposedly under Communist influence.

tian Democrats that year were at the expense not of the PCN but of the other opposition parties. In San Salvador department, for example, the PDC increased its share of the vote from less than 25 percent in 1967 to almost 60 percent in 1968, while the fringe parties dropped from a total of 35 percent to less than 7 percent. The revocation of the PAR's legal registration following the 1967 election no doubt contributed to this process; only in two departments did the MNR match or exceed its predecessor's showing of the previous year. By contrast, the official party gained or virtually held its own in eight of the fourteen departments. In five of the six remaining, its decline clearly benefited the Christian Democrats and no other. Only in Ahuachapán department, where the conservative PPS gained a remarkable 335 percent over its showing in 1967, did a fringe party gain on both the PCN and the PDC. Principal scene of the peasant revolt of 1932, Ahuachapán was the most likely center for a regionally based conservative party. Its local elite historically has been extremely sensitive to the issue of communism and its relations with the PCN have not always been smooth.

As a result of the 1968 election, the Christian Democrats reinforced their status as *"la oposición,"* that is, the party most readily identified in El Salvador with the very concept of opposition.[62] The PCN, on the other hand, found its position weakened, especially in the Legislative Assembly. The official party leadership moved quickly to deal with one of the immediate consequences of the strengthened opposition in the assembly. Whereas traditionally a two-thirds vote had been necessary to organize the house each time a new assembly convened, a party spokesman announced that henceforth a simple majority would suffice.[63] The PCN could not circumvent other difficulties as readily, however. Constitutionally, bills concerning foreign treaties and agreements (including international loans) also required a two-thirds vote. To pass these, the government would be obliged to cultivate the good will of the Christian Democrats.

Thus the PDC, in 1968, was in its strongest position yet. Its experience of the previous four years seemed to confirm the government's florid claims that El Salvador was coming of age as a de-

62. A role once enjoyed by the PAR. *El Salvador Election Factbook,* 17.
63. *Prensa Gráfica,* March 15, 1968.

mocracy. If the *oficialistas* were willing to allow the opposition to challenge seriously their domination of the assembly, reasoned one North American correspondent who watched these developments with great satisfaction, then perhaps by 1972 they would be willing to surrender the presidency.[64] Such a prediction assumed a greater institutionalization of the electoral process than had actually occurred. It overlooked the government's relationship with the army and the oligarchy. Although neither of these elements was monolithic and there was no necessary agreement between them, their combined influence was a matter of great concern to the regime. The army in particular retained its capacity and disposition to act independently of the electorate. The recent emergence and growth of the PPS suggested as well that many conservatives now lacked confidence in the PCN. In emphasizing the official party's vulnerability, the 1968 election may well have helped to encourage an increase in such defections.[65] One North American political scientist who examined El Salvador in the 1960s for evidence of "political development" cited increased voter registration, increased participation, and the growth of parties and meaningful competition as indications of heightened awareness and institutionalization of the political process. But he warned that such changes, once begun, develop a life of their own.[66] The real question facing El Salvador in 1968 was not whether the opposition would continue to make gains, but what the PCN would do when the electoral solution became absolutely incompatible with its survival as the dominant party.

64. Giniger, "Salvador's Left Widens Pressure."
65. See, for example, the biting commentary by José Antonio Rodríguez Porth, "Comentarios de un ciudadano: La derrota del PCN," *Diario de Hoy*, March 21, 1968.
66. McDonald, "Electoral Behavior in El Salvador," 406.

Chapter V

The War with
Honduras

When Fidel Sánchez Hernández assumed the presidency of El Salvador on July 1, 1967, he praised the contributions of his predecessor
to democracy and social progress and vowed to continue them.[1] But
Sánchez Hernández inherited more than the office; there were problems as well. In the closing years of Julio Adalberto Rivera's administration the remarkable economic growth that had favored his efforts since 1961 began to slow. Coffee prices dropped on the world
market in 1966 and the effects were felt at home for some time.
Drought and disease hit the cotton crop, while sugar surpluses piled
up for lack of purchasers overseas. Deficits in both the budget and
international payments discouraged private investment, restricted
social welfare programs, and stalled public works projects. Rising
unemployment and worsening economic conditions led to serious
popular unrest. Jobless workers organized street demonstrations
demanding government action to create jobs, control inflation, provide housing, and open land to cultivation. After Sánchez Hernández took office, labor unions joined the general agitation. Workers in
a number of industries, including teachers legally forbidden to
strike, walked off their jobs. The new president reacted to the situation by naming an army officer minister of labor and denouncing the
protests as Communist-inspired.[2]

1. Fidel Sánchez Hernández, *Discursos del Señor Presidente de la República
General Fidel Sánchez Hernández* (4 vols.; San Salvador, n.d.), I, 3–17.
2. Conde Salazar, "El Salvador en 1967," 29; Henry Giniger, "Salvador Regime
Beset by Strains," New York Times, October 19, 1967, p. 20; Henry Giniger, "Slowdown Sweeps Central America," New York Times, January 22, 1968, p. 64; "El nuevo
gobierno de El Salvador y la situación económica," *Estudios Centro Americanos*, XXII
(1967), 636.

The dramatic opposition gains in the 1968 election also complicated the regime's position. Conservatives, unhappy over the president's articulation of reformist ideals and the presence of progressives in his administration, pointed to the PCN's electoral decline
as the result of ideological error. Efforts on the part of Sánchez
Hernández to reassure the Right served only to alienate his supporters on the left. Following the election, Minister of Economy Rafael
Glower Valdivieso resigned his post and joined the small leftist National Revolutionary Movement. While in the government, Glower, a
well-known economist, had authored a number of reform proposals
dealing with banking, finance, and taxation that alarmed monied
backers of the PCN. Bitter over the timid support he received from
the president, Glower accused him of selling out to the reactionaries.
As part of a thorough cabinet reorganization in late April, Sánchez
Hernández filled the vacant position with Alfonso Rochac, a conservative businessman and economist who had served in the same
capacity under Lemus.[3]

At a time when political opposition and failing resources limited
Sánchez Hernández's options, he also faced demands from the military. Embarrassed by an incident on the Honduran border in 1967,
army officers now demanded budget increases and more modern
equipment. In keeping with the changing aims of United States military aid policy, Rivera had sought to deemphasize the martial aspect
of the army's mission. While the government increasingly employed
troops in "civic action" projects, however, it also accepted the North
American offer of counterinsurgency training beginning in 1965.
Despite serious guerrilla activity in neighboring Guatemala, some
critics of the military argued that El Salvador's special circumstances—dense population and lack of wilderness areas—made this
training and its accompanying technology superfluous. Whatever
the actual threat of insurgency, however, the so-called "Football
War" with Honduras in 1969 would make it clear enough there
could be no thought of weakening or undercutting the army in El
Salvador.[4]

Although ill-defined since the earliest days of independence, El

3. Giniger, "Salvador's Left Widens Pressure"; Diario de Hoy, May 1, 1968.
4. Salvador Pérez Gómez, "Desterrada la guerra en C. A. dice Rivera," Prensa
Gráfica, November 12, 1966; Henry Giniger, "Salvador Weighs Role of Military," New
York Times, October 25, 1965, p. 17.

Salvador's northern frontier with Honduras posed no serious obstacle to amicable relations between the two republics until the mid-1960s when a number of social, economic, and political factors merged to precipitate an international crisis.[5] In the 1920s the consolidation of lands into the hands of major coffee growers caused thousands of agricultural workers to abandon their homes in crowded El Salvador and seek employment from the North American banana companies operating on the sparsely settled northern coast of Honduras. After this wave, and especially during the world depression of the 1930s, came thousands more—landless peasants anxious to take advantage of the stretches of unoccupied public acreage available for clearing in the larger but less populous republic to the north. Urban migrants soon joined their agrarian fellows, moving into Honduran cities, taking up trades and opening shops. Estimates of the size of the Salvadoran community in Honduras by the 1960s vary between seventy thousand and three hundred thousand, but whatever their absolute numbers their economic impact was considerable.[6]

Hondurans began to notice and resent the relative economic success and prosperity characterizing the immigrant community, especially in urban areas, when in the 1950s disease, mechanization, and deliberate management decisions to curtail production reduced the banana industry's demand for workers. The resulting unemployment and, later, a general economic stagnation attributed to Honduras's unfavorable position within the Central American Common Market (CACM) combined to produce antagonisms which by 1965 had begun to find xenophobic expression.

Both El Salvador and Honduras had been in the vanguard of the movement for an isthmian economic community. But in the period

5. Except as specified, the general account that follows is based broadly upon Franklin D. Parker, "The Fútbol Conflict and Central American Unity," Annals of the Southeastern Conference on Latin American Studies, III (1972), 44–59; Jorge Arieh Gerstein, "El conflicto entre Honduras y El Salvador: Análisis de sus causas," Foro Internacional, XI (1971), 552–68; Vincent Cable, "The 'Football War' and the Central American Common Market," International Affairs, XLV (1969), 658–71; and Marco Virgilio Carías, et al., La guerra inútil: Análisis socio-económico del conflicto entre Honduras y El Salvador (San José, Costa Rica, 1971).

6. White, El Salvador, 184–85. Factors precluding accurate estimates include the undocumented status of most migrants and the frequency of intermarriage between Salvadorans and Hondurans. The figure three hundred thousand is most commonly cited.

following the signing of the General Treaty of Economic Integration in 1960, it became apparent that its terms favored the relatively more advanced economies of Guatemala, El Salvador, and Costa Rica at the expense of those of Nicaragua and Honduras. While Salvadoran exports to Honduras quintupled in the years between 1960 and 1968, Honduran sales to El Salvador merely doubled. Not only did Honduras run a consistently negative balance of payments with her more dynamic neighbor, but also competition from Salvadoran products served to discourage native industrial development. This was particularly the case since the favored members of the CACM placed more emphasis on the free trade provisions of the treaty than they did on such other aspects as the planned regional allocation of manufacturing concessions that would have given Honduras and Nicaragua a greater share in opportunities for industrial development. Following Nicaragua's lead, Honduras was by 1968 firmly expressing its dissatisfaction with the existing arrangement.

The governments in San Salvador and Tegucigalpa could probably have come to some peaceful accommodation on these issues had not both had domestic problems to consider. In El Salvador, Sánchez Hernández had inherited from his predecessor not only a discouraging economic situation but also a restive military. The capture in May, 1967, of two truckloads of armed Salvadoran soldiers inside Honduran territory led to a series of incidents that cost the lives of five Salvadorans and two Hondurans. The detention of forty-two men by Honduran authorities profoundly embarrassed the high command in San Salvador. Officers blamed old equipment and inadequate logistics and began to agitate for budget increases and more sophisticated weaponry.[7] Relations with Honduras deteriorated steadily with no less than twelve border incidents over the next two years. The Honduran government categorically refused to release the Salvadoran prisoners until June, 1968, when United States concern with the threat to the Common Market became apparent. There was a brief return to harmony on the occasion of President Lyndon Johnson's personal visit to San Salvador in July to meet with Central American heads of state. By this time, however, Salvadoran opposition parties were already joining elements within the military

7. Giniger, "Salvador Regime Beset"; White, El Salvador, 187.

in criticism of the Sánchez Hernández regime's attitude of "weakness" toward Honduras.[8]

In Honduras, meanwhile, Oswaldo López Arellano, who had seized the presidency in a military coup in 1963 and subsequently regularized his position through election, was now nearing the end of his term. López planned to continue in office by whatever means necessary. Opposing his ambitions was the venerable Liberal party, which his coup had deposed, and the powerful Honduran labor organizations, which stepped up agitation throughout 1968, chiefly along the northern coast.[9] One problem López faced that the Salvadoran regime did not was an organized peasantry. To meet the latter's demand for land, he decided to resume implementation of the 1962 agrarian reform law which had lain dormant since his accession to power.

Both labor and peasant groups in Honduras recognized that part of their problem was the large number of Salvadoran immigrants with whom they must compete for jobs and land. The resumption of "agrarian reform" in 1969 intensified the bitterness already present. The lands involved were not the extensive holdings of the United Fruit Company, much of which lay unused, or even the property of native latifundists. Instead, they were government-owned tracts along the Salvadoran frontier. Although officially vacant, much of this area had already been settled by Salvadoran migrants who simply squatted, cleared plots, and began farming. Many had been there for years or even decades, but a provision of the agrarian reform law forbade concessions of public land to non-Hondurans. It is not difficult to imagine the tensions this situation created in local areas. These tensions became international in April, 1969, when Salvadorans began crossing the frontier back into their homeland.

The political and economic differences dividing the two neighbors were quite serious enough by June when a new issue clouded the whole affair. Violence attended a soccer match in San Salvador on the fifteenth between the national teams of Honduras and El Salvador to determine which would challenge Haiti for the

8. *Diario de Hoy*, July 6, 8, 1968. The PDC and MNR, objecting to the government's grant of amnesty to a Honduran held in El Salvador in return for the release, boycotted official functions during the Johnson visit.

9. Rafael Leiva Vivas, *Un país en Honduras* (Tegucigalpa, 1969).

right to represent the Caribbean region at the World Cup games in Mexico City in 1970. El Salvador had narrowly lost the first game of the series in Tegucigalpa the week before, and ugly rumors at home attributed the defeat to noisy crowds outside the team's hotel that deliberately kept the players awake and even to a sinister conspiracy to poison their food. Resentment at these stories combined with indignation over the expulsion of Salvadoran peasants. Crowds in San Salvador greeted Honduran visitors to the capital for the second game with hostility. A mob besieged the team inside its hotel and bombarded the building with fireworks. The weekend disturbances cost at least two lives, both young Salvadorans, and led to a government security crackdown around Flor Blanca stadium that enabled the game to proceed without major incident. Following the Salvadoran victory, Sánchez Hernández praised the team and the fans for their show of civic pride and responsibility. The official version of the weekend's events attributed the violence not to sports enthusiasm or to greater national problems but to "organized groups led, as everyone knows, by known Communist leaders, university agitators, and elements disaffected with the government."[10]

Honduran fans returned home carrying horrifying stories, more elaborate with each telling, of disrespect for the national flag, of assaults and stonings, and of violations of Honduran women. The local press and radio picked up these tales and integrated them into a well-established anti-Salvadoran propaganda campaign. Coinciding as they did with resentment already gathering over other issues, these insults served only to heighten the general sense of impending crisis.

Reports soon reached San Salvador of gangs who roamed the streets of Tegucigalpa and San Pedro Sula smashing windows and sacking and burning Salvadoran-owned businesses. In both cities, crowds stopped and overturned automobiles bearing Salvadoran license plates. Disturbances spread throughout the countryside as well, especially in the Olancho area where the notorious "Mancha Brava," a civilian vigilance organization reputedly encouraged and

10. Defense Ministry press release, *Diario de Hoy*, June 16, 1969. On these events, see also Duarte, "Intipucá"; *Diario de Hoy*, June 6, 14, 15, 16, 18, 19, 1969; *Prensa Gráfica*, June 8, 9, 17, 1969; Adrián Roberto Aldana, "¡Salvadoreños, a ganar con goleada!" *Prensa Gráfica*, June 12, 1969.

led by government officials, terrorized Salvadoran peasants. Streams of refugees pouring across the border tended to lend authenticity and color to the most extreme of these stories.[11]

The initial response of the Salvadoran government to these developments was to advise calm, predicting conditions would soon return to normal. But not all Salvadorans accepted the regime's assurances. As the flood of refugees continued, the press, various interest and civic groups, and the political opposition began demanding action. On June 23, the Sánchez Hernández government released the text of a firmly worded note warning the regime in Tegucigalpa to put a stop to the violence against Salvadoran nationals. Two days later, El Salvador filed a complaint of "genocide" against Honduras before the Inter-American Human Rights Commission, declared a state of emergency, and severed diplomatic relations with Tegucigalpa.[12]

It is not clear at what point the Salvadoran government settled upon a military solution to its difficulties with Honduras. Certainly official rhetoric became more and more martial as the crisis progressed. On June 27, the day of the third and final game of the series—played in distant, neutral Mexico City—Sánchez Hernández, alluding to opposition charges of cowardice and indecisiveness, responded with the assurance that the army was in high morale and prepared to perform its "sacred constitutional mission."[13] The possibility of open warfare on the isthmus alarmed the other members of the Central American Common Market. The foreign ministries of Guatemala, Nicaragua, and Costa Rica offered to mediate the dispute but, while Honduras readily agreed, El Salvador insisted upon conditions extremely disadvantageous to the other side. Salvadoran reluctance to withdraw forces obstructed an effective demilitarization of the frontier and a number of serious incidents occurred along the

11. *Prensa Gráfica*, June 19, 20, 21, 1969. White (*El Salvador*, 188) estimates the number of refugees may have reached twenty thousand to fifty thousand by June 25. Other figures are more conservative. The editor of *La Prensa Gráfica* ("Documentos vivientes del atropello de Honduras," June 30, 1969) speaks of twelve thousand. Parker ("*Fútbol* Conflict," 53n) estimates sixty thousand by the end of the year, but cautions many of these did not leave Honduras until after the war.

12. *Prensa Gráfica*, June 21, 23, 24, 1969; "Actos indignos que desprestigian a Honduras," *Prensa Gráfica*, June 25, 1969; *Diario de Hoy*, June 24, 1969; *New York Times*, June 26, 1969.

13. Sánchez Hernández, *Discursos*, II, 114.

border in early July. Provocations on both sides continued until, on the evening of July 14, Salvadoran troops invaded Honduran territory.[14]

El Salvador's obstinacy before the attempts of the other Central American republics to mediate the affair suggests it did not place a high premium on a peaceful solution.[15] The official reason for the regime's refusal to make concessions was that the matter was one of principle; human rights are not negotiable.[16] There appear, however, to have been a number of other reasons the government might have been disposed to resort to force. First, El Salvador was in no position to reabsorb any large number of refugees from Honduras. These people had emigrated in the first place because of the lack of land and employment in their own country. A sudden, large increase in the number of landless and jobless in El Salvador could well lead to social and political tensions the regime could not easily accommodate. It would surely produce increased leftist pressure for some sort of agrarian reform, easily the most sensitive and dangerous of Salvadoran political issues.

Sánchez Hernández and his advisors must have had to balance this consideration against the virtual certainty that a war would severely damage, perhaps destroy, the Central American Common Market. That they should have been willing to take such a risk is perhaps understandable when one considers that one of the features of economic integration most attractive to El Salvador was the ideal of free circulation of surplus labor. According to the account of José Napoleón Duarte, who attended a number of policy sessions at the Casa Presidencial during the crisis period, only Minister of Economy Alfonso Rochac expressed any real concern about the fate of the

14. *Prensa Gráfica*, June 29, 30, July 4, 12, 1969; *Diario de Centro América* (Guatemala City), July 7, 8, 1969; Adrián Roberto Aldana, "Ejército rechaza a las tropas hondureñas," *Prensa Gráfica*, July 14, 1969; Jay Mallin, "Salvador-Honduras War, 1969: The 'Soccer War,'" *Air University Review*, XXI (1970), 89.

15. The same can be said of the Salvadoran attitude toward OAS involvement. See Mary Jeanne Reid Martz, "OAS Settlement Procedures and the El Salvador-Honduras Conflict," *South Eastern Latin Americanist*, XIX (September, 1975), 1–7.

16. Representative of this position are El Salvador, Ministerio de Relaciones Exteriores, *Posición de El Salvador ante la Comisión Interamericana de Derechos Humanos: Planteamiento y denuncia de las violaciones contra personas y bienes de salvadoreños en Honduras* (San Salvador, 1969); Secretaría de Información de la Presidencia de la República, *La verdad sobre el conflicto bélico entre El Salvador y Honduras* (San Salvador, 1969); and Ministerio de Defensa, *La barbarie hondureña y los derechos humanos: Proceso de una agresión* (San Salvador, 1969).

CACM. Rather, the general consensus was that because of its structural deficiencies the economic union was itself already in trouble and indeed to a great extent to blame for the attitude of Honduras. No matter what the outcome of the current crisis, the Common Market would not survive in its accustomed form.[17]

More immediate considerations probably weighed as well in the government's assessment of its options. Domestically, the regime's political position was not entirely secure. The official party held only a bare majority in the Legislative Assembly and within that majority there was developing an ideological cleavage that would have important consequences in the months following the war. In addition, Sánchez Hernández was himself increasingly the target of criticism by conservative former supporters who opposed his reformist domestic policies.[18] To complicate the situation, horror stories out of Honduras, detailed reporting on the condition of refugees arriving in the country, and the rhetoric of editorialists and opposition politicians tended to arouse public opinion in favor of a firm stand.

The role of the written and electronic media in the crisis merits a separate study.[19] More relevant to the present discussion is the part played by the Salvadoran opposition parties. Because of their gains in the 1968 election these parties, and especially the Christian Democrats, were in a particularly strong position. By the very nature of the political game they were quick to attack the government whenever they sensed vulnerability, as they had demonstrated in the case of the Honduran border incident two years before.

Members of the PDC recall that their party initially opposed a military solution. Public agitation, however, eventually reached such a level that it became virtually impossible to express an opinion

17. Duarte, "Intipucá." In fairness to El Salvador, one must note that Honduras had its own reasons not to welcome a settlement on the basis of the status quo. One scholar describing Honduran dissatisfaction with the CACM characterizes the conflict as a "war of secession." Alain Rouquié, "Honduras–El Salvador, la guerre de cent heures: Un cas de 'désintégration' régionale," Revue Française de Science Politique, XXI (1971), 1305.

18. For an example of the conservative critique of the Sánchez Hernández administration, see the series of articles by Ricardo J. Peralta, former PCN governor of San Salvador department, Diario de Hoy, June 11, 12, 13, 14, 16, 1969.

19. While journalists certainly did not cause the conflict, they did little to prevent it. By the beginning of July, for instance, La Prensa Gráfica had dropped even the pretense of objectivity. The broadcast media are more difficult to assess because of their ephemeral nature, but indications are that their coverage was quite as inflammatory as that of the daily press. Pablo Conde Salazar, "El Salvador 1969," Cuadernos Americanos, CLXVI (September–October, 1969), 7.

against war with Honduras. As early as June 19, Napoleón Duarte wrote Sánchez Hernández requesting an immediate meeting between the president and the leadership of all the political parties to discuss the international situation. The government agreed and, on June 21, the president and his cabinet received delegations from the four major parties. The primary result of this conference was the announcement two days later of the opposition's agreement to unite with the government in a National Unity Front.[20]

In a joint statement setting forth the principles of the National Unity Front, or Unidad Nacional as it was commonly called, the parties explained that an international crisis involving questions of human rights and El Salvador's national dignity required that they place the interests of the nation above those of partisanship. In the wake of this declaration, various interest and professional groups proclaimed their adherence to Unidad Nacional as well. These ultimately included such ideologically separate organizations as the National Private Enterprise Association and the General Association of Salvadoran University Students. Only the small, outlawed Salvadoran Communist party remained aloof.[21]

A burst of bellicose rhetoric in the Legislative Assembly followed the formation of the National Unity Front. On June 24 amid enthusiastic applause from the gallery, the opposition under the lead of the Christian Democrats called for the organization of parliamentary commissions to carry the "truth" about Honduras to neighboring capitals. PDC Deputy Adolfo Rey Prendes attacked both the Honduran government and people, declaring, "Now is the time to act as true Salvadorans. We must demonstrate to Honduras that we are a united people. . . and we must make them respect our dignity." In a unanimous resolution passed the same day, the assembly roundly denounced the "repugnant massacre" in Honduras and called upon the government to "defend our national dignity and the rights of our compatriots, whatever the price."[22]

Thus firm action on the part of the government found broadly based political support by the final week of June, when Sánchez Hernández filed the genocide complaint and broke off diplomatic re-

20. Duarte, "Intipucá"; Prensa Gráfica, June 21, 24, 1969.
21. Prensa Gráfica, June 24, 1969; Diario de Hoy, July 4, 1969.
22. Prensa Gráfica, June 25, 1969, emphasis added; Francisco A. Martínez, "Indemnización por los daños exigirá el país," Prensa Gráfica, June 25, 1969.

lations. This backing was not at first totally unqualified; the Right and Left both found much ideologically at fault with the government's basic approach.[23] But even this relatively minor criticism disappeared in the week or so immediately preceding the outbreak of hostilities as refugees continued to arrive with tales of atrocities, and cries for revenge increased.

Against the immediate possibility of armed conflict, the government began to stockpile rations, medicines, and blood plasma, to mobilize physicians, and to call up reservists. Sometimes in his capacity as national partisan political leader and sometimes as high-ranking civil official, Napoleón Duarte attended a number of meetings with government officials during this period. His task as mayor of San Salvador was to organize the transportation, storage, and distribution of food supplies as well as the defense of the capital's civilian population. On July 13, the mayor's office announced the division of the city into "civil emergency commands" manned by personnel from the municipality's Department of Communitarian Action, university students, and seminarians. One purpose of this civilian volunteer force was to relieve the army of responsibility for securing the capital against Honduran spies, saboteurs, and paratroops. When Duarte first suggested his men be armed, the government refused. Once the war began, however, the regime recognized the necessity of the measure and by the second night of hostilities Duarte had patrolling the city, by his account, some twenty thousand men armed with pistols, rifles, machetes, and clubs.[24]

The PDC and other opposition parties continued their support of the government for several months following the conclusion of hostilities. The Salvadoran delegation to the Thirteenth Meeting of Consultation of Foreign Ministers of the OAS included two leading Christian Democrats, Abraham Rodríguez and Roberto Lara Velado.[25]

23. Partido Popular Salvadoreño, "Cuando el imperio del derecho es letra muerta," *Diario de Hoy*, June 27, 1969; Luis Fuentes Rivera, "El conflicto Honduras–El Salvador: Aspectos políticos, sociales y económicos," in Carías, *et al., La guerra inútil*, 309–11.

24. Duarte, "Intipucá"; *Prensa Gráfica*, July 14, 1969; Fuentes Rivera, "Conflicto Honduras–El Salvador," 308–309.

25. Both men joined the government in declaring El Salvador's narrow escape from censure a diplomatic triumph and total vindication of the Salvadoran position. *Prensa Gráfica*, August 1, 1969; Abraham Rodríguez, "Actuación de la OEA en el conflicto," *Estudios Centro Americanos*, XXIV (1969), 423–32; Roberto Lara Velado, "La batalla diplomática en la OEA," *Prensa Gráfica*, September 3, 5, 6, 8, 9, 1969;

Meanwhile, Duarte continued his own wholehearted endorsement of the national position. Even before the foreign ministers met in Washington he announced his strong opposition to the withdrawal of Salvadoran troops from conquered territory. Such an action, he feared, would lead immediately to the resumption of genocidal practices on the part of the Honduran government. Following the conclusion of the talks, when El Salvador finally agreed to abandon the 1600 square kilometers it held in Honduras in return for OAS guarantees of the lives and property of its nationals, Duarte echoed the combination of satisfaction and suspicion with which most Salvadoran observers greeted the settlement. In the final analysis, he reminded his listeners, the only genuine guarantee was the vigilance of the Salvadoran people and their armed forces. El Salvador must be prepared to resort to force once again should institutional provisions fail to protect human rights in Honduras.[26]

When the troops finally did return on August 6, Duarte joined with Education Minister Walter Béneke Medina to organize their triumphal entry into the capital. An estimated half million Salvadorans lined the seven-mile parade route for six hours to greet the returning trucks with cries of "Long live the army!" and "Death to López Arellano!"[27]

It is difficult to assess in depth Duarte's personal feelings about the war. His attitude toward Sánchez Hernández and his officers is patronizing throughout his account of the episode, yet he seems genuinely proud of his own cooperation and of his participation in the innermost secrets of the war room. Although he at times blames the incompetence and political perfidy of the opposing regimes for allowing conditions to degenerate to the point of violence, Duarte at other times claims it was the PDC who first demanded a declaration of war. Immediately before and immediately after the conflict, his rhetoric was as jingoist as that of any other politician. He never expressed any doubt as to the accuracy of reports of Honduran atrocities or as to the justice of El Salvador's position.[28]

Roberto Lara Velado, "Después de la batalla diplomática: La realidad de este momento," *Prensa Gráfica*, September 10, 1969. For a balanced account of the negotiations, see Martz, "OAS Settlement Procedures."

26. *Prensa Gráfica*, July 23, August 1, 1969.
27. Duarte, "Intipucá"; *Prensa Gráfica*, August 2, 7, 1969.
28. Duarte, "Intipucá"; *Prensa Gráfica*, July 14, 23, 1969.

The war with Honduras lasted only four days (July 14–18, 1969). Salvadoran troops drove quickly and deeply into Honduran territory along two principal lines of advance. One column penetrated some seventy miles along the western frontier with Guatemala, capturing the cities of Nueva Ocotepeque and Santa Rosa de Copán. The other rolled eastward from El Amatillo to Choluteca in an apparent move to cut off Honduran access to the Gulf of Fonseca and lay the basis for a drive against Tegucigalpa. Salvadorans widely compared their successes with those of the Israelis in the Six Day War of 1967, predicted they would capture the Honduran capital within forty-eight hours, and even talked excitedly of cutting and holding a corridor to the Caribbean.

In spite of the first day's spectacular gains, however, Honduras retained air superiority and successfully bombed El Salvador's petroleum storage facilities at Acajutla and at El Cutuco in the East. Continued dominance of the skies by the Honduran Air Force slowed and eventually stopped the Salvadoran push. El Salvador's supply lines became extended and difficult to maintain, while the raid on the oil tanks severely restricted fuel supplies. In addition, both sides quickly ran low on ammunition. As El Salvador's military drive lost momentum, the Sánchez Hernández regime found itself becoming isolated diplomatically. Alarmed by the Salvadoran advance along its border, Guatemala placed its own forces on alert and announced it would not accept any territorial changes in the area. On June 18, El Salvador gave in to United States and OAS pressure and agreed to a ceasefire.[29]

A widely cited figure set the total of war-related deaths at 4,000, including many Honduran civilians. The Salvadoran government placed its own personnel losses officially at 90 dead and 233 wounded. Material damage in El Salvador was relatively light in spite of the bombing. One serious casualty of the war was isthmian commerce which had made extensive use of the Honduran stretch of

29. Thomas J. Dodd, Jr., "La guerra de fútbol en Centroamérica," *Revista Conservadora del Pensamiento Centroamericano,* XXIII (February, 1970), 30–31; Mallin, "Soccer War," 89–90. Other military accounts include Luis Lovo Castelar, *La Guardia Nacional en campaña: Relatos y crónicas de Honduras* (San Salvador, 1971); Orlando Henríquez, *En el cielo escribieron historia* (Tegucigalpa, 1972); José Luis González Sibrián, *Las 100 horas: La guerra de legítima defensa de la república de El Salvador* (San Salvador, n.d.); and Manuel Morales Molina (comp.), *El Salvador, un pueblo que se rebela: Conflicto de julio de 1969* (2 vols.; San Salvador, 1973–1974).

the Pan-American Highway. Not only did El Salvador lose the Honduran market (which purchased $23 million in Salvadoran goods in 1968), but also it found itself temporarily isolated from Nicaragua and Costa Rica as well. The Salvadoran government responded to this difficulty by establishing a permanent ferry service across the Gulf of Fonseca and by seeking new markets outside the isthmus, even in Communist-bloc countries. Abnormally high coffee prices on the world market promised to aid the rapid economic recovery of El Salvador.[30]

A more immediate financial problem than those related to commerce was the expense incurred in fighting the war itself. According to one source, the Salvadoran government spent in a four-day period perhaps $20 million, or an amount equal to one-fifth a normal annual budget.[31] Although of the type commonly, if too simply, described by observers of Latin American politics as "military," the regime traditionally never spent a large percentage of its national budget on the armed forces. Now it called upon the public to subscribe to a large patriotic bond issue to finance major equipment purchases for rearmament. These additional expenditures may have amounted to as much as $11 million between 1969 and 1971.[32]

Perhaps the most serious of all the war's consequences, however, was the loss to El Salvador of the Honduran demographic "safety valve" and the subsequent necessity to provide domestic accommodations for an increasing population. Immediately this meant finding food, clothing, and shelter for the thousands of refugees who would not be returning to Honduras anytime in the near future. Ultimately it meant devising some way to provide a living in the form of jobs or land to a national population that was growing at a rate higher than the Latin American average and was projected to reach ten million by the year 2000.[33] The issues involved here were very

30. *Prensa Gráfica*, August 7, 1969, November 6, 1971; Mallin, "Soccer War," 89; Fuentes Rivera, "Conflicto Honduras–El Salvador," 312; New York *Times*, December 19, 1969; Juan de Onís, "Central America Seeks Integration," New York *Times*, January 26, 1969, p. 60.
31. Fuentes Rivera, "Conflicto Honduras–El Salvador," 336.
32. El Salvador's annual defense budget (less major equipment purchases in the postwar period) averaged 9.2 percent of total central government expenditures between 1967–1971. Gertrude E. Heare, *Latin American Military Expenditures, 1967–1971* (Washington, D.C., 1973), 10.
33. See estimates in Carlos A. Rodríguez and Ricardo Castañeda Rugamas, *El Salvador: Perfil Demográfico* (San Salvador, 1971), 9–10.

complex. Few who conceded the existence of the problem seriously believed it could be solved without far-reaching structural reforms.

In his public statements on the war, Sánchez Hernández refused to attribute any causal role to El Salvador's social structure or demographic expansion. Speaking to a group of veterans in August, he declared, "El Salvador has space for many more inhabitants than it currently has [and] they can enjoy here well-being, employment, and prosperity." The only obstacle to the realization of this magnificent potential was the hate and discontent fomented by international communism among nations and classes. On other occasions, he blamed the United Fruit Company and its operations in Honduras.[34]

Despite the superficiality of the official presidential explanations, it is apparent from other statements of Sánchez Hernández that he did recognize the necessity for change in El Salvador. Sánchez Hernández believed the postwar period provided a fresh opportunity to enact reform measures, not so much because the conflict had aggravated the country's social and economic problems as because it had produced a high degree of multipartisan support for the government. The president expressed the conviction that the National Unity Front was more than merely a defensive alliance against Honduras. Rather, it was the beginning of a single, truly Salvadoran party which, while it might accommodate within itself minor ideological differences, would be united "intellectually, morally, and emotionally" by its sense of nationality and its dedication to a better El Salvador.[35]

While certain statements of PDC leaders indicated a basic sympathy with the ideal of a national effort to overcome poverty and injustice, the party had no desire to surrender its independence or identity. When they first affiliated themselves with the front, Christian Democrats had emphasized that their participation was no more than an imperative response to the common Honduran threat and that it in no way represented "the abandonment of our profound ideological and political differences with the PCN which, in fact,

---

34. *Prensa Gráfica*, August 25, 1969; Salvador Videgaray, "Habla a SIEMPRE! el presidente de El Salvador Fidel Sánchez Hernández," *Siempre!* (Mexico City), April 15, 1970, p. 59.
35. *Prensa Gráfica*, August 25, 1969.

have recently deepened."[36] As it seemed more and more that the regime was abusing Unidad Nacional as a basis to question the patriotism of its critics, the PDC came to the conclusion that the continued maintenance of an atmosphere of crisis could benefit only the PCN. The war itself had been extremely popular and no party, certainly not the PDC that had supported it so wholeheartedly from the beginning, could now gain politically by condemning it. Still, to continue in support of the government much longer would render the very concept of "opposition" meaningless. With popular identification with the government at an all-time high as a result of the conflict, the Christian Democrats recognized the need to plan early and well for the upcoming assembly and municipality elections in March, 1970. In the light of these considerations, the party leadership announced on October 22 that, the National Unity Front having outlived its usefulness to the republic and become an instrument for the suppression of dissent, the PDC was formally dissociating itself from the government and returning to its accustomed role of open opposition. The Casa Presidencial reacted immediately, charging the Christian Democrats with cowardice and treachery in the face of the enemy. But the PDC's action broke the spell; the multipartisan alliance rapidly fell apart.[37]

While it permitted the resumption of open criticism, the collapse of the National Unity Front did not rule out the possibility of continued cooperation between the PDC and elements of the official party in the Legislative Assembly, where circumstances since 1968 had forced members of the two factions to work together on certain issues. The assembly of 1968–1970 with its large opposition minority was likely the most independent in Salvadoran history. PDC deputies led a number of legislative attempts to seize the initiative from the executive on important issues. Progressive members of the government party were often in sympathy with these efforts and

36. *Diario de Hoy*, June 30, 1969. On the PDC view of Unidad Nacional as a "common association of dissimilar ideas and efforts" working together for the national good, see statements of Deputy Héctor Dada Hirezi, *Prensa Gráfica*, August 10, 1969.
37. Secretaría de Información de la Presidencia de la República, "Mantengamos la Unidad Nacional," *Prensa Gráfica*, October 23, 1969; Partido Demócrata Cristiano, "La unidad nacional no es sumisión al gobierno," *Prensa Gráfica*, October 25, 1969.

only a strongly conservative PCN house leadership kept them in line. The price the government paid for the maintenance of party discipline was the failure of its own reform measures to clear the assembly's committee structure. A number of bills first introduced during the Rivera administration remained stalled in committee in 1969.

To be successful in his attempt to capitalize upon the recent popularity of the government and army to resume the reformist initiatives he had been compelled to abandon the year before, Sánchez Hernández would have to confront and overcome the resistance of the traditional PCN leadership to change. The fact that his natural allies in this effort, the PCN progressives and like-minded members of the opposition, tended to emphasize their independence from the executive promised to complicate his task. The major battles in this domestic war would be fought over the issue of agrarian reform.

On August 14, the Sánchez Hernández administration revealed in general terms a broad program of reform legislation, the most significant element of which was to be a "democratic program of agrarian reform." The announcement gave no details but described the projected reform as one which would "focus upon the problem in its totality . . . [and be] oriented in an integral manner toward a more just distribution of land and greater agricultural productivity." Such a measure, the government explained, had always been a pressing necessity but the recent crisis now made it more urgent than ever.[38] At the end of August, the Agriculture Ministry secured legislative authorization to create an agrarian reform commission to undertake a thorough study of Salvadoran agriculture and make recommendations for its reform. The commission included Ricardo Falla Cáceres, one of the civilian members of the "leftist" junta of October, 1960.[39]

The government's use of the term "agrarian reform" was itself something of a departure from a long-standing Salvadoran political taboo. Agrarian reform was traditionally something only left-wing opposition parties advocated. Conservatives generally identified the concept with international communism in general and in particular with the 1932 revolt in the West. Official vagueness regarding the

38. Casa Presidencial press release, Prensa Gráfica, August 15, 1969.
39. Prensa Gráfica, August 28, 1969. Later that year Falla became manager of the Salvadoran Coffee Company. Prensa Gráfica, November 1, 1969.

regime's intentions contributed to elite uneasiness.[40] Although Sánchez Hernández described his program as "democratic"—an adjective which in Latin American political usage often means "antipopular"—he had also, after all, spoken of "a more just distribution of land." The government appeared to move away from this position in October when Agriculture Minister Enrique Alvarez Córdova assured the national convention of Junior Chambers of Commerce that the primary goal of reform would be increased production rather than distribution.[41] Still, the minister's remarks left many questions unanswered. It was possible the government planned to "reform" marginally productive lands through capitalization, mechanization, and integration into the world market for agricultural exports. A transformation along these lines might please the large agricultural interests, but it would mean more unemployment among subsistence farmers and would not change the basic orientation of Salvadoran agriculture. If the government's intent, on the other hand, was to "reform" agricultural production by redirecting it from the external market to domestic consumption requirements, then it must necessarily involve a high level of coercion and interference with private property rights. No Salvadoran capitalist, whether directly involved in agriculture or not, could take this possibility lightly.

In raising the issue of agrarian reform itself, the regime provided the opposition an opportunity to call for basic structural revisions in the agrarian sector with the added justification that the traditional ban on the topic had at last fallen. The Christian Democrats quickly proposed a program of their own. When the PDC made its first announcement on this matter in late August, it appealed to the patriotism of the Salvadoran people. The Honduran crisis, the party claimed, was far from over. World opinion blamed the conflict on the unjust system of land tenure in El Salvador and, according to the Christian Democrats, world opinion in this regard was correct. There was no excuse for a country as small and crowded as El Salvador to maintain such a "liberal"—to use the PDC's word—policy toward land use and tenure. Under current land laws there were virtually no

40. The government's position was that any discussion or criticism was premature while the matter was under study by the Agrarian Reform Commission. "Silencio alrededor de la reforma agraria," *Prensa Gráfica*, October 15, 1969.
41. *Prensa Gráfica*, October 16, 24, 1969.

restrictions as to who could hold land, how much, or for what purpose. The existing structure made the Salvadoran peasant "one of the most oppressed in Latin America and . . . one of the poorest and most unjustly treated."[42]

According to the PDC, a successful agrarian reform must give equal priority to social justice, human development, and national economic development. In developing their own proposal, the Christian Democrats touched upon a theme they would employ frequently, especially in the 1972 presidential campaign. This was the assertion that there could be no such thing as an effective reform that dealt only with the issues of land tenure or use. Along with land reform must also come banking reform to provide agricultural credit facilities, technical reform to increase productivity, tax reform to encourage innovation, investment, and the diffusion of wealth and property, and educational reform to prepare the peasant population both technically and morally for integration into modern society. Heretofore, the PDC argued, individualistic values regarding landholding and production had kept the *campesino* on the margin of the national economy; now the country required a government-sponsored transformation of consciousness away from an individualist orientation toward a collective or "communitarian" one. The political goal of the PDC land reform, however, was through the elimination of both latifundia and minifundia to create a substantial class of small and medium-sized independent farmers to serve as the constituency for a vigorous democracy.[43]

Thus by September, 1969, both the government and the Christian Democrats had announced plans to introduce significant agrarian reform legislation. The current assembly leadership, of course, was unlikely to receive either program with much enthusiasm. Mildly indicative of the obstacles a substantive land reform might expect in the legislature was the fate of a bill introduced by the Christian Democrats as early as 1965 calling for a minimum agrarian wage of 2.25 colones daily plus meals. The assembly's Labor and Social Welfare Committee was still hearing testimony, mostly contrary, on this measure in late 1969.[44]

42. Partido Demócrata Cristiano, "La crisis nacional y la reforma agraria," *Prensa Gráfica*, August 29, 1969.
43. *Ibid.*; Partido Demócrata Cristiano, "Lineamientos generales sobre una reforma agraria en El Salvador," *La Universidad*, XCV (January–February, 1970), 47–48.
44. *Prensa Gráfica*, September 11, 18, 25, 1969.

For some time discontent had been building among both opposition deputies and a significant minority of *oficialistas* over the house
leadership's obstruction of their attempts to enact reforms. Following the war, the small leftist National Revolutionary Movement
(MNR) made several attempts to force bills out of committee. The
Christian Democrats supported the MNR in these efforts and themselves offered measures designed to reform the committee system
and the house rules. One result of this drive was the imposition of a
sixty-day deadline for the reporting by committees of three particular bills, all closely related to the agrarian question: cooperative associations, irrigation and drainage, and credit institutions.

When the deadline passed without action on the part of the house
leadership, a rebellion ensued. At a sparsely attended session on
November 4, a bare quorum of thirty-one opposition deputies and
PCN progressives voted unanimously to depose the old officers and
reorganize the house. The action came on a motion by the Christian
Democrats, but the PDC declined a place in the new leadership, explaining it did not wish to allow critics of the reorganization to
cheapen it with charges of political opportunism. The nine officers
elected included eight progressive *pecenistas* and one maverick
deputy from the ordinarily conservative Salvadoran Popular party
(PPS). A unanimous resolution of the house promised the rapid consideration of "long forgotten laws signifying true human development in the spirit of social justice." In order to accomplish this, the
committees were the next target of reorganization. Of particular importance were two special committees established to report out the
drainage and irrigation and cooperative associations bills. Officers of
the house and Christian Democrats now overwhelmingly dominated
both.[45]

Publicly, Sánchez Hernández accepted the revolt in the Legislative Assembly without expression of approval or disapproval. These
events in fact coincided with a personnel rotation in his own cabinet
that saw, among other changes, the resignation of conservative
Economy Minister Alfonso Rochac and the appointment of the more
progressive Armando Interiano to succeed him.[46] The ascendancy of

45. *Ibid.*, November 5, 7, 1969; *Diario de Hoy*, November 5, 1969; Sidney Mazzini
V., "Análisis político-constitucional: Golpe de mesa," *Diario de Hoy*, November 7,
1969.
46. *Diario de Hoy*, November 10, 1969.

like-minded men in the assembly was not, however, an unmixed blessing. Although the new house leaders expressed their desire to cooperate with the executive branch to facilitate passage of reform measures, their pronouncements made it clear they valued their independence and had no wish to serve as the regime's rubber stamp.[47]

The most dramatic assertion of legislative independence was the convocation on the assembly's own initiative of the National Agrarian Reform Congress, scheduled to meet in San Salvador January 5–10, 1970. The legislature's call described the proposed congress as a forum for the expression of opinions from all sectors of society on an issue of profound national importance and included the executive branch among those agencies, institutions, and organizations invited to send delegations. For purposes of representation, the Legislative Assembly organized the congress into four functional sectors: government, nongovernment, labor, and private (or entrepreneurial). Representing as it did virtually every political position and economic interest, the agrarian congress may well have been the most broadly representative political gathering in Salvadoran history. Labor sector delegates were quick, however, to criticize the absence of representatives from those groups most to be affected by any agrarian reform, the Salvadoran peasantry and rural labor force. The MNR's Guillermo Manuel Ungo, speaking for the nongovernment sector (which included the political parties, universities, professional associations, and the Roman Catholic hierarchy), joined the unions in their objection. There could be no genuine agrarian reform, he declared, as long as El Salvador failed to incorporate its rural population "fully, democratically, into the bosom of the national community."[48]

In spite of their misgivings, labor organizations and leftists generally considered the agrarian congress a major step forward and were willing and enthusiastic participants. The reaffirmation by Sánchez Hernández in his opening address of the regime's commitment to the "unavoidable necessity" of agrarian reform heartened

---

47. Rafael Rodríguez González, apparent leader of the PCN insurgents, described the vote as a blow for legislative supremacy. *Prensa Gráfica*, November 5, 1969.

48. *Ibid.*, January 6, 1970; Guillermo Manuel Ungo, "Discurso pronunciado por el ... vicepresidente de la Directiva del Congreso Nacional de Reforma Agraria por el sector no gubernamental, en el acto de inauguración," *Prensa Gráfica*, January 10, 1970.

progressives of all parties.[49] The attendance of conservative elements, on the other hand, was reluctant from the beginning. Even before the inauguration of the congress, the Salvadoran Institute of Social and Economic Studies (Instituto Salvadoreño de Estudios Sociales y Económicos, ISESE), a front for the major economic interest groups, charged that the new assembly leadership had already committed itself to a "socialist" agrarian reform. The real purpose of the congress, the ISESE claimed, was to make political propaganda for the March elections. The institute's declaration dismissed as "fallacious" the assumption that the present system of land tenure was an obstacle to national development and proposed that, since only agriculturalists fully understood the agrarian problem, they be given more votes than other sectors.[50]

Conservatives argued generally that agrarian reform was a technical rather than a political issue. Since the congress chairman, Juan Gregorio Guardado, a PCN deputy from San Miguel and president of the reorganized Legislative Assembly, insisted that the purpose of the gathering was precisely not to carry out a technical study but to survey the spectrum of national opinion, members of the entrepreneurial sector concluded the entire exercise had little point. Conservatives especially opposed the idea that the agrarian congress should pass resolutions or make recommendations. When, at the first session, the progressives won an important roll call on this issue, the entire private sector withdrew from the congress.[51]

49. Sánchez Hernández, Discursos, III, 49–50.
50. Instituto Salvadoreño de Estudios Sociales y Económicos, "Una advertencia al país sobre el Congreso Nacional Agrario," Prensa Gráfica, January 5, 1970. For a broader statement of ISESE's critique of postwar reformism, see its "No desordenemos nuestra propia casa con el Mercado Común en peligro," Prensa Gráfica, September 17, 1969. Other conservative reactions include Partido Popular Salvadoreño, "¿Hacia una reforma agraria democrática?" Diario de Hoy, January 6, 1970; José Antonio Rodríguez Porth, "Discurso pronunciado por el . . . vicepresidente de la mesa directiva, en representación del sector empresarial, en el Congreso Nacional de Reforma Agraria, el día de su inauguración," Prensa Gráfica, January 6, 1970; and José Enrique Córdova, "Los comentarios del Dr. Rodríguez Porth al Congreso de Reforma Agraria," Prensa Gráfica, January 26, 1970.
51. Juan Gregorio Guardado, "Palabras del señor presidente de la Asamblea Legislativa . . . en ocasión de celebrarse el primer Congreso Nacional sobre Reforma Agraria," Prensa Gráfica, January 8, 1970; "Declaración de los delegados del sector empresarial acreditados ante el Congreso de Reforma Agraria, al pueblo salvadoreño," Prensa Gráfica, January 7, 1970; Diario de Hoy, January 7, 1970. The conservatives had been successful on an earlier roll call, but the Christian Democrats present employed a parliamentary technicality to overturn the result and hold another vote in which assembly deputies voted individually as ex-officio members of the congress.

While conservatives mounted a sustained campaign of attacks and criticism from the outside, the three remaining sectors continued their work. Upon adjourning, the congress voted a list of resolutions and recommendations which set forth in general terms its consensus on the various issues related to a projected Salvadoran agrarian reform. While this outline had ample precedent in Latin American experience, to conservatives it must have represented the most irresponsible radicalism. The delegates reasoned from the premise, long honored in Hispanic economic thought, that El Salvador's failure to develop resulted from its failure to mobilize adequately its existing resources. The goal of any agrarian reform must be to encourage the most economic use of the nation's limited supply of arable land through the improvement of technology and credit facilities, to insure a higher level of income to peasants and agricultural laborers whose poverty hindered the development of an internal market for national industry, and, finally, to promote an increase in agricultural production for the domestic market without jeopardizing the export sector upon which the national economy depended.

Few observers could have found these goals objectionable in themselves, but the congress went even further. It identified the existence in El Salvador of latifundia and minifundia as the major social evil obstructing the optimum employment and development of national resources, whether human or material. The delegates concluded that, given this situation, it was "not only a right of the state but a duty" to undertake "massive expropriation in favor of the common good."[52] Like many Latin American charters written since the Mexican Revolution, the Salvadoran constitution already provided for the expropriation of property that could be shown to perform no "social function." The National Agrarian Reform Congress defined within that category land whose concentration into a few hands impeded the right of individual Salvadorans of access to resources sufficient to guarantee their personal well-being or prevented the creation of small or medium-sized farm properties, unexploited land or land exploited in an inefficient manner or a manner

52. "Resoluciones y recomendaciones del Primer Congreso Nacional de Reforma Agraria, realizado del 5 al 10 de enero de 1970," Economía Salvadoreña, XXVIII (1969), 109. For other documents from the congress, see the entire number of La Universidad, XCV (January–February, 1970).

that resulted in its physical deterioration, and, finally, land whose owners violated the laws governing labor relations. The delegates specified, however, that except under circumstances already established in the constitution, the state must indemnify the owners of expropriated properties. Such indemnification might be in cash or in government bonds, but should in no event be spread over a period longer than twenty years.[53]

From the spectre of expropriation, the congress passed to another Salvadoran political taboo—rural labor organization. The only guarantee of an effective and irreversible agrarian reform, the delegates declared, would be active popular participation in the process. To this end the government must restrain the landholders and their collaborators within the armed forces, while defending and promoting the right of peasants and agricultural workers to organize into unions and cooperatives. Once free to form associations, the *campesino* could "take his destiny into his own hands and participate directly, actively, and creatively in national development."[54]

In the PDC's August call for agrarian reform, the party had expressed its willingness to join with all sectors and interests, especially those involved in agriculture and economic planning, to draft a general plan. The National Agrarian Reform Congress seemed at least a partial fulfillment of this promise. Certainly the Christian Democrats were among the most dynamic participants. But there were present as well delegates, such as those from the MNR, with much more advanced views. The final resolutions agreed in many particulars with earlier PDC statements on the issue. Christian Democrats, for instance, had always supported the right of agricultural workers to organize. But the congress placed more emphasis on direct expropriation as the specific instrument to accomplish the desired distribution of property than the PDC customarily had. In accepting these resolutions, the Christian Democrats moved significantly beyond their 1967 presidential program.

The National Agrarian Reform Congress lasted one day longer

---

53. "Resoluciones del Congreso de Reforma Agraria," 117. Of particular interest is the position paper presented by the delegation from the National University of El Salvador, "Legislación de Reforma Agraria," *La Universidad*, XCV (January–February, 1970), 93–115. This paper examines the constitutional basis of the question and includes comparative appendices on the concept of "social function" in other Latin American countries.
54. "Resoluciones del Congreso de Reforma Agraria," 114.

than the Honduran War had and, although it did not gain international attention, it too had serious political consequences. The congress set large propertied interests openly and frankly on the defensive in a way very few events—among obvious exceptions, the violence of 1932—ever had. It showed that opposition parties could work smoothly together with elements of the PCN to promote progressive ideas. Finally, it demonstrated that the Legislative Assembly, heretofore the bulwark of civil obstruction, could under the wrong leadership proceed independently of the executive and take the initiative in reform legislation. The increasing isolation and alienation of the conservatives along with the swelling confidence of the progressive opposition would produce major problems for the PCN in the years immediately to come.

Symptomatic of the increasing polarization of Salvadoran politics was the enthusiastic participation of the Roman Catholic hierarchy in the National Agrarian Reform Congress. The Salvadoran episcopacy, long noted for its social and political conservatism, underwent a dramatic transformation in the mid-1960s and especially by the time of the 1968 Conference of Latin American Bishops in Medellín, Colombia. Church declarations on social issues now regularly cited Pope Paul VI's encyclical *Populorum Progressio* and Archbishop Luis Chávez y González, formerly a quite conservative figure, emerged as a major defender of peasant rights and advocate of social and economic reform. Chávez named a group of progressive priests to represent the Metropolitan Curia in the agrarian congress and vigorously defended their performance against all critics. In El Salvador as elsewhere in Latin America, the hierarchy's abandonment of its traditional role as defender of privilege led to acts of physical intimidation against the clergy. The abduction of a young priest in San Salvador during the congress may have been entirely unrelated to this issue, but it led the church to voice even more firmly its commitment to reform.[55]

Another sign of trouble was the continued contraction of the official party's appeal. The Party of National Conciliation was losing the

55. *Prensa Gráfica*, January 30, 1970; "Pronunciamiento de la delegación de la Curia Metropolitana," *Prensa Gráfica*, January 10, 1970; "Pronunciamiento del clero ante el secuestro del Padre Alas," *Prensa Gráfica*, January 12, 1970; "Declaración conjunta del Episcopado Salvadoreño," *Prensa Gráfica*, January 15, 1970.

universality it claimed by virtue of its name. The defection in 1968 of Economy Minister Glower Valdivieso to the MNR and the increasingly obvious independence of the progressives in the assembly emphasized the PCN's weakness on its left. In addition, the erosion of conservative support accelerated following the war and the National Agrarian Reform Congress. The party lost two key conservatives with the resignation in November, 1969, of its secretary-general, Justice Minister Francisco Peña Trejo, and of the recently deposed assembly president, Benjamín Interiano. Both men expressed dissatisfaction with the regime's tolerance of what they considered the "illegal" reorganization of the legislature. In addition, Interiano criticized the president's leadership of the party, charging that Sánchez Hernández had never called a meeting of the current executive council. Hinting darkly at the possibility of Communist infiltration, Interiano denounced the official party itself as a crowd of traitors where one could expect "no comradeship, no unity, nothing." What was worse, the Christian Democrats and their turncoat allies were now running the country.[56]

The steadily growing strength of the opposition also complicated the PCN's position. It was not at all impossible that the PDC and MNR together might deprive the official party of control of the assembly in 1970. The Christian Democrats in particular approached the elections with confidence. Reviewing the decade since its foundation in 1960, the PDC cited with pride its record of consistent growth from a handful of dedicated men to "the most significant political force in the history of the country." Along with the party's own emergence as a permanent, truly national organization, came the awakening of the political consciousness of the Salvadoran people, the disappearance of *caudillismo*, and the progressive weakening of the forces of fraud, imposition, and officialism. It was "undeniable," the party maintained, that the great majority of Salvadorans were "totally firm in their decision to entrust to the Christian Democratic Party the representation of their dearest interests."

56. *Prensa Gráfica*, November 8, 11 (quotation), 1969. Unlike the office of the same name in the PDC, the PCN's secretariat-general was not the party's highest office. Sánchez Hernández as "coordinator-general" was senior. Originally a Christian Democrat, Benjamín Interiano moved to the PCN following the defeat of the conservative faction in the PDC's first national convention in 1961.

The PDC's message at the beginning of the new decade was one of "hope and optimism" that a "new dawn" was about to break upon Salvadoran history's "most brilliant and promising chapter."[57]

A possible indication of PDC sanguineness regarding the strength of its organization and appeal was the decision of José Napoleón Duarte to retire from the mayoralty of San Salvador. Easily the party's best known and most popular national leader, Duarte had contributed a crucial element of charisma to each of the PDC's successful municipality campaigns, and his absence from the presidential ticket in 1967 may well have accounted for the party's unexpectedly poor showing in San Salvador that year. Duarte's retirement was ostensibly to return to his engineering firm, but in reality to prepare his race for the presidency in 1972. According to his own account, the decision was made in active consultation with the party leadership.[58]

The task of choosing Duarte's successor fell to the PDC's national convention in January, and the name of virtually every senior party leader came under consideration. From the beginning, however, the narrow favorite seems to have been municipal secretary Carlos Herrera Rebollo who ultimately won the nomination, defeating Juan Ricardo Ramírez on the second ballot. Although less prominent than his opponents, Herrera had been a founding member of the PDC and possessed a long record of faithful service to the party. Son of a noted educator and married to a medical doctor, the thirty-five-year-old labor lawyer was representative of the young middle-class professionals who dominated the national leadership of the PDC. A student opponent of the Lemus regime, Herrera had been active in the University Catholic Action group as well as the Law Students' Association. Before 1970 he served mostly in party leadership positions rather than seek public office himself. During his association with the party and the Duarte municipal administration he had studied local government and community development in Europe and Chile.[59]

One political actor no one could ignore during this period was

57. Partido Demócrata Cristiano, "Mensaje de esperanza y optimismo," Prensa Gráfica, January 8, 1970.

58. Duarte, "Intipucá."

59. Prensa Gráfica, October 15, 1969; Partido Demócrata Cristiano, "Herrera Rebollo ¡Alcalde!" Prensa Gráfica, February 8, 1970; Duarte, "Intipucá."

the army. It was clear from Salvadoran experience since World War II that the military would intervene if the civil mechanisms for control should break down. Such a breakdown increased in likelihood as the opposition strengthened and the executive lost support. When Sánchez Hernández organized his plans for the 1970 election, he therefore built his strategy upon the two key elements whose support he must retain—the officer corps and the remaining loyal leadership of the PCN. Such a strategy did not necessarily imply a moderation in the pursuit of reform, but it did call for less solicitude for the political rights of opposition parties and in general a more authoritarian approach to civil questions in the future.

The primary goal of the regime was to reduce the opposition margin in, and therefore the independence of, the Legislative Assembly. The issue the government and the PCN chose to emphasize in the election was the one upon which they were least vulnerable, the Honduran War. The official party's 1970 campaign consequently stressed nationalism, the honorable mission of the armed forces, and the need for continued unity and preparedness. One way in which Sánchez Hernández sought to exploit these issues was to employ military men in the campaign. The most visible of these was the commander of the First Infantry Brigade, Colonel Mario de Jesús Velásquez, the party's candidate for the mayoralty of San Salvador. Although seemingly unsuited to the sedentary routine of municipal administration, the bearded, robust popular hero of the Honduran conflict campaigned enthusiastically. Making triumphant public appearances throughout the city, Velásquez dressed in civilian clothes but retained his characteristic black beret with death's head insignia. In the markets, a center of Christian Democratic strength, Velásquez emphasized his role as patriot, family man, and Catholic. He attacked Duarte for what he called six years of ineffectiveness and promised a number of things the PDC had already delivered. His promise of new, clean markets was particularly gratuitous as it came almost immediately following final assembly approval of Duarte's market project.[60]

Not unexpectedly, the opposition parties objected strongly to Na-

60. *Prensa Gráfica*, December 23, 1969; Partido de Conciliación Nacional, "Señoras de los mercados recibieron a su 'héroe' como él se lo merece," *Prensa Gráfica*, March 1, 1970; V. Emmanuel O., "El Diablo una mala interpretación," *Diario de Hoy*, March 3, 1970.

tional Conciliation's employment of soldiers. The Christian Democrats denounced the tactic as the desperate resort of elements just coming to recognize the approaching collapse of their power, and charged the action would compromise a heroic institution in the eyes of the people as well as undermine its readiness in the event of renewed hostilities with Honduras.[61] Minister of Defense General Fidel Torres answered this and similar accusations with the explanation that all officers participating in the election had temporarily separated from active duty and consequently acted as individual citizens rather than as representatives of the armed forces. The PCN itself characterized as antidemocratic the "infantile lamentations" of the opposition, since their effect would be to deny a citizen public office on the sole grounds of his profession.[62]

In addition to military participation, the government sought in other ways to capitalize upon nationalist sentiment. Advertisements compared the PCN to the victorious national soccer team and described it as an "authentically Salvadoran party" completely independent of foreign models or direction. The essential difference, the PCN insisted, between the reforms it proposed and those offered by the PDC was that the Christian Democrats took their inspiration from an international, and therefore un-Salvadoran, movement. One notice closed with the frankly patriotic exhortation "Be a good Salvadoran, vote PCN!"[63]

Particularly beneficial to the regime was a timely renewal of border provocations between El Salvador and Honduras. By the end of January, Salvadoran papers were full of reports of gunfire and expulsions—all very reminiscent of the immediate prewar period. Bilateral negotiations arranged under the auspices of the OAS, CACM, and Organization of Central American States collapsed in mid-February, apparently to general public satisfaction on both

61. Partido Demócrata Cristiano, "Llamado a la conciencia del pueblo y del ejército," *Prensa Gráfica*, January 3, 1970.
62. *Prensa Gráfica*, January 6, 1970; Partido de Conciliación Nacional, "PCN contra la demogogia," *Prensa Gráfica*, January 8, 1970.
63. Partido de Conciliación Nacional, "Patria," *Prensa Gráfica*, January 10, 1970; Partido de Conciliación Nacional, "Vota por el PCN," *Prensa Gráfica*, January 16, 1970. Many conservatives were not impressed by the PCN's claims to authenticity. One commentator described the official party as a thrall of Washington, following "socialist and socialistoid [policy lines] left by Kennedy and his Marxist advisors." Enrique Henríquez Azurdia, "Partidos criollos e internacionales en la lid," *Diario de Hoy*, March 4, 1970.

sides. At home, the Salvadoran opposition parties reacted in anger and confusion, alternating between charges that the incidents were politically motivated fabrications on the one hand and on the other that the government was not doing enough to curb the Honduran menace. At a public meeting called at the request of the opposition, Defense Minister Torres rejected suggestions that the government cease publicizing border incidents until after the election. Torres insisted the regime had no desire to alarm unduly the Salvadoran people, but denied it had a right to keep these matters secret.[64]

In addition to the Christian Democrats and the PCN, three other parties participated in the 1970 election. The National Revolutionary Movement (MNR) claimed to be heir to the left-wing radical tradition of the "New Line" PAR. It was a very small party, however, and still suffered internal organizational problems on the eve of its second electoral experience. In spite of its claim to be "revolutionary," the MNR's attitude toward the government and its program was generally one of constructive, although tough and incisive, criticism. Party pronouncements were highly intellectualized and blasted the PDC for opposing government policies merely to win votes. The MNR also criticized the Christian Democrats for their exclusivism and their alleged failure to recognize that El Salvador's problems were not those of Chile or Venezuela.[65]

In 1967, the conservative Salvadoran Popular party (PPS) had run fourth in a field of four on a rigid appeal to orthodox principles of laissez-faire capitalism. By 1970, party leaders seemed to be attempting to broaden their following. Possibly inspired by a North American "conservative revival" that culminated in the election of Richard M. Nixon to the presidency in 1968, the PPS began to appeal to a sector of Salvadoran society it called—as had Nixonian Republicans in the United States—the "silent majority." These were supposedly the hard-working, taxpaying, home-owning Salvadorans too busy earning their livings to involve themselves in politics and, therefore, ignored by the major parties. The party's emblem, a house, sought to

<hr>

64. *El Mundo* (San Salvador), January 31, 1970; *Prensa Gráfica*, January 30, February 5, 1970; Martz, "OAS Settlement Procedures," 5.

65. Movimiento Nacional Revolucionario, "Carta política . . . al pueblo salvadoreño y al presidente de la república," *Prensa Gráfica*, December 11, 1969. A founding member who quit the MNR in late January charged the leadership with antilabor sentiments and ties to the PCN. *El Mundo*, January 31, 1970.

evoke an entire complex of emotional responses centering upon the ideals of property, family, law and order.[66]

New to party politics was the Nationalist Democratic Union (Unión Democrática Nacionalista, UDN). Describing itself as the "non-Communist" Left, the UDN was in reality a quasi-personalist vehicle organized and led by former vice-president Francisco Roberto Lima. The presence of junior military officers in its ranks as well as the party's early criticism of the government's handling of the war led to constant problems with the authorities. Lima's attempt to return to political office as a deputy from San Salvador collapsed when, following the election, the Central Council of Elections retroactively disqualified his entire departmental slate on a technicality.[67]

The outcome of the March 8 election was calamitous for the heretofore optimistic opposition parties. The damage was particularly serious in the municipal races. In the period 1968–1970, the Christian Democrats controlled seventy-eight municipalities including the three most important. Following the 1970 election, they found themselves reduced to a mere eight, of which only the capital was at all significant. Despite the defeat of Colonel Velásquez by the lawyer Herrera in San Salvador, the PCN swept 252 of the country's 261 municipal councils. The PPS lost all its mayoralties; there was indeed a silent majority in El Salvador, but it was made up of landless peasants rather than taxpaying homeowners. The UDN triumphed only in the city of Usulután. The PDC fared much better in the assembly races, dropping only three seats from nineteen to sixteen. Unfortunately for the opposition, however, the *oficialistas* virtually wiped out the fringe parties, giving the PCN a substantial majority in the new legislature.[68]

66. Roberto López Trejo, "La mayoría silenciosa," *Diario de Hoy*, March 7, 1970.

67. *Prensa Gráfica*, October 7, 1969, March 13, 1970; Unión Democrática Nacionalista, "Primera carta política," *Prensa Gráfica*, October 4, 1969; Unión Democrática Nacionalista, "Segunda carta política," *Prensa Gráfica*, October 15, 1969; *Diario de Hoy*, March 4, 1970. A PDC leader explained to the author in 1976 that "everyone knows" the UDN fronts for the outlawed Salvadoran Communist party.

68. *Prensa Gráfica*, March 12, 13, 15, 1970; *Diario de Hoy*, March 14, 1970. The municipalities taken by the PDC in addition to the capital were Ciudad Delgado (San Salvador department), Cuscatancingo (San Salvador), Jocoatique (Morazán), El Tránsito (San Miguel), Chalchuapa (Santa Ana), Zaragoza (La Libertad), and Puerto El Triunfo (Usulután). The new Legislative Assembly composition was: PCN, 34; PDC, 16; UDN, 1; PPS, 1.

Many Salvadorans offered explanations for the sudden reversal in the opposition's fortunes. Sánchez Hernández cited the consolidation of democracy as a Salvadoran political tradition, a process that presumably could work only to the benefit of the PCN. The Christian Democrats, on the other hand, charged fraud and imposition. In an open letter to General Torres at the Defense Ministry, Duarte claimed he had received numerous reports of official abuses in the provinces. These included a case in El Paisnal where the local commander had allegedly assembled a group of local citizens early on the morning of election day, armed them, and dispatched them to the frontier to repel a supposititious Honduran invasion. All of the men thus deceived, according to Duarte, belonged to the PDC and many were scheduled to serve as poll commissioners. He demanded an investigation and due punishment for the officer responsible.[69]

Streetcorner experts expressed a number of opinions on the election. Some believed there had indeed been extensive fraud; others attributed the PCN's massive victory to general satisfaction with its performance in power. A number of people interviewed the day following the election, however, focused upon what appears to have been the fundamental factor, the prospect of renewed hostilities with Honduras. Many expressed the belief that only the official party, given its experience in government and its close tie to the armed forces, could guarantee national security.[70] Government propaganda had stressed the PDC's abandonment of Unidad Nacional and its extra-Salvadoran ideological ties. What is more, a speech critical of the government's role in the war made by Abraham Rodríguez on national television in late February may have tended in the minds of some voters to confirm official charges of Christian Democratic antipatriotism.[71] The PCN no doubt also profited from the government's customary use of the brief "dead period" between the legal end of the campaign and election day to publicize its own accomplishments as well as the latest developments along the frontier.

Evidence of the importance of the Honduran situation to the out-

69. *Prensa Gráfica*, March 10, 1970. For a catalog of PDC charges regarding the election, see Partido Demócrata Cristiano, "¡La gran estafa del 8 de marzo!" *Prensa Gráfica*, March 16, 1970.

70. *Diario de Hoy*, March 10, 1970.

71. *Prensa Gráfica*, February 25, 1970; J. de Caballero, "A los pensamientos del Dr. Abraham Rodríguez," *Diario de Hoy*, March 2, 1970.

come of the election is the fact that, of the five departments having significant frontiers with Honduras, the official party carried four with more than 70 percent of the vote—La Unión, Cabañas, Chalatenango, and Morazán. The remaining department, San Miguel, contained a major urban center and a strong PDC organization. Even so, the PCN carried San Miguel with almost 63 percent of the vote and recaptured the mayoralty of the departmental capital as well. While its performance was most spectacular along the frontier and in traditional strongholds, the PCN also made serious inroads into Christian Democratic territory. Nowhere did the official party fail to increase its share of the vote substantially over 1968. Only in San Salvador department, which the PDC barely carried with 46 percent of the vote, did the PCN fall short of an absolute majority.[72]

Considering the magnitude of the PDC's defeat, the retention of the mayoralty of San Salvador was an important psychological consolation.[73] Even here, however, there was slippage. The PDC's share of the vote dropped considerably from 1968 when it had won easily with nearly 60 percent. The decline was of great importance because the department of San Salvador had traditionally been the key to the party's national strength. Besides the PDC's weakened position in this populous department, another factor served to limit San Salvador's value to the party in 1970. This was an increased voter participation in the provinces relative to the capital. Whereas in 1964 San Salvador department had contributed more than one-fourth the total national vote, and in 1972 would yield nearly 30 percent, its share in 1970 was barely 18 percent.[74] Assuming the PDC's enthusiastic seizure of the banner of agrarian reform following the war to have been part of a design to improve the party's showing in rural areas where it had never been particularly strong, the strategy yielded no visible benefit in 1970.

72. *Prensa Gráfica*, March 13, 1970; *Diario de Hoy*, March 14, 1970.
73. The isolated victory of Herrera over Velásquez gives ample indication of the location of the PDC's hard-core, residual support. When asked to explain the war hero's defeat, former president Osmín Aguirre commented acidly, "the street women beat him." Lilo Saavedra, "El Cnel. Osmín Aguirre y Salinas comenta derrota de Cnel. Velásquez," *Diario de Hoy*, March 10, 1970. There was a story at the time, and a PDC member repeated it to the author in 1976, that the PCN deliberately sacrificed Velásquez in order to frustrate his presidential ambitions.
74. Compare returns, *Diario de Hoy*, March 20, 1964; February 26, 1972.

The war with Honduras was in many ways a major watershed in the modern political history of El Salvador as well as in the development of its opposition parties. In the aftermath of war it was necessary for the republic to question its traditional views both of itself and the world. Most immediately, El Salvador faced the economic problems occasioned by the loss of its trade with Honduras. In addition, it had to absorb into the national economy tens of thousands of refugees—no easy task in a country already suffering serious rural unemployment and whose entire population of industrial workers numbered less than one hundred thousand. The government sought to meet these challenges by renewing its oft-stated commitment to social and economic reforms. In late 1969, it placed great emphasis upon agrarian reform. There were dangers inherent here, of course. Land reform was a red flag to most conservatives, while the progressive opposition demanded the government be more specific about its aims and proceed more rapidly. The strength of the opposition in the Legislative Assembly afforded that body sufficient independence from the executive to chart its own course. The National Agrarian Reform Congress forced the government publicly to choose sides on an issue that threatened to hasten the process of alienation among its rightist and capitalist supporters. Although the administration identified itself with the popular sector by its participation in the congress, it could not afford to permit the continued growth in prestige of the progressive parties. An opposition victory in 1970 might lead to the sort of political tensions that could threaten not only the survival of the regime but of the "electoral solution" itself. Patriotism and preparedness in the face of a continuing Honduran menace provided the PCN leadership with an issue that cultivated the loyalty of the armed forces while distracting the electorate from more embarrassing political, social, and economic questions. In its campaign the government stressed this issue to the virtual exclusion of all others, with the dramatic success noted above.

A PCN manifesto following the election had charged that the Christian Democrats had learned nothing in ten years of political activity and still did not understand the democratic system. The people had toppled the PDC's "card castle of ambitions," the official party boasted, and "converted it into a B-league team."[75] For their part, however, the Christian Democrats soon put the insults of 1970 behind them and began to prepare for a rematch in 1972. The unexpected reversals had provoked only the second major internal ideological dispute in the PDC's ten years of existence. Two currents of opinion regarding the party's future emerged from postelection discussions among its leaders. One faction favored a mere reorganization of the party's campaign structure in order to increase its ability to penetrate traditional provincial strongholds of the PCN. Another, younger, group advocated radicalization of the party's doctrine and programs. As he had done in the past on occasions when internal divisions threatened the party, José Napoleón Duarte now sought to avoid personal identification with either side. He resigned his position as secretary-general in favor of former San Salvador city attorney Pablo Mauricio Alvergue. Alvergue's judicious leadership guided the party through this period of crisis with a minimum of disruption. Working together with long-time party regulars Juan Ricardo Ramírez and Adolfo Rey Prendes, he mapped out a compromise course of action that preserved the authority of the party's traditional leaders while at the same time it involved both a rethinking of electoral strategy and a continued deliberate ideological shift to the left.[76]

75. Partido de Conciliación Nacional, "El fin de la estafa (el PDC se quita la careta)," Prensa Gráfica, March 18, 1970.
76. Duarte, "Intipucá." Ramírez and Rey Prendes were both members of the legendary "Eight" of 1960–1961. Of the other six, Italo Giammattei had joined the PCN, while León Cuéllar devoted himself to university faculty politics. Duarte, Roberto Lara Velado, and Abraham Rodríguez all served at one time or another as secretary-general. Guillermo Ungo, honored as dean of the party, died of a heart attack in 1966.

Chapter VI

Painful Options:
The Elections of 1972

The political crisis that effectively ended El Salvador's experiment in openness in 1972 resulted from the fact that the government party very nearly lost the presidential election that year. This happened for two reasons. First, the leading opposition party, the Christian Democrats, overcame in the aftermath of their serious reversal of 1970 their long-standing objection to coalitions and successfully organized the other progressive parties into a single front. Equally as important, a growing number of rightists, continuing a trend that had begun in 1966 with the appearance of the PPS, came to the conclusion that they no longer enjoyed a sympathetic protector in the National Conciliation party.

A number of important developments combined in late 1970 and 1971 to encourage an exodus on the part of the privileged and their clients from the columns of the PCN to those of right-wing splinter parties. For one thing, the municipality and Legislative Assembly race of 1970 was not the only election that had captured attention in El Salvador that year. In Chile in September, Salvador Allende at the head of a Communist-backed coalition of left-wing parties defeated the conservative Jorge Alessandri and the Christian Democrat Radomiro Tomic to become the first legally elected Marxist president in Latin America. While Allende's sympathizers and other admirers of Chilean democracy around the world marveled at the peacefulness and legality of the transfer to socialist rule, conservative observers in El Salvador were less enthusiastic. In particular, they were quick to point out that the preceding Chilean regime had been Christian Democratic. Eduardo Frei, they charged, had through the enactment of irresponsible social reforms undercut the foundations of Chilean society and thus prepared the way for the Communist enslavement of the country. The often explicit conclusion was that El Salvador could expect an identical fate should the PDC ever achieve power. Salvadoran Christian Democrats angrily denied that the situations of the two countries were in any way comparable, but they were clearly embarrassed by the poor showing of the Chilean PDC of whose historic victory in 1964 they had boasted as though it had been their own.[1]

The Christian Democrats were not the sole targets of conservative jeremiads on the lesson of Chile. The government suffered its share of criticism as well. One writer noted the traditional Salvadoran respect for Chile's long record of stable democracy. In fact, it used to be said that the one serious breach in that record in the twentieth century—the military intervention led by Carlos Ibáñez in 1924—resulted from wicked habits Ibáñez had acquired during his tour as a military advisor in El Salvador. Now it seemed Chile was having its revenge, that Chileans were teaching Salvadoran leaders how to be soft on communism.[2]

Conservative displeasure with Sánchez Hernández increased after the 1970 election as a result of the fact that, although the progressive opposition found itself considerably reduced, the president chose to regard the vote as an endorsement of his reformist initiatives. Opening the new assembly in July, Sánchez Hernández announced his intention to continue pursuit of agrarian reform legislation "affecting the property system for lands not in use or poorly exploited."[3] During the months that followed, the government repeatedly emphasized its commitment to reform in three major areas of national life—agriculture, education, and governmental administration. To the alarm of oligarchs, the new PCN-dominated assembly proved to be nearly as quick as its hated predecessor to pass "irre-

1. Among many pronouncements of Salvadoran conservatives, see three articles by Carlos Sandoval: "La sepultura de la democracia cristiana," *Diario de Hoy*, September 11, 1970; "Democracias en regresión," *Diario de Hoy*, October 21, 1970; and "Las sorpresas de las afinidades ideológicas," *Diario de Hoy*, October 26, 1970. For the PDC's reply, Partido Demócrata Cristiano, "El caso chileno y el P. D. C. de El Salvador," *Diario de Hoy*, October 7, 1970.
2. Alfredo Parada (h.), "Más sobre la lección chilena y los 'kerenskys' lugareños," *Diario de Hoy*, October 14, 1970.
3. Sánchez Hernández, *Discursos*, IV, 3–13.

sponsible" measures. A common theme in attacks upon the government was that haste in making reform was dangerous. The conservative Salvadoran Institute for Social and Economic Studies (ISESE), for example, called for the leisurely, detailed consideration of all measures. The republic, it argued, had plenty of time and there was no necessity for the government's unseemly hurry. Such precipitous "social reformism," the institute claimed, had been the cause of Chile's "tragic collapse."[4]

The ISESE's attack on the Sánchez Hernández administration came in response to the president's message of September 15, 1970, the one hundred forty-ninth anniversary of Central American independence. Setting aside themes traditional to the occasion, such as the deeds of national heroes, Sánchez Hernández had proclaimed independence a meaningless concept so long as social justice remained a distant aspiration rather than a reality. Necessary reforms, he warned, could no longer be delayed: "The Salvadoran people are noble; they have trusted and continue to trust their leaders. But they have now reached their limit. At this moment, the reforms under consideration are like a rock teetering on the edge of a precipice that no one and nothing can prevent from falling." Sánchez Hernández reminded conservatives that his reforms were not vindictive—he had no desire to see oligarchs reduced to operating elevators in Miami Beach hotels—but they were necessary and would come through violence and terror if the "fierce opponents of evolution" did not permit his government to accomplish them in a peaceful and orderly fashion.[5]

Although he predicted a hostile reaction to his Independence Day message, Sánchez Hernández was sorely offended by the ISESE's suggestion that his government's policies served the Communist cause. History showed, he snapped to reporters, that the privileged had always defended their advantages against any attempt at reform. The same conservatives who now yearned for the days of Hernández Martínez or Osorio had conveniently forgotten how they hated them at the time for their efforts toward social and economic justice. Still, the president argued, the best evidence that

4. Instituto Salvadoreño de Estudios Sociales y Económicos, "El despojo y la imposición como 'reformas sociales,'" *Diario de Hoy*, October 9, 1970.
5. Sánchez Hernández, *Discursos*, IV, 15–21.

he personally was "no Marxist, [but] an enemy of totalitarianism of whatever color," was the climate of liberty that prevailed in El Salvador. The conservatives were completely free to publish whatever they liked about him, but they should remember that other people had rights as well. His duty as president, elected not merely by the minority interests but by all the people, was to see that those rights were vindicated. During this spirited defense of his government's performance, Sánchez Hernández referred to his program as one of "reform in liberty," a direct paraphrase of the Christian Democrats' "revolution in liberty."[6]

A primary issue in the confrontation between conservatives and progressives in late 1970 was the long delayed irrigation and drainage law (ley de riego y avenamiento). This legislation, first introduced by the Rivera government and consistently supported by the Christian Democrats, proposed to establish irrigation districts in areas where land was poorly exploited and to promote development through both private and state investment. One stated goal was increased food production for the domestic market. It was also hoped that the allocation of resources for improvement of conditions in the countryside would mean better employment prospects for rural workers and thereby tend to discourage migration to the cities. In its ideal form, the irrigation law would also attack the twin evils of minifundia and latifundia since upper and lower limits on property size would be set individually for each district. The government's rationale for the latter provision was that irrigation was an expensive undertaking that would require large amounts of public funding. It was hardly just that only a privileged few should benefit from it.[7]

Large propertied interests of all sorts objected vehemently to this proposal and their opposition kept it stalled in committee for years. Essentially, conservatives argued that the measure was unconstitutional because it infringed upon the right to hold property. Such an argument derived from an extremely narrow reading of the constitution of 1962, since both it and the charter of 1950 upon which it was

6. *Diario de Hoy*, October 10, 1970.

7. A. Mendizábal, "De Morazán: Presidente FSH explica lo que es Ley de Avenamiento y Riego," *Prensa Gráfica*, November 11, 1970; Partido Demócrata Cristiano, "Frente a la Ley de Avenamiento y Riego," *Prensa Gráfica*, November 9, 1970. For the text of the law as ultimately passed, see Decree 153, *Diario Oficial*, CCXXIX (November 23, 1970), 13498–510.

based insisted upon the "social function" of property. Expropriations in the irrigation districts would be duly compensated, and in many cases were necessary for the construction of canals, pumping stations, and other works essential to the project itself—a form of state intervention that would be considered justified in the most capitalist of systems. The real objection of conservatives was that these modest undertakings, if allowed to proceed unchallenged, would ultimately provide the legal precedent for a more comprehensive agrarian reform. They saw this threat not only in the fact that the legislation contemplated the establishment of minimum and maximum property sizes in the districts, but also in the repeated assertions especially of the PDC that the irrigation law must be only a beginning.[8]

A special fifteen-man committee finally reported the bill favorably to the full house in mid-November, 1970, and within two days the Legislative Assembly had enacted it into law. Such rapid action after so many years of delay led to angry conservative accusations of reckless reformism. Critics denounced members of the special committee as puppets of the executive and charged all sorts of procedural irregularities. Rumors abounded of a coup d'état to prevent implementation of the law, but Sánchez Hernández signed it on the twenty-third and no crisis ensued. Government officials explained that a new mentality characterized the armed forces and that the irrigation law was a technical rather than a military matter. Still, once the act had become law the government proved in no particular hurry to put it into operation. It was not until January that the first irrigation district was established and that was in the Zapotitán basin, an area lying between the San Salvador and Santa Ana volcanoes and centering upon a large *hacienda* the government had acquired in the 1930s and subsequently developed over the years as a showplace for various programs in agricultural and agrarian reform.[9]

Politically, Sánchez Hernández was probably wise to moderate his approach to land reform after securing passage of the irrigation law. Conservative displeasure with his regime was becoming serious

8. Partido Demócrata Cristiano, "Frente a la Ley de Avenamiento"; *Prensa Gráfica*, November 12, 1970. On the concept of "social function" in the constitution of 1950, see Gallardo, *Constituciones de El Salvador*, II, 227.

9. *Prensa Gráfica*, November 10, 12, 14, 24, 1970, January 21, 1971. On Zapotitán, see Browning, *Landscape and Society*, 277–80.

on a number of other fronts. In early 1971, the coffee interests began one of their periodic publicity campaigns alleging the imminent collapse of coffee culture, and therefore of the national economy, because of the government's failure to defend and protect the interests of the growers to the exclusion of all others. The immediate cause of this particular "crisis" was a decline in the price paid for Salvadoran coffee in the world market from the abnormally high level it had reached in 1969–1970 due to an outbreak of blight in Brazil. Although the lower prices were in fact considerably above the level necessary to make a profit, growers' organizations demanded state action to secure a higher quota from the International Coffee Organization, expressing the hope that the government would not aggravate an already dangerous situation through further ill-conceived reformist adventures. What the interests had in mind in this regard was a pending labor code which included among its provisions the legalization of peasant unions. The right of workers in industry and commerce to organize had been restored by Osorio, but no regime had yet dared to offend the rural economic elite by extending this benefit to agricultural workers. This new threat brought landowner interests of all types together to oppose the measure. While the coffee growers complained that unionization of agricultural workers at a time of low prices would seriously endanger the economy, the cattlemen charged that the measure would subject uncultured peasants to the exploitation of unscrupulous demagogues who would use the new unions to bring the country to a state of "absolute anarchy."[10]

The prospect of "absolute anarchy" in the countryside was not a welcome one to those who recalled the Communist-inspired peasant revolt of 1932. A number of developments in late 1970 and early 1971 served to heighten consciousness—not that it required much heightening—of a "Red threat" in El Salvador. One such incident was the public funeral held in San Salvador for Communist party leader Raúl Castellanos Figueroa who died in Moscow in November.

10. Asociación de Ganaderos de El Salvador, "A la Asamblea Legislativa . . . sobre la sindicalización campesina," *Prensa Gráfica*, June 16, 1971; Junta Cafetalera Departamental de La Libertad, "A la Honorable Asamblea Legislativa . . . sobre la sindicalización campesina," *Prensa Gráfica*, June 25, 1971; and many more. On the coffee "crisis," see Slutzky and Slutzky, "Explotación cafetalera," 101–105; and for a very different viewpoint, Comité de Vigilancia y de Defensa de los Derechos de los Cafetaleros Salvadoreños, "El comité . . . se dirige a los cafetaleros," *Diario de Hoy*, February 9, 1971.

Castellanos's death and the public activities and pronouncements concerning it served to remind the public that the Salvadoran Communist party (PCS), although legally barred from participation in politics, still existed. The fact that Castellanos was at the time of his death a professor of journalism at the National University added emphasis to an increasingly popular tendency to denounce academic subversion—an issue that would become extremely important in the months and years to follow.[11] Salvadoran conservatives did not trouble themselves to distinguish among the various lines within the international Communist movement and consistently lumped the tame, Moscow-line PCS together with all the wicked forces abroad in a hostile world. Almost forty years after the fact, the PCS had still not overcome its identification with the tragedy of 1932, and the slightest hint of leftist recrudescence was generally enough to send right-wing polemicists to their typewriters to review once again the well-known story. One article, published just a month after Castellano's death, lamented the fate of the "poor Salvadoran Indian, deceived first by the sword and the cross, then four hundred years later by the hammer and the sickle." [12]

Communist party members were not the only subversives whose recent activities alarmed the privileged. Progressive members of the Roman Catholic clergy whose vocal participation in the National Agrarian Reform Congress had drawn such criticism continued their work among the poor and disadvantaged. Since many of these priests were foreigners, their attempts to organize peasants and urban squatters in defense of their rights could be interpreted by their opponents not only as a violation of the separation of church and state but also as foreign intervention in domestic politics. Immigration authorities began deportation proceedings in April, 1971, against seven such clerics accused of "dedicating themselves to activities contrary to social tranquillity and democracy." The archdiocese gave its full support to the seven, however, and the government proved reluctant to take action against them. Interior Minister Humberto Guillermo Cuestas acknowledged the gravity of the charges—"this is not Chile," he said firmly—but declared that even foreign priests who organ-

11. *Prensa Gráfica,* November 2, 1970; "Sale de la clandestinidad el Partido Comunista," *Prensa Gráfica,* November 24, 1970.
12. Ramón López Jiménez, "Agustín Farabundo Martí y la revolución comunista," *Diario de Hoy,* December 1, 1970.

ized peasants had rights under the Salvadoran constitution.[13] In years
to follow, as the effectiveness of progressive political parties operating within an electoral context declined, the clergy displaced them
as the spokesmen for popular aspirations in El Salvador. As the government remained indisposed to quiet them, the privileged would
eventually take matters into their own hands.

Those who warned that El Salvador was on the brink of disintegration could point for substantiation to the country's most sensational crime of 1971, the kidnapping and murder of industrialist Ernesto Regalado Dueñas. Regalado, the thirty-four-year-old son of two
of the country's wealthiest and most powerful families, disappeared
from a sidewalk in the capital's prosperous Colonia Escalón on February 11. His abductors demanded a ransom of one million dollars
which was raised but never collected. A week later, authorities
found the victim's battered body near the roadside not far from the
outlying capital suburb of San Antonio Abad. Regalado's killer had
shot him twice through the head.[14] Violent death is a common
enough occurrence in El Salvador, a small country with a high
homicide rate, but the social position of the victim and the identity
of the suspects gave this particular case important political implications.

Although some early reports suggested the kidnapping was the
work of right-wingers, government investigators soon began un-
tangling a confused web of leftist intrigue at the National University.
Witnesses told of the emergence of an ideologically nonspecific revolutionary cell, called simply the "Group," which united young
Marxists and some of the more radical members of the Christian
Democratic youth movement (Juventud Demócrata Cristiana) in a resolve to seize political power by popular force. The kidnapping of
Regalado, according to this version, had been the abortive first step
in a program of extortion to raise funds to finance the Group's operations. These "revelations"—which may well have had some basis
in truth—received extensive publicity and provided substantiation
for those who claimed the university and the PDC were little more
than legally sanctioned centers for Communist subversion. The

13. *Prensa Gráfica*, April 16, 20, 21, 1971.
14. *Diario de Hoy*, February 20, 1971.

political importance of the case was such that one of the country's most articulate and intelligent conservatives, José Antonio Rodríguez Porth, volunteered his services to the prosecution.[15]

The government's list of suspects in the Regalado case ultimately grew to ten names, including the daughter and son-in-law of the prominent leftist politician Fabio Castillo and a number of young Christian Democrats one of whom was a cousin of party founder Adolfo Rey Prendes.[16] This crisis struck the PDC at a politically inopportune moment. Party leaders condemned the government for exploiting the Regalado tragedy for partisan ends, charging that the large body of testimony upon which the authorities were gradually building their case was obtained through the use of drugs and torture and riven with contradictions. Emphasizing that violence and terrorism were totally alien to everything their party stood for, the officers of the PDC went on to suggest quite strongly that only the official party stood to profit from Regalado's death, since it afforded the government an opportunity to persecute its enemies and further its "plans to continue subjugating this suffering people and maintaining the farce of democracy in which no one but Sánchez Hernández believes."[17]

The Regalado murder must have seemed, not only to oligarchs but also to Salvadorans of all classes who valued social order, like the first trumpet in a campaign of leftist slaughter. Institutional violence was common enough—even accepted—in Salvadoran politics, but the hecatomb of 1932 had placed an enduring stigma upon bloodshed in the pursuit of revolutionary ends. Throughout the 1960s, El Salvador had been fortunate enough to avoid the guerrilla activity, assassinations, and kidnappings that plagued neighboring Guatemala, but now it seemed to be beginning at home as well.

The Regalado case was one of many developments that drew attention to the National University, a microcosm where one could find concentrated in extreme form virtually everything conservatives thought to be wrong in El Salvador in 1971. Under a series of

---

15. *Ibid.*, May 27, 28, 29, July 6, 8, 19, 1971.
16. *Ibid.*, May 27, 1971, February 19, 1972; Duarte, "Intipucá." Most of the suspects remained at large a year later.
17. Partido Demócrata Cristiano, "El caso Regalado Dueñas: La corrupción total del oficialismo," *Prensa Gráfica*, June 17, 1971.

dynamic rectors, the best known of whom was Fabio Castillo, this institution had expanded prodigiously in the 1960s. Between 1962 and 1969, for example, the student population doubled and the university budget nearly quadrupled. One effect of this rapid growth was the democratization of the student body, accomplished through the standardization of admissions procedures among the faculties as well as the institution after 1963 of the first scholarship programs in the school's history. Curriculum reforms designed to deemphasize the traditional narrow professional preparation provoked conflicts among administration, faculty, and alumni, as did a prolonged student strike in *areas comunes*, a controversial new two-year basic preprofessional program, in late 1969 and early 1970.[18]

Because of its newness and formlessness, *areas comunes* represented the most restless division of the university. Its radicalized student leaders viciously attacked traditional leftists in the administration, such as Fabio Castillo, whose resignation as dean of the newly created Faculty of Sciences and Humanities the strikers demanded. Student strikes, nonconformity, and left-wing politics were hardly new at the university, but they no longer seemed the adolescent games of a tiny elite. They disturbed conservatives, especially when viewed in the context of a worldwide pattern of student radicalization and violence, of the dramatic, almost chaotic growth of the institution, and of the what must have seemed extravagant budgets the government lavished upon this nest of Red subversives. What particularly concerned critics of the university, besides the apparent laxness of both academic and government officials, was what they perceived as the progressive moral deterioration of the student body. Even university officials complained of long hair on men, sexual promiscuity, venereal disease, and the abuse of alcohol and drugs, particularly marijuana. Allegedly symbolic of this decline in moral standards was a student parade held in December, 1970. This parade, of a type common enough in the past and known popularly as a *bufonada*, featured explicit sexual satire directed at prominent government officials. An ongoing fiscal scandal in the

18. Flores Macal, "Historia de la Universidad," 130–34; George R. and Barbara Ashton Waggoner, *Education in Central America* (Lawrence, Kans., 1971), 67–69.

administration and a widely publicized murder charge against a professor served to complete the picture of uncontrolled decay.[19] Change and disorder in the university had their counterparts in the educational system at large. Sánchez Hernández took a special interest in the problems of schooling and the need for higher levels of basic instruction in any society with pretensions to modernity. Under the demagogic slogan of "build a school a day" and the direction of Education Minister Walter Béneke Medina, the regime poured large amounts of money into programs designed to reform the curricula, increase exposure through expanded enrollments, improve physical facilities, and upgrade the qualifications of instructional personnel. The emphasis was at the traditionally neglected secondary level and especially upon technical as opposed to humanistic subjects, and even included the installation of a controversial educational television network to compensate for the shortage of well-trained secondary teachers.[20]

All of this the government attempted to accomplish as rapidly as possible, working with extremely limited resources. It therefore, from time to time, had to make difficult economic decisions. Among these was the matter of pay and working conditions for the country's expanding corps of schoolteachers, relatively well-educated and articulate men and women with middle-class aspirations who traditionally had enjoyed neither the status nor the material reward society accorded other titled professionals. The late 1960s and early 1970s witnessed a number of confrontations—including the unpleasant strike of 1968—between the Education Ministry and the country's militant teachers' union, the National Association of Salvadoran Educators (Asociación Nacional de Educadores Salvadoreños, ANDES). In July, 1971, ANDES walked out once again to protest, among other issues, a delay in consideration of a new pay

19. Flores Macal, "Historia de la Universidad," 133; Prensa Gráfica, January 22, 1970, January 14, 1971; Guillermo Rivera M., "El foco subversivo de la Universidad Autónoma," Prensa Gráfica, September 11, 1971; Alfredo Parada (h.), "Un insulto a la nación fué desfile de los estudiantes universitarios," Diario de Hoy, December 6, 1970.
20. Waggoner and Waggoner, Education in Central America, 60–63; John K. Mayo, Robert C. Hornik, and Emile G. McAnany, Educational Reform with Television: The El Salvador Experience (Stanford, Calif., 1976), 22–23.

scale bill it had requested. The strike lasted nearly two months and was accompanied by street disturbances. Although the strike was illegal, the government took little overt action against it other than to maintain order in the streets. Once again, conservatives, who saw the fine hand of university Communists behind the troubles, interpreted this as weakness on the part of the regime. Their opinion did not change at all when, through the mediation of Archbishop Chávez y González, the Education Ministry finally reached a negotiated settlement with the teachers.[21]

Commenting upon events in El Salvador in 1971, one diplomatic observer described the Sánchez Hernández administration as follows: "By most standards, this is a conservative Government, but by Salvadoran standards it is pretty progressive."[22] This essentially accurate assessment would have seemed a vast understatement to Salvadoran conservatives who increasingly saw in the regime not only a government that was irrationally hostile to the interests of the more substantial sectors of society, but also one that irresponsibly tolerated and even pampered those whose activities demonstrated contempt for the sacred traditions of Salvadoran society and posed an immediate threat of social disintegration. It must have particularly disturbed oligarchs that there was—in spite of periodic coup rumors that may have represented mere wishful thinking or attempts to offer self-fulfilling prophecies—little evidence of unrest within the military. Progressive members of the officer corps appeared to be in ascendancy. To some, the horrors of the left-wing military regime in Peru seemed a possible omen of things to come closer to home. A prevailing sense of "betrayal" by the government party, the military, and the church must account in great part for the massive conservative defection from *oficialismo* which, along with a new unity among the Left, produced the crisis of 1972.

It seemed to conservatives that leftist agitation was rampant in the country, whether due to the government's lack of vigilance or to its active encouragement. Those who feared El Salvador was about to

---

21. Mayo, Hornik, and McAnany, *Educational Reform*, 127; *Diario de Hoy*, July 18, August 11, 28, 1971; *Prensa Gráfica*, September 1, 1971. For a thorough, intelligent analysis of the 1971 strike, see Universidad Centroamericana José Simeón Cañas, *Análisis de una experiencia nacional* (San Salvador, 1971).

22. *New York Times*, October 17, 1971, p. 21.

go the way of Chile found confirmation for their misgivings when the progressive opposition parties began to form themselves into an electoral coalition in preparation for the presidential and Legislative Assembly elections of 1972.

As early as March, 1971, there were unofficial reports that the Christian Democrats, the MNR, the UDN, and even the PPS were discussing the possibility of offering a single candidate to oppose the official party. These rumors reflected an important departure in electoral strategy on the part of the PDC, a departure resulting from the extensive reassessment of the party's position that had taken place following the disappointing election of 1970. The new Christian Democrat secretary-general, Pablo Mauricio Alvergue, accompanied by party leaders Juan Ricardo Ramírez and Adolfo Rey Prendes, had called upon the leaders of the other legally inscribed parties carrying a message of simple arithmetic. The opposition would be in a stronger electoral position with respect to the government if it were united. Negotiations among the parties had actually been underway nearly a year when in May, 1971, the PDC held a public reception for the other parties at its headquarters in San Salvador. Nothing was decided at this meeting, but it afforded a chance to publicize the talks. Throughout this period, the various parties also issued a number of joint manifestoes on national issues.[23]

A major obstacle to a final agreement on coalition may well have been the attempt to comprehend within it the conservative Salvadoran Popular party. Any chance of PPS participation had evaporated, however, by September, 1971, when there emerged within that party a new group of leaders that included such disenchanted *pecenistas* as Roberto Quiñónez Meza and Constantino Novoa. Quiñónez and Novoa were both wealthy businessmen and long-time vocal conservatives who had participated in the early Christian Democratic study groups but for obvious reasons never found a home in the PDC.[24]

In September, therefore, the progressive parties—the Christian Democrats, the MNR, and the UDN—decided to proceed alone. Declaring the official party to be in league with the oligarchy and imperialism, "the two faces of the hateful coin of dependence," these

23. *Diario de Hoy*, March 20, May 22, 1971; Duarte, "Intipucá"; Duarte, taped interviews, reel no. 7.

24. *Prensa Gráfica*, September 28, 1971; Duarte, "Intipucá."

three parties announced their intention to form a permanent union to lead the popular struggle against oppression and injustice. The participating parties denied that the coalition was a matter of electoral convenience to be discarded once its purpose had been served. On the other hand, they also denied that it was a fusion; each party would maintain its ideological identity and integrity: "We have a common goal capable of transcending the problem of differences of ideology and strategy; we desire a positive change in the existing structures of political and economic power which have demonstrated their injustice and have had a clearly retrocessive effect upon our development."[25]

In spite of this grand proclamation, there were still problems to be resolved. The PDC had to obtain approval of the plan from its national convention in October, and the member parties had to work out a division of benefits and responsibilities as well as agree upon a presidential and vice-presidential candidate and a joint campaign platform. There was some opposition to the coalition at the Christian Democratic convention, especially from some of the more conservative party members who argued that the two smaller parties were Communist fronts and that to cooperate with them would open the PDC to subversion, and ultimately to the fate of the old PAR. This objection was apparently not taken very seriously as the convention delegates gave the coalition an overwhelming endorsement.[26]

One reason that the alliance, which called itself the National Opposing Union (Unión Nacional Opositora, UNO), won ready acceptance from the Christian Democrats was surely that they recognized that their party, so much more powerful than the other two, would inevitably be the senior partner. This circumstance guaranteed that participation in the coalition would not jeopardize the identity of the party or its ideological integrity and independence. The dominance of the PDC could be seen clearly in the division of the UNO electoral slate among the member parties. Besides the presidential election,

25. Movimiento Nacional Revolucionario, Partido Demócrata Cristiano, and Unión Democrática Nacionalista, "Manifiesto al pueblo salvadoreño," Prensa Gráfica, September 3, 1971.

26. Diario de Hoy, August 15, 1971; Prensa Gráfica, October 4, 5, 1971. Duarte (taped interviews, reel no. 7) speaks of an attempt by "Communists" to seize control of the UDN at this time. According to him, much of the convention voting strength that turned back the Marxist assault was composed of regular Christian Democrats on loan to the non-Communist UDN leadership for the duration of the crisis.

there would also be a municipality and assembly election in 1972.[27] The coalition members agreed to distribute the electoral slate by dividing the various offices at stake among themselves according to each party's strength in previous elections. The Christian Democrats received the greatest share of the municipalities, including San Salvador, Santa Ana, and San Miguel—the three most important. The UDN and MNR received fewer and less significant ones. In the Legislative Assembly, the PDC retained for itself thirty-two of the fifty-two seats available. In San Salvador department, where the opposition could expect to be strongest, out of nine seats the Christian Democrats kept five and the other parties divided the four remaining.[28] In addition to the PDC's clear dominance on the legislative and municipal tickets, the party also received the right to designate the coalition's presidential nominee. For this honor, the party's convention unanimously chose José Napoleón Duarte.[29]

Duarte, like most other Christian Democrats who had experienced the UPD disaster of 1961, had long been outspokenly opposed to coalitions. A decade later, however, he and the others now recognized that the opposition's greatest weakness was its disunity. But, before he would accept the nomination, Duarte insisted that certain conditions be met. First, fearing the possibility of assassination, he requested that the Christian Democrats purchase a life insurance policy for him so that his death would not leave his family destitute. He also asked the PDC to provide his wife and children with living expenses for the duration of the campaign. In addition, he insisted that

27. Under the 1962 constitution, El Salvador elects a president every five years, and renews its Legislative Assembly and municipal governments every two. Once every decade, therefore, a presidential and assembly election should occur in the same calendar year. In 1972 the government scheduled the presidential vote for February 20 and the assembly election for March 12.

28. *Prensa Gráfica*, December 14, 30, 1971, January 1, 1972. What is more, under proportional representation, a candidate's actual position on the ticket was of extreme importance. Voters voted only for the party. As the results were tabulated, seats were awarded to a party's candidates in the order they appeared on the slate. In San Salvador, the five positions the PDC reserved for itself were the first, second, fourth, sixth, and ninth. This meant that, if the UNO won only four seats in this department, three would be filled by Christian Democrats; and that the coalition would have to win at least three seats before either of the junior parties received one. The first and second positions on the San Salvador slate went to Juan Ricardo Ramírez and Pablo Mauricio Alvergue, respectively. In San Miguel with its five seats, the Christian Democrats received the first, third, and fifth positions.

29. *Ibid.*, October 5, 1971.

the campaign be organized in all fourteen departments and that there be no Communist participation whatsoever.[30] He further demanded that, should he become president, he be allowed complete freedom in the matter of ministerial appointments. A joint committee representing the three parties would draw up the coalition's platform. Duarte insisted that the member parties promise to support any action he might take as president to carry out the program and to agree not to ask for anything in the future that had not been included in the program.[31]

Duarte presented his conditions to the leadership of the PDC and left for Guatemala on a vacation conveniently timed to have him out of the country while the Christian Democrats discussed his terms with the other parties. The MNR and UDN agreed to Duarte's stipulations and duly nominated him. As his vice-presidential candidate, Duarte asked for and received Guillermo Manuel Ungo, the forty-year-old secretary-general of the MNR. Ungo, a lawyer and close friend of Duarte's, was the son of the late Guillermo Ungo, revered as a founder of the Christian Democratic movement in El Salvador. Duarte admits he would have preferred a PDC member for the second place on the ticket. In young Ungo he came as close as possible without betraying the ideal of coalition.[32]

As early as July, 1971, negotiations had begun on the question of a coalition platform. Each party appointed a committee to draft program suggestions for final synthesis at the coalition level. The PDC's program committee included Duarte, Alvergue, Ramírez, Rey Prendes, Lara Velado, Abraham Rodríguez, and Julio René Vargas—all members of the traditional established leadership of the party.[33] Not surprisingly, the program finally agreed upon looked very much like the PDC's original with a few modifications. It continued the Christian Democrats' emphasis on electoral democracy and individual

30. The Salvadoran Communist party did, in fact, support the UNO but could not legally have participated in it. Shafik Jorge Handal, "El Salvador: A Precarious Balance," *World Marxist Review*, XVI (June, 1973), 46–50.
31. Duarte explains his concern for continued support by citing Frei's experience in Chile where elements, particularly conservatives, who supported him during his campaign ceased to do so once he was in office. Duarte's conditions applied only in the case of coalition. If he ran as the candidate of the PDC alone, he would do so unconditionally. Duarte, taped interviews, reel no. 7; Duarte, "Intipucá."
32. *Ibid.*
33. Duarte, "Intipucá."

liberty as well as the party's stress on pluralism and popular organization at the community level. It reasserted the PDC's faith in the efficacy of "scientific" economic planning and its belief in the necessity of industrialization. But it for the first time adopted the "dependency" theory of underdevelopment, blaming "oligarchy and imperialism" for El Salvador's problems and accusing the PCN of *entreguismo* (literally, "surrenderism"). The 1972 program was much more nationalistic than previous Christian Democratic pronouncements and advocated more independent economic and foreign policies.

A major departure from earlier PDC programs was the coalition's agrarian reform proposal. Whereas in 1961 the Christian Democrats had given redistribution a low priority among approaches to the agrarian problem, and in 1967 had supported the government's projected gradualist agricultural reform, the 1972 UNO platform called for a legal limitation to the size of landholdings and a positive program to destroy latifundism. Even here, however, the traditional Christian Democratic moderation and caution were evident. The platform explained that the new government would decide the size limitations only after considerable study of individual cases which would take into account the nature of the land involved, the type of crop, and the efficiency of exploitation. In practice, only the very large landholders with sizable tracts out of cultivation would be in any real danger of expropriation. If this program represented a step leftward for the PDC, it also constituted a retreat of sorts for the MNR from the radical land reform tradition it inherited from its predecessor, the now defunct "New Line" PAR.

Generally, the UNO platform remained faithful to the PDC's belief in private property. Its scheme of development reserved a dominant role for private sector investment and it contained a call for measures to encourage and protect small and medium entrepreneurs and landholders. Above all, it emphasized that development must be gradual and evolutionary. There were no simple panaceas. No particular reform merited priority over any other. Land reform would be meaningless without technological and educational reform. Educational reform would be meaningless as long as Salvadoran children were ill-housed, ill-clothed, and ill-fed. That the UNO was not proposing a revolution is clear from the very wording of its platform:

"We do not promise to create a paradise overnight. We intend merely to start the country down a road different from that which it has followed for so long and which has brought it to such grave and overwhelming difficulties." [34]

As his predecessor had done, President Sánchez Hernández named his own successor and imposed that choice upon the party and the army. The man he chose was his own secretary, Colonel Arturo Armando Molina, a forty-four-year-old career officer and, like the president himself, a political moderate. There were reports at the time that the choice of Molina was not entirely popular in the army and that the regime had had to undercut resistance in the officer corps through transfers and changes of command. There was in fact such a reorganization in late 1971, but Defense Minister Fidel Torres, of course, denied that it was at all political. There were also reports that the partywide favorite within the PCN was United Nations Ambassador Reynaldo Galindo Pohl, a civilian who had been a member of the Junta of 1948 and whose choice by Osorio to succeed him in 1956 the army had vetoed. It was no more likely in 1972 that the army would accept a civilian, and Galindo let it be known that he did not wish his name to be considered. [35] Two individuals who apparently would have liked to be considered were another civilian, Foreign Minister Francisco José Guerrero, and the commander of the National Guard, General José Alberto Medrano. Of Medrano, there shall be much to say later. When Guerrero's ambitions became too

34. Unión Nacional Opositora, "Programa de gobierno de UNO," *Prensa Gráfica,* January 17, 1972. For a concise expression of the UNO's proposals, see Unión Nacional Opositora, "Texto de las respuestas entregadas por los representantes de la UNO," *Estudios Centro Americanos,* XXVII (1972), 49–67. This was UNO's reply to a questionnaire sent by *ECA* to all four parties involved in the 1972 election. Only the PCN declined to respond. For an analysis of the ideological content of the various party programs, see Román Mayorga Quirós, "Crítica de las ideologías económico-sociales en la campaña presidencial de El Salvador," *ibid.,* 71–100. Mayorga Quirós classifies both the UNO and the PCN as "neo-liberal"; their economic programs are nonsocialist, but they do recognize the necessity for the state to intervene in the economy as investor, promoter, director, and regulator. He places the UNO to the left of the PCN within this limited spectrum, but concedes that comparison is difficult since the official party prefers to discuss accomplishments rather than proposals. The UNO itself charged the PCN had no program.

35. Duarte, "Intipucá"; Duarte, taped interviews, reel no. 7; *Prensa Gráfica,* December 7, 1971; *New York Times,* October 17, 1971, p. 21; Elam, "Appeal to Arms," 149–50.

obvious, Sánchez Hernández dismissed him from both his cabinet and party posts.[36]

Molina, two years younger than Duarte, was probably not as attractive a candidate as the Christian Democrat. He was neither as handsome nor as personable as Duarte, and he tended to be uneasy when speaking publicly. But he did possess great personal energy and could be expected to conduct a tough campaign. The PCN's choice of civilian party regular Enrique Mayorga Rivas as Molina's vice-presidential candidate contributed little color to the ticket. The party's selection, however, of a woman, Yolanda de Novoa, to oppose Carlos Herrera Rebollo's bid for reelection as mayor of San Salvador represented a shrewd, although ultimately vain, attempt to penetrate the Christian Democrats' large feminine following in the capital.[37]

Molina promised that, while his predecessor had given priority to education, he would emphasize a "dignified" settlement with Honduras, and a solution to the agrarian problem. Although he refused to give details, Molina advocated peasant cooperatives and an effort to pass legislation "adapted to the needs of the country." Of course, he continued, "all struggle in favor of the peasant must be undertaken without demagoguery." Caught between the opposition coalition on its left and oligarchic desertions on its right, the PCN emphasized its middle-of-the-road position and called upon the electorate to avoid either ideological extreme.[38]

Against Duarte and Molina, the new leadership of the Salvadoran Popular party sponsored the return to active politics of José Antonio Rodríguez Porth. Rodríguez Porth, a classic laissez-faire liberal, had resigned the Directorio Cívico-Militar in 1961 in protest against Rivera's reform programs. More recently he had led the conservative opposition in the National Agrarian Reform Congress and had at-

36. New York Times, October 17, 1971, p. 21; Prensa Gráfica, June 30, 1971; Diario de Hoy, July 1, 1971; Herman Alas, "Del momento: Incógnitas de la campaña política," Diario de Hoy, July 5, 1971.

37. Duarte, "Intipucá"; Duarte, taped interviews, reel no. 7; Diario de Hoy, February 10, 1972. Señora de Novoa was the wife of Fidel Novoa, Duarte's predecessor as mayor.

38. Prensa Gráfica, September 30, October 15, 1971; Héctor Manuel Salazar Castro, "Al pueblo salvadoreño: ¿ Por quién votaré? Y por qué," Diario de Hoy, February 17, 1972.

tempted, under the guise of assisting the prosecution, to make an anti-Communist and anti-Christian Democrat crusade of the Regalado murder investigation. The PPS as usual vowed to fight international communism, defend private property, and promote "harmony" between labor and capital. What is more, it loudly denounced the agrarian reform proposals of both the UNO and the PCN as "socialist."[39] Rodríguez Porth, vice-presidential candidate Roberto Palomo (a San Salvador psychiatrist trained in the United States), and capital mayoralty candidate Roberto Quiñónez Meza all campaigned in shirtsleeves, claiming to represent the ordinary working man. Given the fact that many of the new leaders of the PPS were factoryowners and that Rodríguez Porth devoted much of his law practice to representing management in labor disputes, few voters were likely to take this appeal seriously—especially since opponents of the party waged a lively campaign to expose its true nature.[40]

The fourth and final presidential candidate to appear in the campaign of 1971–1972 was General José Alberto Medrano, former commander of the National Guard and a hero of the Honduran War. Medrano was the nominee of a new conservative splinter from the official party called the United Democratic Independent Front (Frente Unido Democrático Independiente, FUDI). This party, which applied for legal registration in July, 1971, responded to landowner discontent with the government's coffee policy as well as its position on agrarian reform and its "soft-line" approach to normalization of relations with Honduras. The FUDI appears to have drawn its leadership and support from the landed elite of the country's western zone, especially the powerful Salaverría family of Ahuachapán which until its defection in 1971 dominated the PCN party hierarchy in that department.[41]

39. *Prensa Gráfica*, November 13, December 14, 1971; Partido Popular Salvadoreño, "Reforma agraria," *Prensa Gráfica*, January 15, 1972.

40. See, for example, Roberto Jesús Navarrete, "Una advertencia a la clase trabajadora y el pueblo en general sobre el Partido Popular Salvadoreño," *Prensa Gráfica*, January 8, 1972.

41. *Prensa Gráfica*, June 9, 1971; Frente Unido Democrático Independiente, "FUDI dirígese al CCE," *Diario de Hoy*, July 28, 1971; New York Times, October 17, 1971, p. 21. Mayorga Quirós finds little difference between the ideological orientations of the FUDI and the PPS, but cautions that the personality of Medrano was of greater importance than the party's ostensible program. Mayorga Quirós, "Crítica de las ideologías," 75. The major difference between this group and the PPS seems to have been that while the FUDI represented primarily agricultural interests, the Sal-

Mystery and intrigue attended Medrano's every move in this period. He is reputed to have aspired to the PCN's presidential nomination, but his atavistic image as a populist conservative *caudillo* was unsuited to the increasingly technocratic and nonpersonalist official party. He may have already begun to conspire with the Salaverrías and their allies in late 1970 for, on December 2, the Defense Ministry suddenly announced his dismissal as director general of the National Guard and the appointment in his place of Colonel Oscar Gutiérrez, a confidant of Sánchez Hernández. The government characterized its action as "disciplinary" but refused to specify the offense involved. Rumors abounded that Medrano intended to lead a coup or otherwise seek national political power, and the press linked his name prominently to various factions and personalities. In February, the government decided to exile him, naming him to the Salvadoran consulate in San Francisco, California.[42]

Before Medrano could leave to assume his new duties in the United States, however, he was arrested in the early morning hours of February 12 and charged with the shooting death of a policeman in Colonia Escalón. Medrano at first denied the accusation, but later changed his story and pleaded self-defense, claiming he mistook the officer for an assassin. A jury in Usulután finally acquitted him in June, but many aspects of the case remained unclear. Among these were a number of apparently political arrests that had taken place simultaneously with that of Medrano. Those arrested included one of the Salaverrías, but only Medrano was detained and charged.[43] Perhaps the deepest mystery surrounding the Medrano case was the nature of its relationship to the Regalado kidnapping. General Medrano's fatal encounter with the police had occurred on the night of the day Regalado disappeared. The government later conceded that the officer Medrano shot was in fact assigned to the Regalado investigation. Testimony in the case against the former National Guard

vadoran Popular party, notably in the person of Quiñónez Meza who belonged to the powerful Meza Ayau-Quiñónez familial alliance, spoke for wealthy families that had branched off into industrial entrepreneurship and therefore had different expectations regarding government agrarian policy and normalization of relations with Honduras and the CACM.

42. *Diario de Hoy*, December 3, 4, 6, 1971. At the same time authorities admitted they were investigating an attempt upon Medrano's life.

43. *Ibid.*, February 13, 15, 16, 1971; *Prensa Gráfica*, June 12, 1971.

commander indicated that not only he but also the Salaverrías had been among the initial suspects in the kidnapping. No such charges were ever filed, however, and the investigators turned their attention to the leftist university students.[44]

Following his acquittal of the murder charge in June, Medrano left the country, going first to Guatemala and then on to the United States where he remained some months. His periodic returns from exile were the subject of much political speculation, and there were rumors he was in league with former president Julio Adalberto Rivera, now serving as Salvadoran ambassador in Washington. Other stories linked Medrano with Francisco José Guerrero, the recently dismissed foreign minister. Neither Rivera nor Guerrero emerged as backers of the FUDI, however, and Medrano took as his vice-presidential candidate Raul Salaverría Durán, a representative of one of the country's major coffee producing and exporting families.[45]

Medrano enjoyed significant landowner support as a result of favors done in his days as director of the National Guard. He also, of course, had a number of friends within the officer corps. Founder, and for many years the supreme leader, of the Democratic Nationalist Organization (Organización Democrática Nacionalista, ORDEN), a paramilitary civilian vigilance association composed of many thousand[46] armed peasants with the ostensible mission of combatting communism and defending "democratic" values in the republic's rural areas, Medrano had at his disposal what looked very much like a private army. Although ORDEN had always enjoyed government sponsorship and Sánchez Hernández tried to assert his control over it when the regime broke with Medrano, there was a serious question as to where the members' primary loyalty lay. Although Medrano resigned his formal position with ORDEN following his ouster as National Guard commander, there was continued speculation as to the

44. The suspicion of Medrano and the Salaverrías is clear from Medrano's own formal statement given after his arrest at a time when the Regalado kidnapping was officially a secret. *Diario de Hoy*, February 16, 1971. Months later, when suspicion had shifted to the leftists, Medrano denied under oath any recollection of this aspect of his statement. *Prensa Gráfica*, September 17, 1971.

45. *Prensa Gráfica*, June 9, 13, September 11, October 19, 1971; *Diario de Hoy*, July 28, 29, 1971.

46. White (*El Salvador*, 221) estimates between fifty thousand and one hundred thousand. Other estimates have reached as high as one hundred fifty thousand. *Diario de Hoy*, December 30, 1970.

role the organization would play in his political plans. A year later, the general himself, upon announcing his candidacy under the FUDI banner, expressed confidence that he would receive the votes of all ORDEN members because, thanks to his indoctrination, they loved "democracy" and were undeceived by Communist propaganda.[47]

Duarte had to begin his campaign by assuring local party leaders that the coalition was not really permanent in order to convince them to work amicably with their counterparts from the other member parties, many of whom had until recently been the bitterest of political enemies. The UNO's campaign strategy was to concentrate its fire upon the PCN and its demonstrated inability to solve the nation's problems. The coalition leaders hoped, if at all possible, to avoid all reference to, or contact with, the reactionary fringe parties. Duarte and his advisors recognized that victory was unlikely, but they hoped to make as impressive a showing as possible in the hope that some of the coalition's electoral support would carry over to the assembly and municipal elections in March.[48]

Duarte's campaign schedule called for him to campaign throughout the republic. He spent the greater part of the three-month period traveling El Salvador's back roads by automobile, visiting more than two hundred towns and making more than six hundred speeches. Most of the UNO's limited campaign budget went into these personal tours and into radio and television spots. The coalition made little use of newspaper advertising until the closing weeks of the campaign. The official candidate also toured the country—although by helicopter. Much of Duarte's campaign rhetoric involved an attempt to force a televised confrontation between him and Molina, but Molina repeatedly and disdainfully refused the challenge.[49]

47. White, El Salvador, 207; Diario de Hoy, December 30, 1970; Prensa Gráfica, November 20, 1971.
48. Duarte, "Intipucá." Duarte could foresee only two possible outcomes in the event he should win: 1) the army would not allow him to take office; 2) the army would allow him to take office but his policies would soon anger the privileged sectors and the army would overthrow him.
49. See, for example, Partido de Conciliación Nacional, "El coronel Arturo Armando Molina, candidato de las mayorías, definió categóricamente su posición frente a las pretensiones electoreras de un candidato," Prensa Gráfica, December 17, 1971. Molina declared he would not waste his time or the people's appearing on television with a demagogue who wanted to be a caudillo. Recalling the PDC's abandonment of Unidad Nacional after the Honduran War, Molina questioned Duarte's sincerity, credibility, and patriotism.

The broad administration of the UNO's effort fell under a national command made up of representatives of the three component
parties. Duarte's twenty-year-old son, José Alejandro, handled general coordination for his father. Propaganda was the province of Sig-
frido Munés, a European-trained professional publicity agent who
had directed PDC campaigns since the beginning.[50] Coalition leaders felt there was sufficient danger to the candidates' physical safety
to warrant the establishment of a security corps. They detailed a
force of twenty unpaid volunteers to the protection of Duarte, Ungo,
and their families, and placed them under the supervision of PDC
Deputy Xavier Penagos Pellesser, who administered this phase of the
campaign until his death in a traffic accident in late January.[51]

Throughout the campaign, Duarte was the subject of numerous
accusations and innuendos that appeared to have had two major
objectives: 1) to portray Duarte personally as dishonest and incom-
petent; and 2) to identify him and the coalition in the minds of the
voters as Communists. Most of these attacks were carried out anony-
mously or through agents or fronts. Most appear to have been the work
of the conservative fringe parties, but others were obviously sponsored by the PCN. In November, for example, Foreign Minister Walter Béneke went on television to challenge Duarte's assertion that
conditions had grown worse, if anything, under PCN rule. Béneke
produced an array of statistics designed to prove conclusively that
the UNO candidate was a liar and that his coreligionaries were nothing but "demagogues . . . frustrated magicians [who] want . . . to pull
hospitals, schools, and housing from their sleeves, not to solve problems but to win applause."[52] In Béneke's defense it must be conceded that Duarte opened himself to such criticism by making some
rather reckless promises. On one occasion he declared that his gov-

50. Duarte, "Intipucá." The UNO's National Command in 1971–1972 included:
from the PDC, Pablo Mauricio Alvergue, Julio Adolfo Rey Prendes, Juan Ricardo
Ramírez Rauda, Julio René Vargas, José Ovidio Hernández Delgado, and Roberto Lara
Velado; from the UDN, Manuel de Paz Villalta and Octavio Velasco Miranda; and from
the MNR, Melitón Barba and Luis Alonso Posada. Prensa Gráfica, December 10, 1971.
51. Duarte, "Intipucá"; Prensa Gráfica, January 29, 30, 1972.
52. Walter Béneke, "El ministro Walter Béneke refuta las mentiras y acusaciones
del Sr. Ing. José Napoleón Duarte al gobierno de la república." Prensa Gráfica, November 20, 1971. This is the script of one of several anti-Duarte television speeches
Béneke made during the campaign. Béneke had moved up from the Education Ministry upon the dismissal of Francisco José Guerrero.

ernment would achieve an 8 percent annual growth rate in GNP without inflation. One not unfriendly observer concluded that such an appeal was based more upon an appreciation of the immediate political climate than upon a careful study of El Salvador's social and economic possibilities.[53] It is, of course, the privilege of parties in opposition to make the things they advocate sound easy. Parties in power must of necessity be more cautious.

Another phase of the attack on Duarte's character sought to convince workers that, in spite of his many professions to the contrary, the UNO candidate was in reality antilabor. A group calling itself the Labor Action Political Front (Frente Político de Acción Laboral, FEPAL) charged not only that Duarte was guilty of unfair labor practices in his engineering firm but also that he was a Communist agent. A number of former municipal employees, dismissed for one reason or another, placed advertisements alleging that Duarte had fired them for refusing to join the PDC.[54]

The Red-baiting phase of the campaign against Duarte and the UNO found several distinct expressions. One was an attempt to link the coalition to the new "socialist" progressive trends within the church. Many of the PDC's oldest antagonists joined the effort to spread the word of the coalition's "Communist" connections with the leftist clergy. Ricardo J. Peralta, one-time PCN governor of San Salvador department but in recent years a critic of the regime, described Duarte as a traitor and a liar, a demagogue who was simply a tool of the progressive clergy and their masters in the international Communist movement. He labeled the UNO a "Marxist-Christian coalition" and charged that the new leftist tendencies in the church were merely a "Trojan Horse" with which to introduce communism into Latin America. Peralta compared the UNO's leaders with Quisling, Miramón, Pétain, Frei, and Allende—all men, he said, who had sold out their countries to foreign domination. The conservative friar

53. Manuel Enrique Hinds C., "La imagen del país que se desprende del presente proceso electoral," Estudios Centro Americanos, XXVII (1972), 116.

54. Frente Político de Acción Laboral, "Segundo pronunciamiento de FEPAL," Prensa Gráfica, December 23, 1971. Among many notices alleging political harassment of municipal workers, Herminio Aniano García, "¡Duarte ... Ud. es un mentiroso ... !" Prensa Gráfica, January 13, 1972; Roberto Araujo Batres, "¡Señor Duarte, yo también compruebo que Ud. es mentiroso!" Prensa Gráfica, January 15, 1972. For a reply, see Unión Nacional Opositora, "UNO responde a los falsarios!" Prensa Gráfica, January 22, 1972.

Ricardo Fuentes Castellanos declared support for the UNO inconsistent with true Catholicism and charged further that the Christian Democrats were not really Christians at all but merely front men for the Communists, atheists, and other materialists who wished to dominate El Salvador.[55]

Opponents of the UNO also waved the "bloody shirt" of the 1932 peasant uprising, charging that false demagogic promises of agrarian reform (presumably like those the coalition was now making) had caused that tragic outbreak. The general theme of these attacks was that left-wing "deceit" of the masses, not oppression or exploitation, led to social violence. The Salvadoran Institute of Social and Economic Studies elaborated upon this idea, charging that the mere preaching of "social redemption" could throw a society into turmoil. It cited Nazi Germany, Fascist Italy, and various Communist regimes as examples of how the cry of "social justice" had served to enslave the masses. The institute also sponsored a television documentary which, it announced, clearly demonstrated how agrarian reform had ruined the Cuban economy.[56]

A series of unsigned notices appeared in the press in February playing on these and other themes. These attacks characterized Duarte as "the puppet of the opportunistic and deceitful leaders of the Salvadoran Communist Party" and warned workers that they would be slaves under a Communist dictatorship should the UNO

55. For example, Ricardo J. Peralta, "En defensa de la libertad: Miremos hacia atrás," Diario de Hoy, February 4, 1972; Ricardo J. Peralta, "Carta a un candidato," Diario de Hoy, February 9, 1972; Ricardo Fuentes Castellanos, "Tema del momento: Quién vota a la alianza cristiano-comunista, vota al comunismo," Diario de Hoy, February 17, 1972. Like Peralta, Fuentes Castellanos was also a critic of the government party. He disdained the PCN's program as "socializing" and saw both the PDC and the PCN as dominated by new "techno-bureaucratic" cliques trained in revolution at the Communist-infested university. He called upon the FUDI and the PPS to develop a counterrevolutionary ideology to combat this nefarious subversion. Fuentes Castellanos, "Alrededor de las elecciones: La tecno-burocracia y la política," Diario de Hoy, March 1, 1972.

56. Instituto Salvadoreño de Estudios Sociales y Económicos, "Trés programas políticos y un mismo epílogo," Diario de Hoy, February 7, 1972; Instituto Salvadoreño de Estudios Sociales y Económicos, "Un documento fílmico de palpitante actualidad: Cuba antes y después de Castro," Diario de Hoy, January 13, 1972. On the 1932 theme, see Ramón López Jiménez, "El espectro de 1932 se alza amenazante: Los ofrecimientos de reparto de tierras," Diario de Hoy, February 7, 1972; Sidney Mazzini V[illacorta], "La historia, ¿vuelve a repetirse?" Diario de Hoy, February 10, 1972; Arturo Morales Z[avaleta], "Prevención: Engañar a los campesinos es sumamente peligroso," Diario de Hoy, February 14, 1972; and Julio César Escobar, "Sí soy reaccionario, mi querido doctor," Diario de Hoy, February 17, 1972.

win. The advertisements charged also that vice-presidential candidate Guillermo Manuel Ungo was a "fellow traveler"—in the most literal sense as he had accompanied Fabio Castillo on his notorious trip to Moscow to hire Communist professors for the university. The singular logic of the anonymous authors of these accusations managed somehow to convert the UNO's pronouncements in favor of effective labor unions into threats to confiscate the means of production. No charge was too outrageous or unlikely for inclusion in this campaign. The notices even accused the leadership of the PDC of deliberately conspiring to lose elections by dropping out of Unidad Nacional, engaging in criminal and terrorist activities, allying with the PCS, and failing to qualify its candidates properly.[57] The PPS, through a front group, picked up this last theme and added the elaboration of a conspiracy between Duarte and Sánchez Hernández to keep the PCN in power and maintain Duarte in his role as leader of the opposition. Together they could then continue to burden the republic with big-spending socialist projects like the municipal markets they began when Duarte was mayor and Sánchez Hernández minister of the interior.[58]

The first anniversary of the kidnapping and murder of Ernesto Regalado Dueñas, which fell conveniently in the last week before the election, provided yet another issue for anti-UNO propagandists. Regalado's friends and conservatives in general commemorated the occasion with touching remembrances and jeremiads on the evils of left-wing terrorism, going even so far as to accuse the PDC's leadership of direct complicity in the "criminal" activities of their student colleagues.[59]

57. Particularly, "La UNO se quita la careta," *Diario de Hoy*, February 9, 1972; "El ingeniero Duarte sigue mintiendo," *Diario de Hoy*, February 12, 1972; "¡¡Increíble pero cierto!!" *Diario de Hoy*, February 16, 1972; and "Por cuarta vez la democracia cristiana traiciona a sus correligionarios," *Diario de Hoy*, February 14, 1972.

58. Unión Cívica Salvadoreña, "Duarte defrauda a los demócrata cristianos en toda la república," *Diario de Hoy*, February 16, 1972.

59. See editorial, "Un aniversario trágico: La irrupción del terror en el país," *Diario de Hoy*, February 18, 1972; Ricardo Fuentes Castellanos, "Insigne ciudadano: Aniversario de la muerte de Ernesto Regalado," *Diario de Hoy*; José Antonio Rodríguez Porth, "Ernesto Regalado Dueñas," *Diario de Hoy*. For the accusation of PDC complicity, see "Por cuarta vez la democracia cristiana traiciona." The theory of guilt by association also inspired a similar charge against Ungo since Luisa Castillo de Sol, one of the suspects, had gone with her father and Ungo on their trip to Moscow. "¡¡Increíble pero cierto!!"

The cherished myth of Salvadoran "civic loftiness" (altura cívica) that the government had nurtured and the opposition at times celebrated since 1964 was never much more than a myth. Elections were relatively free and open in urban areas, especially in San Salvador where unobstructed campaigns and honest counts were the rule; but in small towns and rural areas oficialista interference, imposition, intimidation, and ballot-box stuffing continued unhindered. In contrast to the relative political sophistication of even the poorest urban worker, who at least may have understood the purpose of the ballot and the choice of candidates available, the rural laborer's understanding of the electoral process was extremely limited. In a world view defined by personal relationships, the campesino often regarded his vote as simply part of the tribute owed his patrón. Rural voters, more so than urban, were willing to accept "guidance" in their civic duty from local authority figures, and the local authority figures—landlords, alcaldes, Guard commanders—tended in the vast majority to be oficialistas.[60]

In addition to its control of the local sources of influence in the rural areas, the government party had other important tools at its disposal as well. One of the most powerful was its control of the Consejo Central de Elecciones (CCE). Elected by the PCN-controlled Legislative Assembly, the three members of the CCE were the final arbiters of the meaning of the electoral law. They decided who participated in an election, who voted, and how the votes were counted.[61] The old PRUD had used the CCE extensively to exclude opposition candidates and parties from the electoral process through disqualification. The PCN, in contrast, made relatively little use of

60. White (El Salvador, 206) gives this factor more importance in the chemistry of PCN victories than outright fraud. That he is probably right is suggested by the large peasant vote won by the antiagrarian reform FUDI in precisely those areas (especially Ahuachapán) where landlord support for Medrano, himself a particularly important authority figure to the rural Salvadoran, was greatest. It can be argued as well that urban voters are not much less dependent upon authority figures but that in the cities these individuals—municipal administrators, professionals, schoolteachers, etc.—are more likely to be oposicionistas.

61. The members of the CCE in 1972 were José Vicente Vilanova, chairman, Carlos Aguilar Chavarría, and Gerardo Ramos. All were oficialistas. Vilanova had once been a member of the PDC but left to help form the PCN in 1961. The Christian Democrats had filed a motion in the Legislative Assembly to dismiss Vilanova, Aguilar, and Ramos following the 1970 election. When that motion was ultimately tabled and the three reelected for another term, the PDC briefly threatened to abstain from the presidential race. Diario de Hoy, March 24, 25, 26, 1971.

this procedure after the early 1960s. The major difference between the two official parties perhaps was that, whereas the PRUD craved unanimity, the PCN was content with a majority. As the opposition grew stronger, however, majorities became more difficult to achieve. By 1968–1970, the PCN was in danger of losing control of the Legislative Assembly. The government enjoyed a brief reprieve in 1970 due to nationalist fervor associated with the "Football War," but by 1972 the peril was definitely too great. The Left was united, the PCN had lost support, and a serious opposition had appeared on the right.

The *oficialistas* did not anticipate the loss of the presidency,[62] but the fear that they would fall short of a majority in the assembly was quite real. Consequently, the regime undertook its first serious use of disqualification as a political weapon. Basing its actions upon legal technicalities and formalities, the CCE tossed out the UNO's assembly slates in the departments of San Salvador, San Miguel, Usulután, Sonsonate, La Unión, and San Vicente.[63] The most significant losses here were San Salvador and San Miguel. San Salvador, especially, was of crucial importance. It was the nation's most populous department and voted heavily Christian Democratic. The large PDC delegations from San Salvador traditionally formed the core of the opposition's forces in the Legislative Assembly. Without San Salvador, there was absolutely no danger that the UNO would capture a majority of the deputies' seats.

Tales of actual physical intimidation were less common than reports of official harassment, but there was one serious incident at the end of December in the small town of Intipucá in La Unión department. Duarte's campaign tour was to finish up the old year with a rally in San Miguel on December 30. The party spent the night of the twenty-ninth at a beach resort and the following morning sent a caravan of sound trucks to the towns of Chirilagua and Intipucá to announce that the UNO candidate would address meetings there later in the day. As the column left Intipucá, a sniper opened fire from an overlooking bluff, mortally wounding Miguel Angel Barrera López, the driver of the lead vehicle. President Sánchez Hernández

---

62. A clear majority was necessary for election. No one thought Duarte would do that well. A disputed election would go to the Legislative Assembly for decision and that body, elected in 1970, was heavily *oficialista*.
63. *Diario de Hoy*, February 12, 15, 17, 1972.

immediately condemned the killing and ordered a thorough investigation. The UNO blamed the National Guard, but Director-General Colonel Oscar Gutiérrez denied these charges, pointing out that the weapon used was a .22 calibre rifle—not Guard issue.[64]

Whatever the truth of the matter, the UNO turned the incident into a campaign issue. Duarte began publishing open letters to Sánchez Hernández, giving his campaign itinerary for the week and asking the president to take the necessary steps to insure that no one shot at him in the places listed.[65] Miguel Angel Barrera López was the only martyr the Christian Democrats had after almost a dozen years of political struggle and they were determined to exploit his death as fully as possible. Duarte named his political memoir "Intipucá" after the little town and dedicated it to Barrera, "who gave his life while delivering a message of peace and hope to the Salvadoran people."

The outcome of the presidential voting February 20 aggravated the polarization caused by the Barrera shooting, the cancellation of the UNO assembly slates, and the bitter polemics of the campaign. Early returns from outlying departments gave Molina a commanding lead. With seven out of fourteen departments reporting, he was enjoying a clear majority with 54 percent of the vote. With the arrival of totals from more populated areas, however, the UNO began to close the gap. Molina suffered his most severe losses in San Salvador department (home of 30 percent of the republic's registered voters) where Duarte defeated him by a margin of two to one. The results from San Salvador spread consternation through PCN headquarters, where some leaders began resignedly to predict defeat. The government reacted to the worsening situation by banning the broadcast of election returns. All through the night the outcome remained in doubt. On the afternoon of the following day, the CCE announced that Molina had indeed defeated Duarte by a margin of 22,000 votes. Even in faraway London, the prestigious *Economist* noted the pecu-

64. Duarte, taped interviews, reels no. 7 and 8; Duarte, "Intipucá"; *Prensa Gráfica*, December 31, 1971, January 4, 1972. Duarte places the killing one day later than it actually occurred. The investigation ordered by Sánchez Hernández came to nothing. Duarte (taped interviews, reel no. 8) speculates that the fatal shooting was accidental, that the National Guard was merely trying to frighten his workers.

65. For example, José Napoleón Duarte, "Señor Presidente de la República," *Prensa Gráfica*, January 13, 1972.

liarity of this procedure and commented on how "coincidental [it was] that the government's position began to improve only when the results stopped being announced on radio and television."[66]

The UNO did not accept the government's count and announced figures of its own which showed Duarte ahead of Molina by 9,500 votes. The UNO claimed that its figures came from the departmental tabulating boards and that the CCE had arbitrarily adjusted the count after receiving its figures from the same boards.[67] The question was academic since the PPS and the FUDI scored well over 100,000 votes between them and, therefore, neither of the leading parties would have had the necessary majority under either set of returns. Duarte conceded that it was "inevitable" that the Legislative Assembly would choose Molina, regardless of whether or not he had won a plurality. Asked whether he would accept the assembly's decision, Duarte refused to comment, adding only that he opposed recourse to violence and that it would be "the people who decide[d]." The CCE reacted to the UNO's announcement by reminding the public that, under the law, only it could issue official returns and that any returns from any other source should be considered suspect.[68]

In the wake of opposition protests, the official candidate, expressing his certainty that there had been no fraud, agreed to an official recount. With Abraham Rodríguez observing for the UNO, the time-consuming retabulation began under heavy military guard; but it was of little consequence. Duarte and Ungo convened a press conference to announce their intention to challenge the entire election. They would, they declared, petition the CCE to nullify all the results and schedule a new election. At the same time, they announced an opposition drive within the Legislative Assembly to reorganize the CCE itself. They vowed to go so far as a general strike "to secure for the people the triumph they legally obtained at the polls."[69]

66. "Votes in the Night," The Economist, February 26, 1972, p. 42; New York Times, February 22, 1972, p. 24, February 24, 1972, p. 11; Diario de Hoy, February 22, 1972; Duarte, "Intipucá"; Duarte, taped interviews, reel no. 8.

67. Diario de Hoy, February 22, 1972. The UNO's figures were Duarte, 326,968 to Molina's 317,535, or a difference of 9,433. The official figures, as announced by Vicente Vilanova of the CCE on February 21, had given Molina 314,748 to Duarte's 292,621. For the UNO's description of the fraud involved, see Unión Nacional Opositora, "Importante communicado de la UNO," Diario de Hoy, February 25, 1962.

68. Diario de Hoy, February 23, 1972.

69. Ibid., February 25, 1972.

Not wishing to allow more time to pass, the government hastily convened the Legislative Assembly to meet on the afternoon of February 25 for the purpose of electing Molina to the presidency. The surprise call—the assembly was not supposed to meet until March 2—caught many opposition deputies unawares and quite a few had not yet arrived when the gavel fell shortly after 3:00 P.M. Adolfo Rey Prendes, PDC deputy from San Salvador, took the floor to request a recess to allow the rest of the minority deputies a chance to arrive, but assembly president Salvador Guerra Hércules overruled him and proceeded with the business at hand. A heated argument followed and, when the PCN majority brought the question of the presidency to a vote, the opposition walked off the floor in protest. The thirty-one remaining *oficialista* deputies then unanimously elected Arturo Armando Molina president of the republic for a five-year term to begin July 1, 1972. Precisely one hour and one minute after the opening of the session, they filed out of the chamber congratulating themselves on having done "what was best for the tranquillity of the country." While the assembly met in what observers described as "the most important plenary session in [Salvadoran] history," military and police units surrounded the Palacio Nacional and closed it to the public.[70]

While President-elect Molina, promising a "government of conciliation," set off to tour the country and meet the people, conservatives expressed satisfaction that the voters, in defeating the UNO, had dealt a grievous blow to communism.[71] Meanwhile, bitterness over the disputed presidential election continued to grow. The fragile Salvadoran democracy appeared irreparably weakened as the country healed almost immediately into another round of elections—this time to choose municipal councils and a Legislative Assembly—on March 12.

The disqualification by the CCE of the UNO's assembly ticket for

70. *Ibid.*, February 26, 1972. On the same day, the government announced the final, official results of the recount. They bore small resemblance to either of the disputed sets of figures: PCN, 334,600; UNO, 324,756; FUDI, 94,367; PPS, 16,871. The total vote was 770,594, of which 385,298 would have constituted a majority. The representatives of the UNO and the FUDI declined to sign the results.

71. *Diario de Hoy*, February 29, 1972. For representative opinions on the outcome of the elections, see "El voto anti-comunista en las elecciones del 20," *Diario de Hoy*, February 25, 1972; Ricardo J. Peralta, "Partido de oposición: Nunca admitirá su derrota," *Diario de Hoy*, February 29, 1972.

San Salvador promised the official party an easy victory, but not necessarily a peaceful one. In the presidential voting the UNO had carried San Salvador department with 129,262 votes to the PCN's 66,024, according to the government's own official returns. The coalition hoped to employ this large reserve of voter support in the department to put the lie to the *oficialistas'* pretensions of democratic triumph. It began a campaign to convince its supporters in San Salvador to deface their assembly ballots in protest against the UNO's exclusion from the race there. Under the Salvadoran electoral law, officials counted defaced ballots as null votes. Any election in which null votes outnumbered the total number of valid votes was itself theoretically null and required a new election. While the UNO plotted this popular assault on the PCN's pretensions in San Salvador, the FUDI's mayoral candidate, Mercedes de Rodezno, dropped out of the race explaining that she did not believe the government would allow a fair count.[72]

A series of unsavory incidents contributed to the general discontent and the unpleasant atmosphere that pervaded the early days of March. San Salvador's mayor, Christian Democrat Carlos Herrera Rebollo, accused the National Police of attempting to assassinate him in early March. Shortly afterward, authorities discovered a homemade bomb concealed in an attaché case at a meeting where the featured speaker was to be Yolanda de Novoa, Herrera's PCN opponent. Elements of the National Police disarmed the device before it could explode. A government spokesman attributed it to "subversive elements" who wished to disrupt the elections.[73]

Political violence unconnected with the activities of the two major parties was also on the increase. Far leftist elements at the university had from the beginning repudiated the moderates of the UNO and their participation in the electoral process.[74] Now, when

72. *Diario de Hoy*, February 26, March 7, 1972; Unión Nacional Opositora, "UNO condena," *Diario de Hoy*, March 7, 1972; Frente Unido Democrático Independiente, "Comunicado," *Diario de Hoy*, March 8, 1972.
73. Concejo Municipal de San Salvador, "El concejo . . . condena enérgicamente: El acto criminal de agresión de que fué víctima el alcalde . . . doctor Carlos Antonio Herrera Rebollo," *Diario de Hoy*, March 7, 1972; Dirección General de la Policía Nacional, "La . . . Policía Nacional, ante las acusaciones . . . ," *Diario de Hoy*, March 8, 1972.
74. Corresponsal, "Las autoridades de El Salvador intervienen la Universidad Nacional," *Estudios Sociales* (Guatemala City), no. 7 (August, 1972), 27–28.

that process appeared to be breaking down, extreme leftists seized the opportunity to launch a campaign of terrorist attacks and arson. On the evening of March 2, a group of guerrillas attacked a party of National Guardsmen in San Salvador, killing one and wounding another. The assailants stole the guardsmen's weapons and escaped in the general direction of the university. Authorities tracked them as far as the Dental Faculty but lost them there after causing considerable disruption and arousing the resentment of the students. The government claimed that police found Communist literature at the scene of the attack and blamed the incident on "red terrorists." The official party condemned the attack and challenged the opposition to do likewise, insisting that their silence would represent "satisfaction with or complicity in the execrable deed." Fires and incidents of terrorism continued to plague the capital and the nation until Sánchez Hernández found it necessary to deny rumors that the government was behind the wave of disorders. It was not true, he insisted, that his regime was attempting to create the conditions for military intervention in the form of a "self-coup" (autogolpe).[75]

Conditions worsened following the election itself. Incomplete returns gave the UNO only 8 seats in the Legislative Assembly and only 17 of the republic's 261 municipalities. That the coalition would have fared much better in a normal election is suggested by the fact that Herrera easily won reelection in San Salvador and that PDC candidates running under the coalition's banner recaptured from oficialista incumbents the municipalities of Santa Ana and San Miguel.[76]

In San Salvador department, the UNO's ballot-defacing campaign was quite successful.[77] Out of little more than 144,000 votes cast, almost 75,000 were nulls, compared with the less than 70,000

75. Diario de Hoy, March 3, 4, 10, 1972; Juventud Odontológica Salvadoreña, "Denunciamos," Diario de Hoy, March 6, 1972.

76. Diario de Hoy, March 13, 14, 17, 1972.

77. Duarte ("Intipucá") justifiably insists that the success of this campaign depended not only upon the firmness of popular support for the UNO but also upon the political sophistication of San Salvador's voters, since it required them to vote UNO on their municipal ballots while defacing their assembly ballots. The PPS, on the other hand, saw the matter as further proof of a UNO-PCN conspiracy since it was bound to provoke disorders that would justify further repression and imposition. Partido Popular Salvadoreño, "El P. P. S. ante el fraude, la farsa y el engaño," Prensa Gráfica, March 18, 1972.

valid votes which the PCN divided with the PPS.[78] The UNO demanded that the government nullify the election and hold another. Meanwhile, Duarte addressed an open circular to the diplomatic corps condemning the Sanchéz Hernández regime's "anti-democratic" practices. A UNO manifesto published on March 15 declared democracy dead in El Salvador and charged the regime had chosen the "path of political gangsterism." The UNO described Sánchez Hernández and his government as "oppressive, cynical, antipopular, and mafioso." [79]

Disturbances and difficulties continued to plague the embattled regime. Among these was the case of the newly elected UNO councilman (regidor) of San Marcos who disappeared from his home on the eighteenth. Relatives of Alfonso Rigoberto Alvayero said that National Guardsmen had come to the house and taken him away. He was recuperating from surgery at the time of his arrest and his family was concerned about his health. Officials at National Guard headquarters admitted the capture had taken place, but claimed they had released Alvayero on the same day. On the evening of March 20 his body, with all identification removed, was discovered in the road leading into town. An autopsy suggested an automobile had run him down.[80] Alvayero's family and his colleagues within the opposition demanded an explanation of his death from the regime. But the regime had run short of explanations. It was beginning to recognize that it had woefully miscalculated the political situation and pushed the opposition too far. It was in danger of losing control and the army was becoming restless.

In the week following the death of Alvayero, the political situation continued to deteriorate. The departmental electoral board in San Salvador accepted the UNO's petition and on March 22 invalidated the election for deputies and ordered another. The official party appealed the decision immediately and the following day the

78. Unión Nacional Opositora, "UNO pide nulidad," Diario de Hoy, March 18, 1972. Actual figures: total votes cast, 144,101; nulls, 74,922; valids, 69,179; PCN, 54,140 (7 deputies); PPS, 15,039 (2 deputies). These are the UNO's figures. The government never contested the assertion that a majority of the votes were nulls.

79. Unión Nacional Opositora, "El oficialismo se quitó la máscara," Diario de Hoy, March 15, 1972; Diario de Hoy, March 13, 1972.

80. Diario de Hoy, March 22, 1972; Unión Nacional Opositora, "¡Todos unidos contra la represión!" Prensa Gráfica, March 23, 1972.

CCE reversed the lower body's ruling and declared the results official.[81] Two days later, elements of the army went into open rebellion.

At 1:30 A.M. Saturday, March 25, the residents of San Salvador awakened to the sound of gunfire. Without lights or telephones, all was confusion in the city as the rebelling units went efficiently about their business of securing strategic positions and sealing off approaches to the capital. As the hours passed, it became clear that the coup d'état was the work of the two major military installations in San Salvador, the Zapote barracks across from the Casa Presidencial and the San Carlos barracks on the other side of town. In undisputed command of the uprising was Colonel Benjamín Mejía, the forty-eight-year-old commander of artillery at Zapote. After daybreak newsmen found Mejía at Zapote directing the revolt. He announced to them the formation of a new "Junta Revolucionaria" and declared himself its president.[82]

Before dawn, Mejía's second-in-command, Colonel Manuel Antonio Núñez, led a party of soldiers from San Carlos to the private residence of President Sánchez Hernández in San Salvador's Colonia Layco. The attackers dispersed the president's guard with gunfire, stormed the house and captured Sánchez and his seventeen-year-old daughter Marina. With the capital and the president in his hands, Mejía had reason to be confident. He announced—somewhat prematurely as it turned out—the fall of San Vicente and Santa Ana and the impending capitulation of San Miguel. "We have triumphed," he declared. "It is the triumph of the military youth [juventud militar]."[83]

But even before Mejía's boastful proclamation, Salvadoran Air Force planes began to rain bombs on the capital. Mejía and his fellow conspirators had succeeded in mobilizing the army in San Salvador against the regime, but the Air Force, the National Police, the Treasury Police (Policía de Hacienda), and the National Guard all remained loyal. While the pilots kept up the bombing, National Guard

81. *Diario de Hoy*, March 23, 24, 1972; Duarte, taped interviews, reel no. 8. The departmental electoral junta contained one *oficialista*, one Christian Democrat, and one "neutral."

82. Joining Mejía on the Junta were Major Arturo Guardado and the civilian Manuel Rafael Reyes Alvarado. *Prensa Gráfica*, March 26, 1972; *Diario de Hoy*, March 27, 1972; Duarte, "Intipucá."

83. *Diario de Hoy*, March 27, 28, 1972; *Prensa Gráfica*, March 26, 1972.

units from all over the country, and especially from Sonsonate and San Miguel, converged upon the capital under the stubborn command of Colonel Oscar Gutiérrez. Rebel antiaircraft artillery on a nearby hilltop fired upon the attacking planes but to little effect. Citizens poured out of the city in taxis, in light vehicles, and on foot, while the corridors of the Military Hospital and the Hospital Rosales filled with the wounded and dying. A twelve-year-old girl and a female attendant perished when loyalist bombs meant for rebel headquarters flattened a children's home instead. Soldiers from both sides swarmed the streets of the city. Reporters stopped a patrol and asked them whether they were loyalists or rebels. "They awakened us at eleven o'clock last night," they replied. "We don't know what's happening."[84]

As the initially orderly takeover degenerated into a bloody battle for San Salvador, rumors swept the city as to the identity of Mejía's sponsors. Some said he acted on his own account, that he was bitter because the PCN had not offered him its nomination or because the army had not made him a general. Others said the rebels were loyal to General Medrano. Still others said they were leftists. A radio speech proclaiming victory for the coup made over a rebel-held station at mid-morning by left-wing politician René Glower Valdivieso leant some credence to the latter view. But there was no hint of UNO or Christian Democratic involvement until shortly after noon when listeners to San Salvador's station YSC heard the voice of José Napoleón Duarte call upon them to resist the loyalist forces. Duarte warned residents of the area surrounding El Zapote to evacuate their homes as rebels were about to begin an artillery bombardment to prevent loyalist troops from advancing upon their position. He also advised the National Guard to surrender and called upon his supporters to erect barricades to obstruct the movement of government forces.[85]

84. Guillermo Peñate Zambrano, "Para la historia: El frustrado golpe militar del sábado," Diario de Hoy, March 27, 1972, Suplemento Cívico. See also, New York Times, March 27, 1972, pp. 1, 19; Diario de Hoy, March 27, 1972. If the soldiers questioned were indeed awakened at 11:00 P.M., they were obviously rebels; but, given the mechanics of the truly professional coup d'état, it was perfectly natural that no one had told them so. Edward Luttwak, Coup d'Etat: A Practical Handbook (London, 1968).

85. Diario de Hoy, March 27, 28, 1972; Peñate Zambrano, "Para la historia"; Duarte, "Intipucá."

Fighting in San Salvador continued on into the afternoon. Dead soldiers lay in the city's streets. Reports spoke of 100 killed and another 200 wounded. The rebels resisted the loyalist onslaught valiantly, but little by little their position began to crumble. While the Air Force continued its bombing, guardsmen retook the telephone exchange, the Military Academy, and the General Staff. Finally, at 4:15 P.M., a white flag fluttered above the walls of Zapote and the insurgents conceded defeat. Released by his captors, Sánchez Hernández assumed command of his forces and declared martial law.[86]

All over the city, persons who had reason to fear reprisals began disappearing into foreign embassies. Before the collapse of the revolt, rebel officers warned Napoleón Duarte of a supposed government plot to assassinate him and advised him to seek asylum. Heeding their admonition, he took refuge in the home of the first secretary of the Venezuelan embassy, Gonzalo Espina. Later in the evening a group of plainclothes policemen backed by soldiers with bayonets arrived at the house. They forced their way in, ignored Espina's protests of diplomatic immunity, manhandled him and his wife, and arrested Duarte who was hiding in a bedroom. The ruffled diplomat later complained that the policemen had beaten their prisoner in his living room while his small sons watched.[87]

The capture of Duarte brought an immediate and angry protest from Venezuelan Ambassador Aquiles Certad who summoned a meeting of the diplomatic corps to discuss the situation. The Salvadoran government denied that the home of a first secretary was a legitimate sanctuary, but the regime in Caracas was not prepared to bend when the fate of a fellow Christian Democrat was at stake. Word reached San Salvador that Venezuelan president Rafael Caldera intended to break off diplomatic relations unless Sánchez Hernández agreed to set Duarte free.[88]

Meanwhile, the government was neither confirming nor denying that it had Duarte in custody. It did announce, however, that it was making plans to court-martial and shoot the leaders of the coup on

86. Diario de Hoy, March 27, 1972; New York Times, March 27, 1972, p. 19.
87. Duarte, taped interviews, reel no. 8; New York Times, March 29, 1972, p. 29.
88. Duarte, taped interviews, reel no. 8; Duarte, "Intipucá"; Diario de Hoy, March 27, 30, 1972; Prensa Gráfica, March 28, 1972; New York Times, March 28, 1972, p. 3; New York Times, March 29, 1972, p. 29. The Venezuelan embassy later denied there had been a threat to break off relations.

charges of "sedition, treason, and rebellion." Learning of this, the diplomatic corps nominated the ambassadors of the United States, Italy, and Brazil to intercede with the Foreign Ministry on Duarte's behalf. Sánchez Hernández cancelled plans to execute the rebels and decided, instead, to ship them into exile. On March 28, while the president was still denying any knowledge of Duarte's whereabouts, a Salvadoran Air Force plane deposited the former presidential candidate in Guatemala City. Joined there by his family, he went first to Miami and then to Caracas where he ultimately took up residence.[89]

Citing his broadcast in support of the rebels, the government claimed that Duarte had been a leader of the coup. That is unlikely. He claims that he knew nothing of the orientation of the movement until 9:00 A.M. when Colonel Mejía called to inform him of it. Later, Glower Valdivieso telephoned to advise him that all was not well and that the rebels required his assistance. Having no particular love for the existing regime and fearing its reprisals whether or not he cooperated with Mejía, Duarte concludes, he agreed to make the radio speech.[90] Nothing is known of Mejía's intentions had he maintained himself in power. None of the visible leaders of the coup attempt was politically prominent or identified with any particular party. Colonel Núñez was almost certainly dissatisfied for career reasons. He was one of the officers the government inactivated when it reshuffled the army in December.[91] Without any firm evidence of the involvement of Duarte or any other leader of the PDC or the UNO in the plotting and execution of the attempted overthrow, it seems safest to conclude that it was a classic example of officers with personal ambitions to fulfill taking advantage of a disordered political situation that momentarily disposed their colleagues toward rebellion.

Successful or not, the mere fact of the revolt provides ample evi-

89. *Diario de Hoy*, March 28, 29, 30, 1972; *Prensa Gráfica*, March 29, 1972; New York *Times*, March 27, 1972, pp. 1, 19; Duarte, taped interviews, reel no. 9; Duarte, "Intipucá."

90. Duarte ("Intipucá") explains also that he feared that if Mejía was successful he would take reprisals against the PDC for its refusal to cooperate. A military court acquitted Duarte *in absentia* in November. White, *El Salvador*, 258n.

91. *Prensa Gráfica*, December 7, 1971. In an interview, Sánchez Hernández described Mejía as an old friend about whom he had been receiving disturbing reports but of whom he had never thought as a "traitor." He added that Mejía was ambitious to be a general. *Prensa Gráfica*, March 29, 1972.

dence of the depth to which the prestige of the PCN and of the electoral solution itself had fallen. However, it simultaneously afforded the triumphant *oficialistas* a new opportunity to cast the opposition as scapegoats. The regime boasted that it had beaten down a "leftist" attempt at revolution and proceeded to characterize the UNO as insurrectionary and antidemocratic.[92]

With its most important leader in exile, and itself stigmatized as revolutionary, the future of the progressive opposition and particularly of the Christian Democratic party appeared to hold little promise in 1972. Long before the coup, the regime's actions had made it clear that the halcyon days of the mid-1960s were no longer. The function of the official party had never been to compete for power. Its founders organized it from a position of power to maintain themselves in power. Beginning in the administration of Julio Adalberto Rivera, the government allowed and even encouraged formal opposition through alternative political parties. This much-heralded "liberalization" of the 1960s was in reality, however, an attempt to co-opt dissident sectors of the politically articulate population by allowing them minority representation on the national level and limited access to power and patronage in certain local areas. It counted among its advantages that it fostered an image of democracy and political "maturity" and that it contributed to political stability by channeling the expression of dissent into peaceful and legal avenues.

As long as the Christian Democratic party remained within the bounds established by those who instituted the electoral solution of the 1960s, the solution encouraged its growth. The PDC was particularly suited to its role as leader of the legal opposition. It differed from the parties that had come and gone before it in that it was an ideological rather than a personalist party. This circumstance favored the degree of permanence necessary to become the nucleus of an established opposition movement. Furthermore, it was a party whose ideology, while it called for social and economic reform, emphasized domestic peace and political and social stability. This meant that, at least in formal terms, opposition to the government

92. See comments by Sánchez Hernández, *Prensa Gráfica*, March 29, 1972. A Salvadoran journalist who covered the coup attempt was hesitant to categorize it as leftist. Peñate Zambrano, "Para la historia."

did not involve questioning the legitimacy of the government's power. It certainly precluded the pursuit of power through violent or extraconstitutional means as long as the electoral solution remained viable. To this extent, the party offered little offense to those in power and proved attractive to those who, for whatever reason, opposed them but were content to confine the expression of their dissent to peaceful means.

Taking advantage of President Rivera's apparently sincere belief in the electoral process, the Christian Democrats began fielding candidates earnestly in 1964. That year they captured the mayoralty of San Salvador, which they held until 1976, and broke the government party's monopoly of the Legislative Assembly. By 1968, combined opposition strength in the assembly came within two seats of that of the government party. The Christian Democrats, with nineteen of the opposition's twenty-five deputies, constituted its largest single bloc. The elections of 1968, however, represented the peak of opposition power. The governing party and the military manipulated patriotic and nationalistic fervor in the year following the Honduran War to deal the PDC and lesser opposing parties a serious reversal in the 1970 elections. In 1972, the PDC returned to mount a strong challenge to the government party's control of the presidency and the assembly by coalescing with two smaller parties to its left. By that time, however, the regime of Fidel Sánchez Hernández had begun to revive certain techniques of electoral manipulation common to pre-Rivera governments.

The commitment of the governing party to the experiment in openness lasted only as long as there was no danger of the opposition's gaining total control. The logical flaw of the electoral solution of the 1960s was that it encouraged an active opposition but, by definition, forbade that opposition to come to power. It also required the official party repeatedly to win elections. In the early period, this was easy. And it remained so in the country's rural areas where the *oficialistas* were able to combine the relative lack of sophistication of the voters with appeals to respect for authority and a liberal employment of bribery, fraud, coercion, and imposition. For various reasons, not the least of which was the greater sophistication of the city, this was decreasingly possible in the urban areas as the years passed. San Salvador, and later Santa Ana and San Miguel, became important centers of opposition voting strength. By 1970, it was no longer a question of "allowing" the Christian Democrats a few seats. It became a matter of preventing them from assuming power.

One consequence of the "liberalization" begun by Rivera was the creation of a large sector of the population sophisticated in its understanding of the ballot and *oposicionista* in its political mentality. Unfortunately for the government, these voters were largely concentrated in the capital and the republic's major cities. The ruling party became more and more populist in its appeal in an attempt to keep them from the Christian Democrats, but the PDC was always slightly ahead of it. Eventually, this leftward drift cost the PCN a major component of its support—members of the landed, capitalist oligarchy. Convinced that they could go no further to the left, the *oficialistas* decided in 1972 to circumvent the will of those they once had courted, using their control of the electoral machinery. To do this without arousing the urban masses to bitterness and perhaps to violence was a delicate task, and the government survived ultimately only through repression.

Because of the paradox of the Salvadoran PDC's position as a strong opposition party within what is in reality a one-party system, it is difficult to assess its relevance to the experience of Christian Democratic parties elsewhere in Latin America. To a great extent it owed its success to arbitrary decisions on the part of the country's rulers as to the extent of opposition they would allow. Why this particular party, rather than any one of the several other fledgling parties that appeared and disappeared in the early part of the decade, should have become the major opposition force is also difficult to say. As noted, it may in part have been because the Christian Democrats possessed a coherent and systematic ideology and offered a definite program. It may also have been because their most important leader, José Napoleón Duarte, proved ultimately to be a man of considerable charismatic appeal.

Unfortunately, the intriguing and crucial question of the type of Salvadoran who joined and voted for the Christian Democratic party lies largely beyond the scope of this study and the documentation upon which it is based. On the simplest level, it is clear that the PDC developed substantial followings in urban areas, particularly in San Salvador. It is also clear that the leadership of the party consisted almost exclusively of university-educated professionals. It is not clear, however, that the government party recruited its leaders from substantially different sectors of the population. The most obvious contrast between the two parties is the presence of military officers and large landowners in the official party and their relative absence from the Christian Democratic party. This fact has led critics of the government party to conclude that it has been merely the agent of right-wing militarism and landowner interests. The political behavior of the Salvadoran military has, however, been essentially tactical rather than ideological, and the alliance between the governing party and the traditional economic oligarchy since 1961 has been an uneasy one. In 1972 there was clear evidence that substantial elements of the oligarchy felt they had lost political influence. Significantly, their anxiety found expression in legal partisan activity rather than in military action. When elements of the military did move against the government in an unsuccessful attempt to overthrow it, they appeared to be acting on behalf of the progressive rather than the conservative opposition.

El Salvador, 1972–1977

One student of El Salvador has suggested that the country's political history in the twentieth century has been the story of a series of governments seeking the optimum balance between concession and repression.[1] No less than his predecessors, Arturo Armando Molina had to face upon his assumption of the presidency the necessity to calculate the political benefits of continuing to meet popular demands in even the gradual and minimal manner of Sánchez Hernández against the costs inherent in marginalizing the oligarchy and rightist elements within the officer corps. His options were made no easier by the fact that the relative political order that characterized the 1960s now seemed definitively a thing of the past. Political expectations, particularly in urban areas, had been raised to such a point that they could not readily be deflated without serious cost, and the blatant employment of legal and extralegal electoral controls in 1972 had contributed to the alienation of the opposition and severely damaged the prestige of the democratic solution. Many youths had already chosen to express their dissent through revolutionary violence. The events of the 1970s would encourage not only the growth of leftist guerrilla movements but also right-wing paramilitary organizations, and El Salvador would experience in the 1970s the sort of political warfare—clandestine armies of the ideological extremes attacking visible enemies of the center such as the church, the government, and the opposition parties—that Guatemala had suffered in the 1960s.

1. White, *El Salvador*, 95.

The narrowness and suspiciousness of his electoral victory weakened Molina's position from the beginning.[2] Before he even assumed office, there was a military challenge to his legitimacy in the form of a coup attempt that enjoyed at least some support from representatives of the civilian opposition. The new president survived this test, but he needed an issue upon which he could base his right to govern and he found it in "law and order" and "anticommunism." Virtually Molina's first official act was to join the government to the conservative assault upon the National University. On July 19, explaining that the institution "had fallen into the hands of the Communists," Molina secured a decree from the Legislative Assembly abrogating the university's organic law and ordered troops to occupy the central campus in San Salvador as well as the outlying regional centers in Santa Ana and San Miguel. Authorities arrested a number of administrators, professors, and students, deported the foreigners among them, and exiled many of the Salvadorans. The university remained closed for more than a year and when it reopened in September, 1973, it did so under tight governmental control with a government-appointed rector.[3]

Although the government's action scandalized academics at home and abroad, it was not entirely unpopular in El Salvador. Politically active students were now seen less as romantic young opponents of tyranny and more as overprivileged, irresponsible, and ungrateful children. In conservative minds, the great wickedness of the university and other centers of permissiveness in Salvadoran society consisted largely in the exposure of youth to corrupting foreign influences. Some of these—manifested in a predilection for Marxist formulas, revolutionary slogans, and the idealization of such heroes of the Left as Ernesto "Che" Guevara and Salvador Allende—clearly came from the traditional enemy camp, the socialist world; but other no less destructive trends—long hair, drug abuse, sexual promiscuity—were seen as imports from the developed capitalist world and, in particular, from the United States. All came together in popular resentment and official rhetoric under the collective rubric "com-

2. On the relationship between narrowness of margin and legitimacy, as well as a consideration of recent trends toward closer elections, see Martin C. Needler, "The Closeness of Elections in Latin America," *Latin American Research Review*, XII (1977), 115–21.

3. Flores Macal, "Historia de la Universidad," 134–35.

munism." The university itself was only the outward symptom of a greater cancer in Salvadoran society, conservatives charged. An advocate of Molina's "reform" declared on the assembly floor that Rivera and Sánchez Hernández had mistakenly believed they could maintain an open society and restrict subversives to the campus, but that events now demonstrated the naïveté of that position. The time had come for forceful action. Clandestine right-wing sources began to advocate a campaign of "sanitation" against Communists wherever they might appear—in the Supreme Court, the Legislative Assembly, government ministries, even the clergy.[4]

Identified as a major conduit for subversive notions from abroad were the progressive members of the Roman Catholic priesthood, who increasingly worked at the organization of the urban and rural poor in defense of their political, social, and economic rights. Many of these priests, especially those of the Maryknoll and Jesuit orders, were foreigners and demands for their expulsion were already common before the election. Here Molina could not move as decisively, perhaps, because the progressive clergy were not as isolated socially as the boisterous students—they in fact enjoyed the full support of the Salvadoran ecclesiastical hierarchy including such men of impeccably anti-Communist backgrounds as Archbishop Chávez of San Salvador and Bishop Aparicio of San Vicente. But, caught between pastoral calls for social change and insistence on the part of conservatives that the clergy be silenced, Molina could not hope to remain neutral for long.

Not surprisingly, conservatives associated the spread of social reformism within the Salvadoran clergy with the political rise of the Christian Democratic party. The international nature of the PDC, its association with popular causes, its alliance with left-wing and even, clandestinely, Communist party elements through the UNO, its near victory in 1972, and its identification in the person of Napoleón Duarte with the coup attempt of that year, all combined to make the most powerful of Salvadoran opposition parties an obvious target for repression. Still the PDC and its partners in the UNO remained intact and legal and participated in the assembly and munic-

4. Corresponsal, "Autoridades intervienen la Universidad."

ipal elections of 1974. These elections, the first since the troubles of 1972, took place in an extremely tense political climate. Brazen acts of political terrorism in the capital—including an armed attack upon the offices of the CCE—indicated that some elements of the opposition had no further interest in electoral politics. And if the Left thus signaled its disenchantment with the democratic experiment, the Right was not silent either. At least one vocal conservative openly advocated the liquidation of the representative system and the establishment of direct military rule.[5]

Electoral manipulation was even more obvious in 1974 than it had been in 1972; the government never got around to publishing official returns, but it claimed the PCN had captured thirty-six seats to the UNO's combined total of fifteen and the FUDI's one. The UNO lost three of the twenty municipalities it held from 1972, although it retained for the sixth time the capital city. Few people took these results seriously. Opposition politicians denounced the fraud, and an experienced student of Salvadoran politics calculated from independent surveys that the UNO would have come out of a fair race with a majority in the Legislative Assembly.[6]

Contributing to the weakness of the PDC's position was the prolonged exile of Napoleón Duarte. Acquitted of charges in connection with the 1972 coup attempt, he was under no legal ban and his continued residence in Caracas was entirely discretionary on his part. Although he explained in 1973 that the "martyrdom" of exile had more political value to him and the party than any role he could play in El Salvador, his expatriation meant that he gradually lost his personal influence in party decision-making, while men of his generation—such as Juan Ricardo Ramírez, Adolfo Rey Prendes, and Roberto Lara Velado—who remained present and active retained theirs. Duarte did return briefly to campaign for the UNO in 1974 and demonstrated that he had lost little of his charismatic appeal or

5. *Prensa Gráfica*, March 7, 1974; *Diario de Hoy*, March 4, 7, 1974; Sidney Mazzini V[illacorta], "Otra vez, ¿va a salvarse El Salvador?" *Diario de Hoy*, March 11, 1974.

6. Unión Nacional Opositora, "El fraude eleccionario demostración palpable de la debilidad del régimen," *Diario de Hoy*, March 19, 1974; Edmundo Víctor Paz, "El Salvador and Honduras: Small Countries with Big Problems," *Latinamerica Press* (Lima, Peru), September 26, 1974.

his capacity to provoke controversy, but on election day he slipped quietly out of the country and returned to Venezuela.[7] As a result of his experience in 1972, Napoleón Duarte had become skeptical of the feasibility of a democratic solution to El Salvador's social and economic problems. And while he certainly did not emphasize these doubts in his public appearances during the 1974 visit, and while neither he nor the party ruled out the possibility that he would run for the presidency again, he had by 1973 come to the conclusion that the future of reform lay with the army, in particular the younger officers. He even speculated about the possibility of a transitional regime that would unite civilian and military progressives.[8]

Those who still believed in pure democracy in El Salvador had less and less cause for optimism as the 1970s progressed. Political violence increased following the elections and two fairly well-defined urban guerrilla movements emerged, the People's Revolutionary Army (Ejército Revolucionario del Pueblo, ERP) and the Farabundo Martí Popular Liberation Forces (Fuerzas Populares de Liberación "Farabundo Martí," FPL). These movements specialized in hit-and-run terrorist raids and financed their operations by kidnapping for ransom members of the country's oligarchic families. Violence from the right was not unknown either, such as the massacre by "security forces" of a group of peasants at La Cayetana (San Vicente) in late November. This last incident in particular contributed to the further extreme polarization of Salvadoran politics. A young progressive priest led a crowd of ten thousand peasants in a protest demonstration before the Casa Presidencial. Molina listened politely to their demands, but a move by the opposition in the assembly to promote a legislative investigation into the truth behind the official version of the events came to nothing.

Following the La Cayetana incident, El Salvador's bishops began to speak out more regularly and more loudly in condemnation of social inequities and of the use of the state's repressive apparatus in the service of landholding interests. In May, responding to the abuse of one of his priests by agents of the National Guard, Bishop Aparicio

7. Duarte, taped interviews, reel no. 9; information from a Christian Democratic party leader, 1976; *Diario de Hoy*, March 11, 1974.
8. Duarte, taped interviews, reel no. 9; José Napoleón Duarte, "La historia está de nuestra parte," *Diario de Hoy*, March 6, 1974.

denounced the guard as a threat to social order and issued a decree of excommunication against the responsible parties. Archbishop Chávez meanwhile devoted a pastoral letter to a call for agrarian reform and peasant mobilization.[9] Molina cautiously endorsed the archbishop's remarks, but he also took care to warn of the danger of a politicized church.

While the social activism of the Roman Catholic clergy emerged as one of the regime's most serious political challenges, trouble began at the university again. In spite of the tight controls imposed when it reopened, the institution had quickly fallen into old patterns. The government-appointed rector, physician and public health specialist Juan Allwood Paredes, resigned in September, 1974, declaring the situation impossible. Strikes and demonstrations were constant. Students demanded, among other things, the withdrawal of police from the campus, the restoration of student participation in naming the rector, and an end to a new government policy limiting the number of places open to students from San Salvador.

The climax of the confrontation between government and students occurred in late July. Students at the regional center in Santa Ana had demonstrated in protest against the priorities shown in the government's massive expenditure on the 1975 "Miss Universe" pageant held in San Salvador. When authorities forcibly broke up this demonstration, some two thousand students at the main campus in San Salvador staged a march on July 30 from the university to Plaza Libertad as a manifestation of solidarity. Along the route, National Guardsmen opened fire on the marchers. Estimates reaching the exterior in spite of government efforts to stifle coverage of the incident placed the student death toll at at least thirty-seven. Many more were injured, arrested, or "disappeared." These events came at a time when political violence was becoming more intense and kidnappings and assassinations more frequent on both extremes of the ideological spectrum.

The opposition parties and the Roman Catholic hierarchy roundly condemned the shootings, and a sullen crowd of as many as fifty thousand capitalites walked in procession on August 1 to honor

9. "El Salvador Bishop's Protest to the Government over Police Conduct," *Latinamerica Press*, June 26, 1975; Luis Chávez y González, "Inflation in El Salvador and the Christian Conscience," *Latinamerica Press*, April 24, 1975.

the memory of the fallen. A large group of workers, university students, and seminarians occupied the cathedral and held it for five days demanding the release of those arrested, while railway workers called for a work stoppage. The government's use of naked force against the students served to create martyrs and to a large extent seemed to reverse public attitudes toward the university. In late 1975, the Molina administration appeared to be entering a crisis resembling those that had precipitated the collapse of Martínez and Lemus.[10]

The Defense Ministry claimed that the demonstrators had initiated the violence of July 30. President Molina blamed the incident on Communist subversion and "revealed" what he described as a master conspiracy on the part of the Salvadoran Communist party to seize political power—ignoring, as was customary, all the evidence of a deep split between the moderate PCS and the younger radicals in the guerrilla movements. Molina declared that elements of the PCS had infiltrated the PDC, the MNR, the UDN, and various antigovernment labor organizations, including the militant teachers' union ANDES. According to this version, PDC deputies had deliberately incited the disturbances at Santa Ana and later in San Salvador, and these incidents would somehow contribute to an overall Communist scheme to split the army along generational lines, form a worker-peasant alliance, and come to power legally in the assembly and municipality elections in 1976. While PDC spokesmen dismissed these accusations with the scorn they deserved on logical grounds, they surely could not have missed the implications of Molina's message for the future of the government's already waning commitment to competitive electoral politics. The president concluded his message by promising an investigation of all political organizations to determine which were in violation of constitutional prohibitions against "antidemocratic" and international parties—a charge to which the PDC was particularly vulnerable.[11]

Whether the PCN government could continue its centrist stand on social and economic policies and long indulge in this sort of destructive rhetoric was extremely doubtful in late 1975. In many ways the government's actions and declarations served to encourage ex-

10. *Central America Report* (Guatemala City), August 1, 8, 1975.
11. *Prensa Gráfica*, August 1, 2, 1975.

tremism of both the Left and the Right. Early in August, a manifesto appeared from a group calling itself the Wars of Elimination Anti-Communist Liberation Armed Forces (Fuerzas Armadas de Liberación Anti-comunista de Guerras de Eliminación, FALANGE). Revealing in its choice of acronym and obviously patterning itself on "death squads" that had emerged in other Latin American countries, notably Brazil and Guatemala, the FALANGE promised to exterminate all Communists and their collaborators in Salvadoran society. It denounced both the government and the church for harboring Reds—bishops, priests, deputies, ministers, even military officers—and concluded with the hope that by taking the vanguard in this struggle it would inspire Molina to come to his senses, clean house, and organize a proper regime modeled upon that of Martínez.[12]

Local speculation linked the FALANGE variously to rightist elements within the military, to powerful landholding families, and to multinational corporate interests. The organization took credit for a number of killings in the weeks that followed, and the left-wing terrorist groups were active as well. The spiral of violence continued to expand. The first week of October reported thirty-eight assassinations on both sides. The campaign of kidnappings continued, newspaper offices were attacked, and unidentified assailants gunned down UDN deputy Rafael Aguiñada Carranza. In the countryside, confrontations between National Guardsmen and peasants left many dead or "disappeared."[13] Molina's greatest achievement during this period of crisis appears to have been to hold the loyalty of the army; it was probably the major factor that accounted for his survival. Rumors that he intended to cancel the upcoming elections were discounted by veteran observers who argued that such an action would constitute an admission of desperation and could lead to the collapse of the regime.

While the escalation of political violence captured attention outside El Salvador and cast Molina in a distinctly unfavorable light, it must be remembered that he attempted during his period to carry forward the developmental, social, and economic goals of previous PCN administrations and, in doing so, attempted to respond to popular pressures through gradual but tangible concessions. Much of his

12. *Ibid.*, August 8, 1975.
13. *Central America Report*, October 6, 1975.

program was threatened by the worldwide economic events of the early 1970s—the dramatic increase in petroleum prices and other inflationary pressures. Molina consequently devoted his attention to measures designed to reduce national dependency. During the Molina period, El Salvador accelerated steps to diversify its markets, its exports, and its sources of capital and technology, negotiating in the process commercial agreements with a number of eastern bloc countries including the Soviet Union. The latter policy, as one can readily imagine, was not without its vocal detractors given the local political issues of the day. El Salvador also sought to decrease its dependence upon imported fossil fuels and in late 1974 moved to increase the power output of the Lempa hydroelectric system with the Cerrón Grande project, to explore the possibilities of geothermic energy—seemingly a natural in a country with so many volcanoes—and to encourage oil exploration on its continental shelf. In addition, Molina undertook to expand and rationalize national control of the country's essential infrastructure, cancelling the concession of the U.S.-owned International Railways of Central America (IRCA), which had not been due to expire until the year 2009, and placing the line, its stock, and port facilities under the management of the Acajutla Port Authority.[14]

The knottiest problems facing Molina's administration were, as always, those related to the development of the rural sector. During his campaign for the presidency, he had promised to seek a solution to these problems, and in particular to improve the lot of the peasant; but any substantial program of change could expect ferocious resistance from landholding interests. This had been demonstrated clearly enough during the regimes of Rivera and Sánchez Hernández, and each had retreated from the full implications of his rhetoric. Molina was already experiencing difficulties with the oligarchy over his agreement in September, 1974, following student and worker demonstrations, to increase the agrarian minimum wage to a magnanimous $1.40 daily for male workers. Furthermore, coffee growers loudly objected to the regime's attempt to win higher world prices by holding the Salvadoran crop off the market, thus pitting the government's concern over declining exchange reserves against individual producers' concern for immediate profits.

14. *Ibid.*, October 11, 25, November 22, 1974.

In such an unpropitious climate, Molina attempted to meet the challenge some Salvadoran government ultimately must—the fact that this smallest and most densely populated of Latin American nations, although priding itself upon the efficiency with which it exploits its limited resources, suffers from massive rural underemployment and malnourishment. To a great extent this is due not simply to the rapid increase in population but to the fact that much of the best agricultural land is devoted to such nonfood export crops as coffee and cotton, or to cattle raising, an industry which, while salutary from the point of view of national diversification, produces a relatively small amount of expensive food per precious acre. In spite of the crowded conditions under which Salvadoran agriculture operates, much land goes totally unexploited, and acreage devoted to food production for domestic consumption is generally cultivated with antiquated, grossly inefficient techniques.

Molina's agrarian program took the form first of a law enacted in late 1974 to provide for the forced rental, or in extreme cases expropriation, of unexploited or inefficiently exploited lands. Another law passed in mid-1975 created the Salvadoran Institute of Agrarian Transformation (Instituto Salvandoreño de Transformación Agraria, ISTA)—agrarian "transformation" apparently being thought more palatable than agrarian "reform"—to replace the old ICR and to supervise the operation of government agrarian programs. This measure aroused much opposition at the time both within and outside the government, but a court challenge failed and on June 29, 1976, the government announced the creation of the first agrarian transformation zone, an area of some 150,000 acres largely devoted to cotton and cattle in San Miguel and Usulután departments to be divided among approximately twelve thousand peasant families. Legislation establishing the zone set minimum and maximum limits on holdings within it of three and thirty-five hectares respectively. Although, in the tradition of distributive agrarian programs since the time of Martínez, this was a modest beginning in global terms, it was a quite radical departure in El Salvador and it met stubborn—and ultimately violent—resistance.[15]

The political timing of the decree was important. It came shortly

15. *Ibid.*, November 22, 1974, July 4, 1975, July 12, August 2, 1976. For analyses and documents dealing with the agrarian transformation controversy, see the entire number of *Estudios Centro Americanos*, XXXI (September–October, 1976).

after the Legislative Assembly and municipal elections of 1976—
elections from which, for the first time since 1962, the opposition
parties abstained en masse. The opposition's action came in protest
against massive manipulation on the part of the government as well
as against "reforms" to the electoral law designed to make it more
difficult to qualify candidates. The refusal to participate on the part
of the member parties of the UNO meant one more formal expression
of discredit with respect to the electoral process; it also meant that
the PDC, MNR, and UDN surrendered without a struggle every public office they held, including the municipality of San Salvador. The
latter was no real loss, explained PDC mayor José Antonio Morales
Ehrlich, who had succeeded Carlos Herrera Rebollo in 1974, since
the Molina government had so interfered in municipal affairs that
the mayoralty had been reduced to a powerless and thankless position.[16] If the government was unwilling to risk aggravating an ongoing political crisis by cancelling elections, the opposition, for its
part, felt no particular need to cooperate.

The creation of the ISTA and of the Usulután–San Miguel zone
were attempts not only to solve a pressing national problem but to
rally popular support to an embattled government and reestablish its
credibility as a progressive force. And the bill did receive the endorsement of many of the regime's severest critics on the left. Even
the outgoing PDC deputies voted for it; party leaders explained they
would support any measure, no matter how minimal, that moved the
country even a step closer to a genuine agrarian reform. But, while
they praised the measure itself, representatives of the legal opposition questioned Molina's motives and expressed the fear that agrarian transformation, like other grand designs to reform the Salvadoran rural sector in the past, would end quietly after the first widely
publicized installment.[17]

Certainly if Salvadoran conservatives had anything to say about
it, that was precisely what would happen. The National Private Enterprise Association (ANEP), along with various coffee and other ag-

16. Unión Nacional Opositora, "La UNO se retira de las elecciones y llama al
pueblo al rescate de la constitucionalidad y conquista de la democracia," Prensa
Gráfica, March 2, 1976.
17. Partido Demócrata Cristiano, "Frente a la transformación agraria," Estudios
Centro Americanos, XXXI (1976), 626–28. ·

ricultural interest groups, mounted a massive publicity campaign designed to block implementation. The deadline for property-owners to sell lands in excess of the legal maximum passed in September and it became clear that while less well-to-do landholders might comply and accept compensation for their lands, the wealthier interests were prepared to fight, tying up the court system with lengthy litigation and exporting surplus capital to more favorable localities. When the flight of capital became sufficiently serious to threaten a devaluation of the colón, Molina agreed to meet with representatives of the interests opposing agrarian transformation. The outcome of these talks was a "compromise" that in fact emasculated the law, exempting lands judged to fulfill a quite lenient definition of "social function," leaving to the discretion of the individual landholder which of his lands still eligible would be expropriated, and accepting the owners' formula for compensation. Commenting on the changes to the law, PDC leaders estimated it would now take from one hundred to two hundred years to achieve its goal.[18]

Reversals such as the one the Molina administration effected in its agrarian policy in late 1976 were common enough in Salvadoran history and in the past were not presumed to have serious political consequences since those whose interests were most damaged, the rural poor, were generally without organization or independent voice. But changes were coming to the Salvadoran countryside in the 1970s, largely as the result of the organizational efforts of opposition parties such as the PDC and of the progressive clergy, and landowners increasingly found themselves having to bargain with spokesmen for such technically illegal groups as the Christian Federation of Salvadoran Peasants (Federación Cristiana de Campesinos Salvadoreños, FECCAS) or the Union of Rural Workers (Unión de Trabajadores Campestres, UTC). The government had, beginning in the late 1960s, sought to counter agitation in rural areas by organizing peasants on its own, first in the paramilitary ORDEN and later in the more socially oriented Salvadoran Communal Union (Unión Comunal Salvadoreña, UCS). The UCS by 1976 claimed as many as eighty thousand members and represented an attempt, like agrarian

18. *Central America Report*, October 18, November 29, 1976; "Power Structure Blocking Salvador Land Reform," *Latinamerica Press*, January 13, 1977.

transformation itself, to create a privileged class within the peasantry that would serve as a buffer and foil to greater popular demands and perhaps at the same time aid the government party in reducing somewhat its political dependence upon the oligarchy.

Landed interests, of course, opposed the very idea of peasant organization outside their own tutelage and recognized that their political victory in San Salvador on the ISTA issue would ultimately prove meaningless failing a restoration of "order" in the countryside. The opportune "disappearance" of fractious peasants at the hands of the National Guard intimidated many but did not treat the source of the problem—the organizational activities of nonpeasants. The shooting death in December, 1976, of a prominent landowner currently involved in negotiations with the FECCAS and UTC led to cries of indignation and calls for draconian measures against progressive priests serving in rural parishes who, landowners charged, preached hatred and actively fomented violent revolution.[19]

The frequency with which elections are conducted in El Salvador under the 1962 constitution insures that virtually no prolonged difficulties of any sort can escape aggravation by the demands of electoral politics. By the time of the troubles over agrarian transformation, the country was already preparing for the presidential election to be held February 20, 1977. The PCN's choice as its candidate of Defense Minister General Carlos Humberto Romero, a specialist in counterinsurgency warfare popularly identified with such acts of repression as the student massacre of 1975 and believed to be unsympathetic to Molina's agrarian reform initiatives, appeared to confirm publicly a shift toward the right on the part of the government party. The right-wing fringe parties of previous years had by now disappeared, and the administration's willingness to accept modifications to the ISTA legislation seemed to help consolidate the conservative position with that of the government. General José Alberto Medrano, who had opposed the PCN in 1972 as a "corrupt band, infiltrated by communists," now cautiously associated himself with its cause.[20]

For its part, the UNO did not turn to its own ranks for its nominee and choose someone, such as Duarte, with a well-established political identity. Instead, it selected a retired military man, fifty-four-

19. "Power Structure Blocking Reform."
20. *Central America Report*, January 31, 1977.

year-old Colonel Ernesto Claramount Rozeville. Claramount, an officer with extensive command and diplomatic experience, was the son of General Antonio Claramount, a prominent military figure of his day and pioneer aviator who had been a presidential contender in 1931 and again in 1944. The UNO's vice-presidential candidate in 1977 was the former PDC mayor of San Salvador, José Antonio Morales Ehrlich. Claramount and Morales campaigned on a platform offering the undeniably attractive ideals of a "return to democracy" and an end to political violence, but few observers believed the election, no matter what its outcome, could do other than worsen the political chaos in El Salvador.

The fact that Romero "won" the election was less surprising to observers than the obviousness of official manipulation. Ballot boxes in some areas were reported already filled when the polls opened. Many UNO observers were arrested or otherwise bodily removed from their stations. Opposition representatives were present to certify the results from only 920 of the country's 3,540 boxes, nearly half of them in the capital area. Observers noted that Claramount defeated Romero handily in these boxes, but received less than a third of the vote nationwide.[21]

As they had in 1972, UNO leaders denounced·the fraud and vowed to take their case to the people. By the evening of election day some fifteen thousand supporters had joined Claramount and Morales Ehrlich in Plaza Libertad, and the defeated presidential candidate announced his willingness to "remain in the plaza as long as the people want me to." By the third night, the crowd was estimated at fifty thousand and there were calls for a general strike. Although Claramount was joined by a number of other retired officers, both in his campaign and now in his protest, there was no indication of sufficient sympathy among active-duty personnel to produce a coup attempt such as the one that had followed the defeat of Napoleón Duarte. On the sixth night of the protest, the government brought in police in armored cars and dispersed the crowd, leaving perhaps forty or fifty demonstrators dead. Claramount and some fifteen hundred supporters fled and took refuge in El Rosario church

21. In the 920 "free" booths, Claramount received 157,574 votes to Romero's 120,972. The official national total gave Romero 812,281 to 394,661 for Claramount. *Central America Report,* February 28, 1977.

adjacent to the square, where friends from the officer corps and representatives of the Red Cross eventually convinced him to surrender and accept exile in Costa Rica. The government imposed a state of siege which lasted throughout the month of March and was renewed in April.[22]

As he left the occupied church in a Red Cross ambulance to be escorted to Ilopango Airport, Colonel Claramount had declared, "This is not the end. It is only the beginning."[23] It certainly was not the end of political violence. From the beginning, the left-wing guerrilla organizations had denounced as "opportunistic" the UNO's participation in the election and had escalated their campaign of terror as the voting approached. Whereas their activities had heretofore largely involved the kidnapping of wealthy private citizens and shootouts with local authorities, they now began to target high government officials. The abduction and murder of tourism director Roberto Poma on January 27 scandalized the capital at a time it seemed few things still could. Following the election, there was a drive by the Right, including assassinations, torture, and "disappearances." A number of progressive priests were subjected to arbitrary arrest and expulsion. On March 12, unidentified gunmen shot and killed the Jesuit parish priest of Aguilares (San Salvador), Father Rutilio Grande, and two companions, as he drove to a nearby town to say mass. Aguilares had been the scene of major electoral abuse in the recent voting, and Grande himself had for some time been accused by such organizations as ANEP of fomenting "revolution" among the peasantry.[24]

Oscar Arnulfo Romero Galdámez, an extremely committed progressive clergyman who had been elevated to the Archbishopric of San Salvador upon the recent retirement at age seventy-five of Luis Chávez, reacted quickly and decisively to the attack on Grande. He and his fellow bishops had already issued a denunciatory report on the government's conduct regarding the election and the violence that followed it. Now the archbishop ordered church schools closed for a two-day period and suspended masses on Sunday, March 20, in

22. *Ibid.*, February 28, March 7, 1977; New Orleans *States-Item*, February 28, 1977, sec. A, p. 3.
23. New Orleans *States-Item*, February 28, 1977, sec. A, p. 3.
24. "Salvadoran Church Leaders Decry Repression and Injustice," *Latinamerica Press*, April 14, 1977.

all the nation's churches except the cathedral in the capital. Romero further demanded an official investigation of the slaying, which Molina was quick enough to promise, and forbade all clerics under his jurisdiction to attend government functions until the case was satisfactorily resolved.[25]

Not surprisingly, the situation in El Salvador caught the attention of the Carter administration in Washington, which had assumed office in January with a controversial avowed commitment to predicate foreign aid upon the observation of "human rights" in recipient countries. There was considerable sentiment in Congress to withhold monies from the Salvadoran government following the 1977 election, and this feeling increased as a result of the Grande assassination. Hearings conducted by Congressman Donald Fraser's House Subcommittee on International Organizations into conditions in El Salvador drew vocal criticism from the Molina regime as a violation of national sovereignty and ultimately a decision on the part of Molina to follow Chile, Uruguay, Argentina, Brazil, and Guatemala in refusing further military aid from the United States.[26]

As the regime in San Salvador seemed increasingly isolated politically at home and diplomatically abroad, extremists of the Left and the Right seemed to vie with one another in the perpetration of sensational crimes. If the killing of Father Grande had been a coup for the Right, the Left replied on April 19 by kidnapping Foreign Minister Mauricio Borgonovo Pohl. The culprits—believed to be the FPL—refused all offers of ransom and demanded instead the release of thirty-seven dissidents they claimed were being held in government prisons. In spite of offers of mediation by both Costa Rica and Panama, Molina refused to concede the terrorists' demands— probably because the prisoners in question had long since "disappeared" and could not be produced. Finally, after three weeks of futile exchanges, the guerrillas announced the "execution" of their hostage.[27]

The killing of Borgonovo provoked rage throughout the Salvado-

25. Kernan Turner, "Rights Confrontation in El Salvador," New Orleans Times-Picayune, April 6, 1977, sec. 3, p. 9.

26. Central America Report, March 21, 1977; Charles Green, "Guatemala Cuts U.S. Arms Aid," New Orleans Times-Picayune, March 18, 1977, sec. 1, pp. 1, 12.

27. Isaac A. Levi, "Troubled San Salvador Turning into Armed Camp," New Orleans Times-Picayune, May 2, 1977, sec. 1, p. 8; New Orleans States-Item, May 30, 1977, sec. A, p. 10.

ran Right. During his captivity, a clandestine paramilitary group emerged and declared it would exterminate all revolutionaries, their families, and their collaborators if Borgonovo was not released unharmed. This White Warrior Union (Unión Guerrera Blanca, UGB) contended that the Jesuits and other progressive priests were responsible for revolutionary violence in El Salvador and that they must be punished. Following the announcement of Borgonovo's death, gunmen on May 12 assassinated a second priest, Father Alfonso Navarro, pastor of Miramonte. Subsequently a general campaign of persecution seemed to be unleashed against the clergy. On the nineteenth, security forces assaulted the town of Aguilares and arrested three Jesuits who had been associated with Father Grande, and the government quickly announced their expulsion from the country. On May 25, two young diocesan priests, the brothers Higinio and Inocencio Alas, fled their parish of Suchitoto (Cuscatlán) after receiving threats from the UGB and went into exile. Retired Archbishop Chávez y González took over duties in the parish as a demonstration of solidarity with his successor's defiance of the government and right-wing terrorists.[28]

General Romero was inaugurated president on July 1, 1977, without major incident. Since there had been as yet no progress in the Grande case—to no one's particular surprise—the clergy boycotted the ceremony. The bishops, in fact, were now preoccupied with an even greater crisis. The UGB had announced in June that, if El Salvador's forty-seven Jesuit priests did not abandon the country by July 21, they would be considered "military targets" and systematically eliminated. This new threat caused a flurry of diplomatic activity from Washington to the Vatican and greatly increased world awareness of the public order situation in El Salvador. Secretary of State Cyrus Vance called in officials from the Salvadoran embassy in Washington to communicate the Carter administration's concern for the fate of the Jesuits. President Romero, who before his inauguration had spoken contemptuously of "Marxist-Leninist priests," now assured church officials that he would tolerate no terrorism of the Right or the Left and agreed to provide troops and police to protect

28. "El Salvador: Puntos sobre las íes," *Diálogo Social* (Panama City), no. 90 (June, 1977), 24–29; Margaret Goff, et al., "Business Groups and Government Combating the Church," *Latinamerica Press*, June 16, 1977.

ecclesiastical lives and property. The "day of death" came and went without the promised massacre, and there was some speculation it had been a grisly hoax. While no one can be certain whether the threat was genuine, the passions it reflected are quite real and exist today in El Salvador.[29]

Carlos Humberto Romero—who described himself as an "anti-Communist all of my life"—promised a regime of peace, tranquility, and social change at home. The odds were not great that he would be able to deliver, although he did show from the beginning a desire for conciliation with the church and the democratic opposition—seen most notably in his firm public commitment to prevent the UGB from carrying out its death threat against the Jesuits. The violence, meanwhile, continued. Kidnappings occurred throughout 1977, and in July the Farabundo Martí Popular Liberation Forces exacted vengeance for a forty-five-year-old crime when they gunned down former president Osmín Aguirre y Salinas, aged eighty-two, as he stood in front of his home talking with his grandchildren. Aguirre, as director of the National Police, had been a key figure in the repression that followed the revolt of 1932, a revolt whose most famous martyr gave his name to the FPL. Amid all this, there was not much talk of elections to come in El Salvador. Following the massive fraud of 1977, José Antonio Morales Ehrlich perhaps best expressed the dilemma of the democratic reformer in contemporary El Salvador. "How can we ever ask [the people] to participate again," he wondered. And "what about us who want to see change effected through the electoral process? We can't all simply become guerrillas."[30]

29. La Hora (Guatemala City), July 20, 1977; New Orleans States-Item, July 22, 1977, sec. A, p. 13; Clarion Herald (Archdiocese of New Orleans), July 14, 1977, p. 2; Alan Riding, "Central America's Violence," New York Times, May 22, 1977, sec. E, p. 4; Central America Report, July 25, 1977.

30. Central America Report, February 28, July 11, 1977; New Orleans States-Item, July 13, 1977, sec. D, p. 13.

BIBLIOGRAPHY

UNPUBLISHED MATERIALS

Duarte Fuentes, José Napoleón. "Intipucá." Ms. in possession of Professor Roland H. Ebel.
————. Taped interviews conducted by Professors Roland H. Ebel, Ralph Lee Woodward, Jr., et al. New Orleans, Louisiana, January 22–February 2, 1973. 9 reels. Howard-Tilton Library, Tulane University.

PUBLIC DOCUMENTS

Consejo Central de Elecciones. Memoria de las elecciones de 1950. San Salvador: Secretaría de Información de la Presidencia de la República, 1951.
————. Memoria de las labores realizadas por el Consejo Central de Elecciones durante el año 1964. San Salvador: Imprenta Nacional, n.d.
————. Memoria de las labores realizadas por el Consejo Central de Elecciones durante el período comprendido entre abril de 1965 y marzo de 1968. San Salvador: Imprenta Nacional, n.d.
Consejo Nacional de Planificación y Coordinación Económica. El Salvador: Su desarrollo económico y su progreso social. San Salvador: n.p., 1966.
Dirección General de Estadística. Anuario estadístico correspondiente al año 1930. San Salvador: Imprenta Nacional, n.d.
Dirección General de Estadística y Censos. Cuarto censo nacional de población: Cifras preliminares. San Salvador: n.p., 1971.
————. Tercer censo nacional agropecuario, 1971. 2 vols. San Salvador: n.p., 1974–75.

————. *Tercer censo nacional de población, 1961.* San Salvador: n.p., 1965.

Heare, Gertrude E. *Latin American Military Expenditures, 1967–1971.* Washington, D.C.: U.S. Government Printing Office, 1973.

Inter-American Development Bank. *Economic and Social Progress in Latin America: Annual Report, 1972.* Washington, D.C.: Inter-American Development Bank, 1972.

————. *Tenth Annual Report, 1969.* Washington, D.C.: Inter-American Development Bank, 1970.

Ministerio de Defensa. *La barbarie hondureña y los derechos humanos: Proceso de una agresión.* San Salvador: n.p., 1969.

Ministerio de Relaciones Exteriores. *Posición de El Salvador ante la Comisión Interamericana de Derechos Humanos: Planteamiento y denuncia de las violaciones contra personas y bienes de salvadoreños en Honduras.* San Salvador: n.p., 1969.

Pensamiento político-revolucionario del teniente coronel José María Lemus. San Salvador: n.p., 1956.

Sánchez Hernández, Fidel. *Discursos del Señor Presidente de la República General Fidel Sánchez Hernández.* 4 vols. San Salvador: Imprenta Nacional, n.d.

Secretaría de Información de la Presidencia de la República. *Por qué estamos con la revolución salvadoreña.* San Salvador: Imprenta Nacional, n.d.

————. *La revolución salvadoreña: Folleto no. 1.* San Salvador: Tipografía La Unión, n.d.

————. *La verdad sobre el conflicto bélico entre El Salvador y Honduras.* San Salvador: n.p., 1969.

Secretaría de Información de la República. *De la neutralidad vigilante a la mediación con Guatemala.* San Salvador: Imprenta Nacional, 1954.

NEWSPAPERS

Clarion Herald (Archdiocese of New Orleans), July 14, 1977.

Diario de Centro América (Guatemala City), July, 1969.

El Diario de Hoy (San Salvador), 1960–74.

The Economist (London), February 26, 1972.

Excélsior (Mexico City), May 19, 1969.

La Hora (Guatemala City), July 20, 1977.

El Mundo (San Salvador), January 31, 1970.
La Prensa Gráfica (San Salvador), 1964–72, 1974–75.
New Orleans *States-Item*, 1977.
New Orleans *Times-Picayune*, 1977.
New York *Times*, 1963–72, 1977.

NEWSLETTERS

Central America Report (Guatemala City), 1974–77.
Latinamerica Press (Lima, Peru), 1972–77.

ARTICLES (Newspapers and Newsletters)

In order to avoid extensive repetition, the following abbreviations are used to cite the most frequently consulted newspapers: DH, *El Diario de Hoy*; PG, *La Prensa Gráfica*; NYT, *New York Times*.

"Actos indignos que desprestigian a Honduras." PG, June 25, 1969.

Alas, Hernán. "Del momento: Incógnitas de la campaña política." DH, July 5, 1971.

Aldana, Adrián Roberto. "Ejército rechaza a las tropas hondureñas." PG, July 14, 1969.

———. "¡Salvadoreños, a ganar con goleada!" PG, June 12, 1969.

Aniano García, Herminio. "¡Duarte ... Ud. es un mentiroso ... !" PG, January 13, 1972.

"Un aniversario trágico: La irrupción del terror en el país." DH, February 18, 1972.

Araujo Batres, Roberto. "¡Señor Duarte, yo también compruebo que Ud. es mentiroso!" PG, January 15, 1972.

Asociación de Ganaderos de El Salvador. "A la Asamblea Legislativa ... sobre la sindicalización campesina." PG, June 16, 1971.

Asociación General de Estudiantes Universitarios Salvadoreños. "El pueblo tiene una cita." DH, April 16, 1962.

Asociación Nacional de la Empresa Privada. "Declaraciones ... en relación a la nueva Tarifa de Arbitrios Municipales." DH, May 7, 1970.

Béneke, Walter. "El ministro Walter Béneke refuta las mentiras y acusaciones del Sr. Ing. José Napoleón Duarte al gobierno de la república." PG, November 20, 1971.

"El boicot radial a la propaganda marxista." DH, January 15, 1967.

Caballero, J. de. "A los pensamientos del Dr. Abraham Rodríguez." DH, March 2, 1970.

Chávez y González, Luis. "Inflation in El Salvador and the Christian Conscience." *Latinamerica Press*, April 24, 1975.

Chez, Ramón. "Al museo todos los disfraces del cnel. Rivera." DH, March 10, 1967.

Comité de Vigilancia y de Defensa de los Derechos de los Cafetaleros Salvadoreños. "El comité . . . se dirige a los cafetaleros." DH, February 9, 1971.

Concejo Municipal de San Salvador. "El concejo . . . condena enérgicamente: El acto criminal de agresión de que fué víctima el alcalde . . . doctor Carlos Herrera Rebollo." DH, March 7, 1972.

Consejo Central de Elecciones. "El Consejo . . . declara sin lugar solicitud de inscripción del 'P. R. A. M.' por tratarse de una agrupación antidemocrática." DH, July 16, 1960.

Córdova, José Enrique. "Los comentarios del Dr. Rodríguez Porth al Congreso de Reforma Agraria." PG, January 26, 1970.

"Declaración conjunta del episcopado salvadoreño." PG, January 15, 1970.

"Declaración conjunta del episcopado salvadoreño ante la situación política.' DH, February 22, 1967.

"Declaración de los delegados del sector empresarial acreditados ante el Congreso de Reforma Agraria, al pueblo salvadoreño." PG, January 7, 1970.

Departamento de Relaciones Públicas, Casa Presidencial. "Es necesario que el Pueblo Salvadoreño conozca a algunos elementos extranjeros contratados expresamente por los líderes de la AGEUS, CGTS y comunistas para masacrar a las personas que honraban a la patria frente a la estatua de La Libertad." DH, September, 22, 1960.

Dirección General de la Policía Nacional. "La . . . Policía Nacional, ante las acusaciones . . ." DH, March 8, 1972.

"Documentos vivientes del atropello de Honduras." PG, June 30, 1969.

Duarte [Fuentes], José Napoleón. "Democracia cristiana y justicia social." DH, March 28, 1961.

———. "Estudios sobre objetivos del Partido Demócrata Cristiano, I: Unidad de gobierno." DH, May 25, 1961.

———. "Estudios sobre objectivos del Partido Demócrata Cristiano, IV: Aumento de la producción nacional." DH, June 3, 4, 1961.

———. "La historia está de nuestra parte." DH, March 6, 1974.

———. "Señor Presidente de la República." PG, January 13, 1972.

"El Salvador Bishop's Protest to the Government over Police Conduct." *Latinamerica Press*, June 26, 1975.

Emmanuel O., V. "El Diablo una mala interpretación." DH, March 3, 1970.

———. "Problemas legislativos: Asamblea unipartidista o proporcional." DH, May 12, 1970.

Escamilla Saavedra, Julio. "¿La 'falsa imagen del comunismo,' Dr. A. Rodríguez?" DH, November 9, 1966.

Escobar, Julio César. "Sí soy reaccionario, mi querido doctor." DH, February 17, 1972.

Frente Político de Acción Laboral. "Segundo pronunciamiento de FEPAL." PG, December 23, 1971.

Frente Unido Democrático Independiente. "Comunicado." DH, March 8, 1972.

———. "FUDI dirígese al CCE." DH, July 28, 1971.

Fuentes Castellanos, Ricardo. "Alrededor de las elecciones: La tecno-burocracia y la política." DH, March 1, 1972.

———. "La democracia cristiana y el marxismo." DH, March 13, 1967.

———. "La democracia cristiana y la propiedad." DH, March 9, 1967.

———. "Democracia cristiana y revolución." DH, March 4, 1967.

———. "Insigne ciudadano: Aniversario de la muerte de Ernesto Regalado." DH, February 18, 1972.

———. "Tema del momento: Quién vota a la alianza cristiano-comunista, vota al comunismo." DH, February 17, 1972.

Giniger, Henry. "Left in Salvador Scores Big Gains." NYT, March 12, 1968, p. 55.

———. "Opposition Gains in Salvador Vote." NYT, March 15, 1966, p. 15.

———. "Salvador Elects President Today," NYT, March 5, 1967, p. 27.

———. "Salvador Fears a Pre-Vote Coup." NYT, December 10, 1966, p. 18.

————. "Salvador is Calm for Voting Today." NYT, March 13, 1966, p. 27.

————. "Salvador Regime Beset by Strains." NYT, October 19, 1967, p. 20.

————. "Salvador Seeks to Push Industry." NYT, November 6, 1965, p. 34.

————. "Salvador Weighs Role of Military." NYT, October 25, 1965, p. 17.

————. "Salvador's Left Widens Pressure." NYT, June 21, 1968, p. 9.

————. "San Salvador's Chaotic Market Reflects the Nation's Problems." NYT, June 26, 1968, p. 12.

————. "Slowdown Sweeps Central America." NYT, January 22, 1968, p. 64.

————. "Street Art Stirs Salvador Voters." NYT, January 21, 1966, p. 12.

————. "Two Leftist Parties Rebuffed in Salvador as Army Colonel Wins Presidency." NYT, March 7, 1967, p. 4.

Goff, Margaret, et al. "Business Groups and Government Combating the Church." Latinamerica Press, June 16, 1977.

Green, Charles. "Guatemala Cuts U.S. Arms Aid." New Orleans Times-Picayune, March 18, 1977, sec. 1, pp. 1, 12.

Guardado, Juan Gregorio. "Palabras del señor presidente de la Asamblea Legislativa . . . en ocasión de celebrarse el primer Congreso Nacional sobre Reforma Agraria." PG, January 8, 1970.

Henríquez Azurdia, Enrique. "Partidos criollos e internacionales en la lid." DH, March 4, 1970.

Imendia, Carlos Arturo. "El conflicto de la oposición." DH, March 5, 1964.

"¡¡Increíble pero cierto!!" DH, February 16, 1972.

"El ingeniero Duarte sigue mintiendo." DH, February 12, 1972.

Instituto Salvadoreño de Estudios Sociales y Económicos. "Una advertencia al país sobre el Congreso Nacional Agrario." PG, January 5, 1970.

————. "El despojo y la imposición como 'reformas sociales.'" DH, October 9, 1970.

————. "Un documento fílmico de palpitante actualidad: Cuba antes y después de Castro." DH, January 13, 1972.

————. "No desordenemos nuestra propia casa con el Mercado Común en peligro." PG, September 17, 1969.

————. "Trés programas políticos y un mismo epílogo." DH, February 7, 1972.

Junta Cafetalera Departamental de La Libertad. "A la Honorable Asamblea Legislativa... sobre la sindicalización campesina." PG, June 25, 1971.

Juventud Odontológica Salvadoreña. "Denunciamos." DH, March 6, 1972.

Kennedy, Paul P. "Salvador Assays Red Labor Drive." NYT, June 13, 1965, p. 25.

Lara Velado, Roberto. "Aclarando posiciones, III: Libertad y justicia." PG, October 10, 1966.

————. "La batalla diplomática en la OEA." PG, September 3, 5, 6, 8, 9, 1969.

————. "La Democracia Cristiana Salvadoreña y sus detractores, II: El partido y la iglesia." PG, October 24, 1966.

————. "La Democracia Cristiana Salvadoreña y sus detractores, III: Los partidos internacionales." PG, October 26, 1966.

————. "La Democracia Cristiana y la remuneración del trabajo." DH, April 25, 1961.

————. "Después de la batalla diplomática: La realidad de este momento." PG, September 10, 1969.

————. "La economía no es independiente de la ética." DH, June 30, 1961.

————. "Las elecciones de 1968." PG, March 29, 1968.

————. "En resumidas cuentas." PG, November 5, 1966.

————. "Ni liberalismo, ni socialismo, sino Democracia Cristiana." DH, June 5, 1961.

————. "Los pronunciamientos sociales de la Democracia Cristiana." DH, March 22, 1961.

————. "Qué es la revolución de los pobres." DH, January 31, 1964.

Larde y Larín, Jorge. "El próximo debate electoral." PG, November 15, 1966.

Lepidus, Henry. "Salvador Cheered by Better Balance of Payments." NYT, April 8, 1963, p. 74.

————. "Salvador is Confident About Future." NYT, January 28, 1966, p. 66.

Levi, Isaac A. "Troubled San Salvador Turning into Armed Camp." New Orleans *Times-Picayune*, May 2, 1977, sec. 1, p. 8.

Lima, Francisco Roberto. "Al pueblo salvadoreño." PG, March 4, 1966.

López Jiménez, Ramón. "Agustín Farabundo Martí y la revolución comunista." DH, December 1, 1970.

————. "El espectro de 1932 se alza amenazante: Los ofrecimientos de reparto de tierras." DH, February 7, 1972.

López Trejo, Roberto. "La mayoría silenciosa." DH, March 7, 1970.

Martínez, Francisco A. "Indemnización por los daños exigirá el país." PG, June 25, 1969.

Martínez Vargas, Isidro. "¿El partido oficial ganará las elecciones?" DH, January 3, 1967.

————. "Más sobre la lección chilena y los 'kerenskys' lugareños."

Mazzini V[illacorta], Sidney. "Análisis político-constitucional: Golpe de mesa." DH, November 7, 1969.

————. "La historia, ¿ vuelve a repetirse?" DH, February 10, 1972.

————. "Otra vez, ¿va a salvarse El Salvador?" DH, March 19, 1974.

Mejía, Ricardo. "Inoficiosa prevención del Consejo Central de Elecciones." DH, January 16, 1967.

Mejido, Manuel, "Hablan cuatro alcaldes centroamericanos: Pesimismo sobre un cambio en las relaciones con EU." *Excélsior* (Mexico City), May 19, 1969, pp. 1, 19.

Meléndez, Joaquín. "Lo irremisible del mañana evitémoslo con la previsión hoy." DH, January 13, 1967.

Mendizábal, A. "De Morazán: Presidente FSH explica lo que es Ley de Avenamiento y Riego." PG, November 11, 1970.

"Mensaje del Comité Femenino Santaneco del Partido Demócrata Cristiano a la mujer salvadoreña." DH, February 19, 1961.

Morales Zavaleta, Arturo. "Peligrosa incitación a la lucha de clases." DH, January 25, 1964.

————. "Prevención: Engañar a los campesinos es sumamente peligroso." DH, February 14, 1972.

Movimiento Nacional Revolucionario. "Carta política . . . al pueblo salvadoreño y al presidente de la república." PG, December 11, 1969.

Movimiento Nacional Revolucionario, Partido Demócrata Cristiano,

and Unión Democrática Nacionalista. "Manifiesto al pueblo salvadoreño." PG, September 3, 1971.

Municipalidad de San Salvador. "La municipalidad de San Salvador
aclara y explica al pueblo." PG, April 30, 1970.

Navarrete, Roberto Jesús. "Una advertencia a la clase trabajadora y el
pueblo en general sobre el Partido Popular Salvadoreño." PG,
January 8, 1972.

Nuila, V., Francisco E. "La patria está en peligro: Partido Acción Renovadora y Partido Demócrata Cristiano." DH, March 1, 1967.

Onís, Juan de. "Central America Seeks Integration." NYT, January
26, 1969, p. 60.

"Otra vez la amonestación de monseñor Aparicio y Quintanilla."
DH, January 23, 1967.

Parada (h.), Alfredo. "Un insulto a la nación fué desfile de los estudiantes universitarios." DH, December 6, 1970.

———. "Más sobre la lección chilena y los 'kerenskys' lugareños."
DH, October 14, 1970.

Partido Accion Renovadora. "Ciudadanos." DH, February 10, 1962.

Partido de Conciliación Nacional. "Con relación a los conceptos."
DH, February 6, 1962.

———. "El coronel Arturo Armando Molina, candidato de las
mayorías, definió categóricamente su posición frente a las pretensiones electoreras de un candidato." PG, December 17, 1971.

———. "El fin de la estafa (el PDC se quita la careta)." PG, March 18,
1970.

———. "El Partido de Conciliación Nacional aclara." DH, January
25, 1964.

———. "Patria." PG, January 10, 1970.

———. "PCN contra la demagogia." PG, January 8, 1970.

———. "Señoras de los mercados recibieron a su 'héroe' como él se
lo merece." PG, March 1, 1970.

———. "Vota por el PCN." PG, January 16, 1970.

Partido Demócrata Cristiano. "El caso chileno y el P. D. C. de El Salvador." DH, October 7, 1970.

———. "El caso Regalado Dueñas: La corrupción total del oficialismo." PG, June 17, 1971.

———. "La crisis nacional y la reforma agraria." PG, August 29,
1969.

———. "La Democracia Cristiana ante el problema social." DH, March 2, 1961.

———. "La Democracia Cristiana y el problema campesino." DH, March 7, 1961.

———. "La Democracia Cristiana y la familia." DH, March 9, 1961.

———. "La Democracia Cristiana y la propiedad privada." DH, March 8, 1961.

———. "Demócrata Cristiano contesta al Conciliación Nacional." DH, February 9, 1962.

———. "Frente a la Ley de Avenamiento y Riego." PG, November 9, 1970.

———. "Frente al paredón comunista." DH, January 24, 1962.

———. "¡La gran estafa del 8 de marzo!" PG, March 16, 1970.

———. "Herrera Rebollo ¡Alcalde!" PG, February 8, 1970.

———. "Llamado a la conciencia del pueblo y del ejército." PG, January 3, 1970.

———. "Mensaje de esperanza y optimismo." PG, January 8, 1970.

———"El Partido Demócrata Cristiano frente a las próximas elecciones." DH, March 5, 1962.

———. "¿Por qué el PRAM rehuye el debate periodístico?" DH, February 20, 1962.

———. "El pueblo nos dió la razón." DH, March 20, 1964.

———. "Reforma Metropolitana." PG, February 27, 1964.

———. "Sexto aniversario celebra el P. D. C." PG, November 25, 1966.

———. "¡¡Traición al pueblo salvadoreño!!" DH, September 4, 1961.

———. "La unidad nacional no es sumisión al gobierno." PG, October 25, 1969.

Partido Popular Salvadoreño. "Cuando el imperio del derecho es letra muerta." DH, June 27, 1969.

———. "¿Hacia una reforma agraria democrática?" DH, January 6, 1970.

———. "El P. P. S. ante el fraude, la farsa y el engaño." PG, March 18, 1972.

———. "Reforma Agraria." PG, January 15, 1972.

Paz, Edmundo Víctor. "El Salvador and Honduras: Small Countries with Big Problems." *Latinamerica Press*, September 26, 1974.

Peñate Zambrano, Guillermo. "Para la historia: El frustrado golpe militar del sábado." DH, March 27, 1972, Suplemento Cívico.

———. "Rivera satisfecho de labor de gobno." DH, January 1, 1967.

Peralta, Ricardo J. "Carta a un candidato." DH, February 9, 1972.

———. "En defensa de la libertad: Miremos hacia atrás." DH, February 4, 1972.

———. "Partido de oposición: Nunca admitirá su derrota." DH, February 29, 1972.

Pérez Gómez, Salvador. "Desterrada la guerra en C. A. dice Rivera." PG, November 12, 1966.

Pineda, Gustavo. "La tragedia comunista de 1932: Hablando de un ex-dictador." DH, January 15, 1967.

"Por cuarta vez la democracia cristiana traiciona a sus correligionarios." DH, February 14, 1972.

Posada, Luis Alonso. "Las declaraciones del Dr. Abraham Rodríguez." DH, March 14, 1967.

"Power Structure Blocking Salvador Land Reform." Latinamerica Press, January 13, 1977.

"Pronunciamiento de la delegación de la Curia Metropolitana." PG, January 10, 1970.

"Pronunciamiento del clero ante el secuestro del padre Alas." PG, January 12, 1970.

Riding, Alan. "Central America's Violence." NYT, May 22, 1977, sec. E, p. 4.

Rivas Cerros, Luis. "La filiación democrática del cnel. Sánchez Hernández." DH, January 12, 1967.

Rivera M., Guillermo. "El foco subversivo de la Universidad Autónoma." PG, September 11, 1971.

Rodríguez Mojica, Maximiliano. "Triunfa psicosis dice A. Rodríguez." DH, March 7, 1967.

Rodríguez Porth, José Antonio. "Comentarios de un ciudadano: La derrota del PCN." DH, March 21, 1968.

———. "Discurso pronunciado por el . . . vicepresidente de la mesa directiva, en representación del sector empresarial, en el Congreso Nacional de Reforma Agraria, el día de su inauguración." PG, January 6, 1970.

———. "Ernesto Regalado Dueñas." DH, February 18, 1972.

Saavedra, Lilo. "El Cnel. Osmín Aguirre y Salinas comenta derrota de Cnel. Velásquez." DH, March 10, 1970.

Salazar Castro, Héctor Manuel. "Al pueblo salvadoreño: ¿Por quién votaré? Y por qué." DH, February 17, 1972.

"Sale de la clandestinidad el Partido Comunista." PG, November 24, 1970.

"Salvadoran Church Leaders Decry Repression and Injustice." Latinamerica Press, April 14, 1977.

Sandoval, Carlos. "Democracias en regresión." DH, October 21, 1970.

———. "La sepultura de la democracia cristiana." DH, September 11, 1970.

———. "Las sorpresas de las afinidades ideológicas." DH, October 26, 1970.

Secretaría de Información de la Presidencia de la República. "Mantengamos la Unidad Nacional." PG, October 23, 1969.

Sector Femenino del Partido Demócrata Cristiano de San Salvador. "Manifiesto." DH, January 19, 1961.

———. "Mensaje a las madres de Cuscatlán." DH, May 9, 1961.

"Silencio alrededor de la reforma agraria." PG, October 15, 1969.

"Sitios definitivos para mercados capitalinos." PG, September 22, 1969.

Suárez, Carmen Delia de. "Peces en el pavimiento y conciliación en el aire." DH, February 15, 1964.

Turner, Kernan. "Rights Confrontation in El Salvador." New Orleans Times-Picayune, April 6, 1977, sec. 3, p. 9.

Ungo, Guillermo. "La Guardia Nacional ganó las elecciones." DH, January 7, 1962.

Ungo, Guillermo Manuel. "Discurso pronunciado por el . . . vicepresidente de la Directiva del Congreso Nacional de Reforma Agraria por el sector no gubernamental, en el acto de inauguración." PG, January 10, 1970.

Unión Cívica Salvadoreña. "Duarte defraude a los demócrata cristianos en toda la república." DH, February 16, 1972.

Unión Democrática Nacionalista. "Primera carta política." PG, October 4, 1969.

———. "Segunda carta política." PG, October 15, 1969.

Unión Democrática Salvadoreña. "Barbudos comunistas invaden soberanía salvadoreña." DH, February 10, 1960.

Unión de Partidos Democráticos. "Un golpe más a la democracia." DH, December 20, 1961.

Unión Nacional Opositora. "El fraude eleccionario demostración palpable de la debilidad del régimen." DH, March 19, 1974.

————. "Importante comunicado de la UNO." DH, February 25, 1972.

————. "El oficialismo se quitó la máscara." DH, March 15, 1972.

————. "Programa de gobierno de UNO." PG, January 17, 1972.

————. "¡Todos unidos contra la represión!" PG, March 23, 1972.

————. "UNO condena." DH, March 7, 1972.

————. "UNO pide nulidad." DH, March 18, 1972.

————. "UNO responde a los falsarios!" PG, January 22, 1972.

————. "La UNO se retira de las elecciones y llama al pueblo al rescate de la constitucionalidad y conquista de la democracia." PG, March 2, 1976.

"La UNO se quita la careta." DH, February 9, 1972.

"Votes in the Night." The Economist (London), February 26, 1972, p. 42.

"El voto anti-comunista en las elecciones del 20." DH, February 25, 1972.

ARTICLES (Journals and Magazines)

Anderson, Charles W. "Central American Political Parties: A Functional Approach." Western Political Quarterly, XV (1962), 125–39.

Arieh Gerstein, Jorge. "El conflicto entre Honduras y El Salvador: Análisis de sus causas." Foro Internacional, XI (1971), 552–68.

Aubey, Robert T. "Entrepreneurial Formation in El Salvador." Explorations in Entrepreneurial History, 2nd ser., VI (1968–69), 268–85.

Cable, Vincent. "The 'Football War' and the Central American Common Market." International Affairs, XLV (1969), 658–71.

Caldera, Rafael. "Democratic Revolutions." Commonweal, October 29, 1965, pp. 120–24.

"Central America: The Seven Presidents." Newsweek, March 25, 1963, p. 59.

Colindres, Eduardo. "La tenencia de la tierra en El Salvador." *Estudios Centro Americanos*, XXXI (1976), 463–72.

Conde Salazar, Pablo, "El Salvador en 1967." *Cuadernos Americanos*, CLV (November-December, 1967), 20–30.

———. "El Salvador 1969." *Cuadernos Americanos*, CLXVI (September–October, 1969). 7–19.

Corresponsal. "Las autoridades de El Salvador intervienen la Universidad Nacional." *Estudios Sociales* (Guatemala City), no. 7 (August, 1972), 18–31.

De la Selva, Mauricio. "El Salvador en 1960." *Cuadernos Americanos*, CXIII (November–December, 1960), 35–46.

———. "El Salvador: Trés décadas de lucha." *Cuadernos Americanos*, CXX (January–February, 1962), 196–220.

"Democracia Cristiana salvadoreña en acción." *Información Democrática Cristiana* (New York), IX (June, 1961), 4–5.

Dodd, Thomas J., Jr., "La guerra de fútbol en Centroamérica." *Revista Conservadora del Pensamiento Centroamericano*, XXIII (February, 1970), 30–32.

Ducoff, Louis J. "Población migratoria en un área metropolitana de un país en proceso de desarrollo: Informe preliminar sobre un estudio experimental efectuado en El Salvador." *Estadística*, XX (1962), 131–39.

Ebel, Roland H. "Governing the City-State: Notes on the Politics of the Small Latin American Countries." *Journal of Inter-American Studies and World Affairs*, XIV (1972), 325–46.

"El Salvador: Fury." *Newsweek*, November 20, 1961, pp. 60–61.

"El Salvador: Puntos sobre las íes." *Diálogo Social* (Panama City), no. 90 (June, 1977), 24–29.

"El Salvador: The Out—And the Ins." *Newsweek*, November 7, 1960, p. 66.

"El Salvador: Vote for Reform." *Newsweek*, January 1, 1962, p. 25.

Flores Macal, Mario. "Historia de la Universidad de El Salvador." *Anuario de Estudios Centroamericanos*, II (1976), 107–40.

Geyer, Georgie Anne. "Latin America: The Rise of a New Non-Communist Left." *Saturday Review*, July 22, 1967, pp. 22–23.

Grieb, Kenneth J. "The United States and the Rise of General Maximiliano Hernández Martínez." *Journal of Latin American Studies*, III (1971), 151–72.

Handal, Shafik Jorge. "El Salvador: A Precarious Balance." *World Marxist Review*, XVI (June, 1973), 46–50.

"The Hemisphere: Two Forward, One Back." *Newsweek*, March 28, 1966, p. 58.

Hinds C., Manuel Enrique. "La imagen del país que se desprende del presente proceso electoral." *Estudios Centro Americanos*, XXVII (1972), 101–16.

Lara Velado, Roberto. "Aspecto socio-económico del control de la natalidad." *La Universidad*, XCII (January–February, 1967), 57–69.

Lima, Francisco Roberto. "La Ley del Impuesto sobre la Renta de 1963." *La Universidad*, XCV (May–June, 1970), 5–24.

Luna, David. "Análisis de una dictadura fascista latinoamericana: Maximiliano Hernández Martínez, 1931–1944." *La Universidad*, XCIV (September–October, 1969), 38–130.

McDonald, Ronald H. "Electoral Behavior and Political Development in El Salvador." *Journal of Politics*, XXXI (1969), 397–419.

————. "Electoral System, Party Representation, and Political Change in Latin America." *Western Political Quarterly*, XX (1967), 694–708.

Mallin, Jay. "Salvador-Honduras War, 1969: The 'Soccer War.'" *Air University Review*, XXI (1970), 87–92.

Martz, Mary Jeanne Reid. "OAS Settlement Procedures and the El Salvador-Honduras Conflict." *South Eastern Latin Americanist*, XIX (September, 1975), 1–7.

Mayorga Quirós, Román. "Crítica de las ideologías económico-sociales en la campaña presidencial de El Salvador." *Estudios Centro Americanos*, XXVII (1972), 71–100.

Needler, Martin C. "The Closeness of Elections in Latin America." *Latin American Research Review*, XII (1977), 115–21.

"El nuevo gobierno de El Salvador y la situación económica." *Estudios Centro Americanos*, XXII (1967), 636.

Oldman, Oliver. "Tax Reform in El Salvador." *Inter-American Law Review*, VI (1964), 379–420.

Parker, Franklin D. "The Fútbol Conflict and Central American Unity." *Annals of the Southeastern Conference on Latin American Studies*, III (1972), 44–59.

Partido Demócrata Cristiano, "Frente a la transformación agraria." *Estudios Centro Americanos*, XXXI (1976), 626–28.

———. "Lineamientos generales sobre una reforma agraria en El Salvador." *La Universidad*, XCV (January–February, 1970), 47–48.

Rama, Carlos M. "La religión en América Latina." *Casa de las Américas*, VI (March–April, 1966), 11–26.

"Resoluciones y recomendaciones del Primer Congreso Nacional de Reforma Agraria, realizado del 5 al 10 de enero de 1970." *Economía Salvadoreña*, XXVIII (1969 [sic]), 97 –122.

"The Rising Force." *Time*, September 18, 1964, pp. 48, 53.

Rodríguez, Abraham. "Actuación de la OEA en el conflicto." *Estudios Centro Americanos*, XXIV (1969), 423–32.

Rouquié, Alain. "Honduras-El Salvador, la guerre de cent heures: Un cas de 'désintégration' régionale." *Revue Française de Science Politique*, XXI (1971), 1290–1316.

Sermeño Lima, José Arnoldo. "El Salvador, 1985–2000: Población y recursos naturales." *Estudios Sociales Centroamericanos*, III (September–December, 1974), 207–54.

Sloan, John W. "Electoral Fraud and Social Change: The Guatemalan Example." *Science and Society*, XXXIV (1970), 78–91.

Slutzky, Daniel, and Ester Slutzky. "El Salvador: Estructura de la explotación cafetalera." *Estudios Sociales Centroamericanos*, I (May–August, 1971), 101–25.

"Socialistas que rezan." *Visión*, July 26, 1963, pp. 24–25.

Téfel Vélez, Reinaldo, Antonio. "Izquierdas y derechas en Latinoamérica y el movimiento socialcristiano." *Revista Conservadora del Pensamiento Centroamericano*, IV (August, 1962), 18–21.

Tugwell, Franklin, "The Christian Democrats of Venezuela." *Journal of Inter-American Studies*, VII (1965), 245–68.

Unión Nacional Opositora. "Texto de las respuestas entregadas por los representantes de la UNO." *Estudios Centro Americanos*, XXVII (1972), 49–67.

Universidad Nacional Autónoma de El Salvador. "Legislación de Reforma Agraria." *La Universidad*, XCV (January–February, 1970), 93–115.

Videgaray, Salvador. "Habla a SIEMPRE! el presidente de El Salvador

Fidel Sánchez Hernández." *Siempre!* (Mexico City), April 15, 1970, p. 59.

Williamson, Robert C. "Some Variables of Middle and Lower Class in Two Central American Cities." *Social Forces,* XLI (1962), 195–207.

Zamora, Rubén. "¿Seguro de vida ó despojo? Análisis político de la transformación agraria." *Estudios Centro Americanos,* XXXI (1976), 511–34.

BOOKS

Adams, Richard N. *Cultural Surveys of Panama—Nicaragua—Guatemala—El Salvador—Honduras.* Washington, D.C.: Pan American Sanitary Bureau, 1957.

Alexander, Robert J. *The Venezuelan Democratic Revolution.* New Brunswick, N.J.: Rutgers University Press, 1964.

Ameringer, Charles D. *The Democratic Left in Exile: The Antidictatorial Struggle in the Caribbean, 1945–1959.* Coral Gables, Fla: University of Miami Press, 1974.

Análisis de una experiencia nacional. San Salvador: Universidad Centroamericana "José Simeón Cañas," 1971.

Anderson, Thomas P. *Matanza: El Salvador's Communist Revolt of 1932.* Lincoln: University of Nebraska Press, 1971.

Barón Castro, Rodolfo. *La población de El Salvador: Estudio acerca de su desenvolvimiento desde la época prehispánica hasta nuestros días.* Madrid: Consejo Superior de Investigaciones Científicas, Instituto Gonzalo Fernández de Oviedo, 1942.

Browning, David. *El Salvador: Landscape and Society.* Oxford: Clarendon Press, 1971.

Caldera, Rafael. *The Growth of Christian Democracy and its Influence on the Social Reality of Latin America.* New York: Center of Christian Democratic Action, 1965.

Capa, Cornell, and J. Mayone Stycos. *Margin of Life: Population and Poverty in the Americas.* New York: Grossman, 1974.

Carías, Marco Virgilio, et al. *La guerra inútil: Análisis socioeconómico del conflicto entre Honduras y El Salvador.* San José, Costa Rica: Editorial Universitaria Centroamericana, 1971.

Choussy, Félix. *Economía agrícola salvadoreña: Producción agrícola e industrias conexas.* San Salvador: n.p., 1950.

Cuenca, Abel. *El Salvador: Una democracia cafetalera.* Mexico: ARR-Centro Editorial, 1962.

Dalton, Roque. *Miguel Mármol: Los sucesos de 1932 en El Salvador.* San José, Costa Rica: Editorial Universitaria Centroamericana, 1972.

Dealy, Glen. "The Tradition of Monistic Democracy in Latin America." *Politics and Social Change in Latin America: The Distinct Tradition.* Edited by Howard J. Wiarda. Amherst: University of Massachusetts Press, 1974.

Ebel, Roland H. "The Decision-Making Process in San Salvador." *Latin American Urban Research.* Edited by F. F. Rabinovitz and F. M. Trueblood. Vol. I. Beverly Hills, California: Sage Publications, 1971.

El Salvador Election Factbook, March 5, 1967. Washington, D.C.: Institute for the Comparative Study of Political Systems, 1967.

Feder, Ernest. *The Rape of the Peasantry: Latin America's Landholding System.* Garden City, N.Y.: Anchor Books, 1971.

Fuentes Rivera, Luis. "El conflicto Honduras-El Salvador: Aspectos políticos, sociales y económicos." *La guerra inútil: Análisis socio-económico del conflicto entre Honduras y El Salvador.* San José, Costa Rica: Editorial Universitaria Centroamericana, 1971.

González Casanova, Pablo. *Democracy in Mexico.* Translated by Danielle Salti. New York: Oxford University Press, 1970.

González Sibrián, José Luis. *Las 100 horas: La guerra de legítima defensa de la república de El Salvador.* San Salvador: Tipografía Offset Central, n.d.

Gross, Leonard. *The Last, Best Hope: Eduardo Frei and Chilean Democracy.* New York: Random House, 1967.

Guandique, José Salvador. *Roberto Edmundo Canessa: Directivo, fundador, ministro, candidato, víctima.* San Salvador: Editorial Ungo, 1962.

Hayes, Carlton J. H. *A Generation of Materialism, 1871–1900.* New York: Harper and Row, 1963.

Henríquez, Orlando. *En el cielo escribieron historia.* Tegucigalpa: Tipografía Nacional, 1972.

Hoopes, Paul R. "El Salvador." *Political Forces in Latin America: Dimensions of the Quest for Stability.* Edited by Ben G. Burnett and Kenneth F. Johnson. Belmont, Calif.: Wadsworth Publishing Company, 1970.

Huezo Selva, Rafael. *El espacio económico más singular del continente americano.* San Salvador: n.p., 1972.

Karnes, Thomas L. *The Failure of Union: Central America, 1824–1960.* Chapel Hill: University of North Carolina Press, 1961.

Kennedy, Paul P. *The Middle Beat: A Correspondent's View of Mexico, Guatemala, and El Salvador.* Edited by Stanley R. Ross. New York: Teachers College Press, 1971.

Krehm, William. *Democracia y tiranías en el Caribe.* Edited by Vicente Sáenz. Mexico: Unión Democrática Centroamericana, 1949.

Leiva, Vivas, Rafael. *Un país en Honduras.* Tegucigalpa: Impr. Calderón, 1969.

Lovo Castelar, Luis. *La Guardia Nacional en campaña: Relatos y crónicas de Honduras.* San Salvador: Editorial Lea, 1971.

López Trejo, Robert. *Realidad dramática de la república: 25 años de traición a la fuerza armada y a la patria.* San Salvador: Editorial Ahora, 1974.

López Vallecillos, Italo. *El periodismo en El Salvador.* San Salvador: Editorial Universitaria, 1964.

Luttwak, Edward. *Coup d'Etat: A Practical Handbook.* London: Allen Lane, 1968.

Macrum, Joseph M. *Themes and Appeals of Christian Democracy in Latin America.* Washington, D.C.: Center for Research in Social Systems, American University, 1967.

Martin, Percy F. *Salvador of the Twentieth Century.* London: Edward Arnold, 1911.

Martz, John. *Central America: The Crisis and the Challenge.* Chapel Hill: University of North Carolina Press, 1959.

Masferrer, Alberto. *El mínimum vital y otras obras de carácter sociológico.* Guatemala: Ediciones del Gobierno de Guatemala, 1950.

Mayo, John K., Robert C. Hornik, and Emile G. McAnany. *Educational Reform with Television: The El Salvador Experience.* Stanford, Calif.: Stanford University Press, 1976.

Méndez (h.), Joaquín. *Los sucesos comunistas en El Salvador*. San Salvador: Imprenta Funes y Ungo, 1932.

Monteforte Toledo, Mario, et al. *Centro América: Subdesarrollo y dependencia*. 2 vols. Mexico: Instituto de Investigaciones Sociales, Universidad Nacional Autónoma de México, 1972.

Morales Molina, Manuel, comp. *El Salvador, un pueblo que se rebela: Conflicto de julio de 1969*. 2 vols. San Salvador: Tipografía Central, 1973–74.

Packenham, Robert A. *Liberal America and the Third World: Political Development Ideas in Foreign Aid and Social Science*. Princeton, N.J.: Princeton University Press, 1973.

Paredes, Jacinto. *Vida y obras del doctor Pío Romero Bosque: Apuntes para la historia de El Salvador*. San Salvador: Imprenta Nacional, 1930.

Parker, Franklin D. *The Central American Republics*. London: Oxford University Press, 1964.

Peña Kampy, Alberto. *El general Martínez: Un patriarcal presidente dictador*. San Salvador: Editorial Tipográfica Ramírez, n.d.

Raynolds, David R. *Rapid Development in Small Economies: The Example of El Salvador*. New York: Praeger, 1967.

Rodríguez, Carlos A., and Ricardo Castañeda Rugamas. *El Salvador: Perfil Demográfico*. San Salvador: Asociación Demográfica Salvadoreña, 1971.

Ross, Stanley R. "Mexico: The Preferred Revolution." *Politics of Change in Latin America*. Edited by Joseph Maier and Richard W. Weatherhead. New York: F. A. Praeger, 1964.

Schlesinger, Arthur M., Jr. *A Thousand Days: John F. Kennedy in the White House*. Boston: Houghton Mifflin, 1965.

Schlesinger, Jorge. *Revolución comunista*. Guatemala: Unión Tipográfica Castañeda, Avila, 1946.

Turner, Frederick C. *Catholicism and Political Development in Latin America*. Chapel Hill: University of North Carolina Press, 1971.

Ventocilla, Eleodoro. *Lemus y la revolución salvadoreña*. Mexico: Ediciones Latinoamérica, 1956.

Waggoner, George R., and Barbara Ashton Waggoner. *Education in Central America*. Lawrence: University Press of Kansas, 1971.

Walker, Thomas W. *The Christian Democratic Movement in Nicara-*

gua. Comparative Government Studies, no. 3. Tucson: University of Arizona Press, 1970.

Wayland-Smith, Giles. *The Christian Democratic Party in Chile: A Study of Political Organization and Activity with Primary Emphasis on the Local Level.* Cuernavaca, Mexico: Centro Intercultural de Documentación, 1969.

White, Alastair. *El Salvador.* New York: Praeger, 1973.

Williams, Edward J. *Latin American Christian Democratic Parties.* Knoxville: University of Tennessee Press, 1967.

Wollaston, Nicholas. *Red Rumba: A Journey through the Caribbean and Central America.* London: Hodder and Stoughton, 1962.

Woodward, Ralph Lee, Jr. *Central America: A Nation Divided.* New York: Oxford University Press, 1976.

THESES AND DISSERTATIONS

Ashton, Raymond Charles. "El Salvador and the 'Controlled Revolution': An Analysis of Salvadorean Development, 1948–1965." M.A. thesis, Tulane University, 1967.

Campbell, Jane. "The Chamber of Commerce and Industry of El Salvador: A Latin American Interest Group." M.A. thesis, Tulane University, 1969.

Elam, Robert Varney. "Appeal to Arms: The Army and Politics in El Salvador, 1931–1964." Ph.D. dissertation, University of New Mexico, 1968.

Gamble, Joyce Elaine. "The Partido Acción Renovadora in the Elections of 1964, 1966, and 1967." M.A. thesis, Tulane University, 1968.

Harrison, Sandas Lorenzo. "The Role of El Salvador in the Drive for Unity in Central America." Ph.D. dissertation, Indiana University, 1962.

Wilson, Everett A. "The Crisis of National Integration in El Salvador, 1919–1935." Ph.D. dissertation, Stanford University, 1969.

Index

225